In the Name of Jesus |

In the Name of Jesus is one of those rare book
foundly important and deeply relevant material but also has you hoping it will
never end. You'll be convinced that your life—and the world—will change after
reading this book. Dr. Clouzet has masterfully combined fascinating stories,
powerful quotes, and the Word of God. You'll wish you could have read this
book many years ago.

—John Bradshaw, president, It Is Written

We believe "at the sound of fervent prayer, Satan's whole host trembles" (*Testimonies for the Church*, vol. 1, 346). Prayer is one of God's chosen weapons in the
great war for people's hearts and minds. Our friend Ron Clouzet has inspired
us so often as he has spent his whole life passionately seeking to reach people
for Jesus. He knows from real-life experience the power of prayer and also the
best practical methods to get us doing it! We have been deeply moved again in
reading this book. We hope and pray every pastor, elder, and member will read
it! Now is the time for us all to move beyond talking and dreaming about the
last great breakthroughs and on to really praying and seeing the change in our
own lives, our families, churches, and the world around us! Read it and watch
the Lord work!

—Jerry and Janet Page, Ministerial Association, General Conference

In the Name of Jesus: Power to Pray for People and Places has inspired and challenged me greatly to consider using prayer as the strategy for mission to the
cities. I highly recommend this book to everyone wishing to enrich his or her
prayer life—every pastor, local church leader, prayer group, and church member. Those with a passion for seeing greater success in preparing the cities of
the world for the second coming of Jesus Christ, including coordinators for
Mission to the Cities, will find this to be a powerful resource.

—Geoffrey G. Mbwana, general vice president, General Conference

Read this book with a prayerful heart, and your life will be transformed! You
will discover powerful insights about prayer from the Word of God, be inspired by stories of prayer in action, and learn practical strategies for living a
prayer-saturated life in the name of Jesus.

—Derek Morris, president of HOPE TV and author of *The Radical Prayer*

As I have been reading *In the Name of Jesus*, chills of excitement have overwhelmed me, and I've had a hard time putting the book down. *This is it!* This is what we've been missing as Christians! Let me just say that *if* you want to take your prayer life and your relationship with Jesus to a whole new level, then *this is* the book for you! In fact, I believe this book should be read by every serious believer as its message has the power to revolutionize our church. This is a truly outstanding book, and I can't wait to share it!

—**Melody Mason**, General Conference United in Prayer coordinator and author of *Daring to Ask for More*

If you are looking for an inspiring book to share with your church on how to really pray from a Seventh-day Adventist perspective, *In the Name of Jesus* is your book. If you feel the need for a strategic revolution in city evangelism and would like to know more about corporate prayer, prayer walking, or intercession prayer in teams, this is your book.

—**Roberto Badenas**, former chairman of the Biblical Research Committee, Euro-Africa Division, and dean of Theology, Collonges-sous-Salève, France

This book takes an in-depth look at fervent prayer, both private and corporate, and the most effective strategies for spiritual revival and evangelism, too often overlooked and neglected. The author clearly and convincingly presents God's Bible prayer promises along with practical illustrations and insightful suggestions, such as prayer walking and intercessory prayer, for people who are living in large, secular cities. I wholeheartedly recommend that this book be seriously read and its methods implemented in our personal lives, our churches, and our church institutions.

—**Jairyong Lee**, former president of the Northern Asia-Pacific Division

This book, *In the Name of Jesus*, is right on time! It is urgently needed now. It is motivational, inspiring, and encouraging, and hopefully, it will be read by Christians everywhere. It can be a help to launch a movement of prayer that will be life-changing. It is interesting, with stories and examples that make you want to read on and to listen to His voice in Scripture and to pray earnestly. I pray that this book will change us to become people of prayer.

—**Ruthie Jacobsen**, author and former Prayer Ministries coordinator, North American Division

What a privilege it is to understand God's plan for our lives and His plan for spiritual commitment in our local churches through the power of prayer. Dr.

Ron E. M. Clouzet, in this attractive and encouraging book, is helping us understand prayer as a strategy and prayer as a spiritual revolution for our lives and churches. He is inviting us to use Heaven's powerful resource to open the hearts of the people in our cities. The Almighty's desire is for us to be much in prayer to make progress in the Christian life.

—**Billy Biaggi**, general vice president,
General Conference of Seventh-day Adventists

The Adventist Church has struggled for years to win souls in Japan. Yet, Christianity remains at less than 1 percent of the population. The book *In the Name of Jesus* is not only practical and powerful but also transformational. This is a *must-read* book that will change your spiritual life in these challenging times. I'd like to see a renewal of prayer life "in the name of Jesus" for every pastor, teacher, leader, parent, youth, and professional Adventist all across Japan.

—**Nozomu Obara**, associate director, Mission Unusual—Tokyo!,
and former president, East Japan Conference

When we're up against seemingly insurmountable spiritual strongholds, accessing the limitless reservoir of prayer often becomes the last defensive option. But Ron Clouzet presents prayer as an offense. This book is an excellent guide for ministry practitioners. It will change your attitude toward the practice of praying.

—**Ivan L. Williams Sr.**, director, Ministerial Association,
North American Division

Perfectly complementary to the Adventist Church's initiatives of "I Will Go," "Revival and Reformation," and "Sabbath School Alive!," Dr. Clouzet's study on prayer walking presents the incredible challenge to reach today's mission field, especially in the cities of both developed and developing worlds. In clarifying the commonly misunderstood aspects of prayer, he states what prayer walking is and what it is not, highlighting the underutilized power of this exercise. Prayerful workers in and for the mission field will benefit from the practical methods, troubleshooting techniques, and thought-probing study-guide questions provided in its chapters.

—**Justin Kim**, editor and assistant director, Sabbath School and
Personal Ministries Department, General Conference

I feel like my eyes have been opened to the privilege and power of prayer since reading this book. Dr. Clouzet's heartfelt appeal for a strategic prayer revolution has both moved me and challenged me to pray more intentionally and to pray more with others. This call to action is a timely reminder of the urgency before us of connecting with God through prayer for the salvation of others. I can't wait to start applying the practical suggestions and sharing them with others.

—**Nina Atcheson**, curriculum manager, Sabbath School and Personal Ministries Department, General Conference, and author of *As Light Lingers*

"Most of us . . . pray little. And many pray without faith." What a poignant reality check by Dr. Clouzet, showing what has become of prayer today. This book is a *must-read* for all Christians! God wants to do so much for us, and through us, if we would just earnestly, genuinely, and consistently pray. My friend Dr. Clouzet systematically teaches us the value of prayer, how to pray, and the powerful results of what real prayer can do! Are you just going through the motions when you pray? This book will revitalize, recharge, and reinspire you to have a vibrant prayer life.

—**Tony Anobile**, vice president for Multilingual Ministries, North American Division

This book is a galvanizing call to prayer and must be read by any serious Christian who wants to see Jesus come in this generation.

—**Moise Ratsara**, Michigan church pastor and former GYC leader

My profound thanks to Dr. Ron E. M. Clouzet for his untiring efforts to complete this work on prayer. *In the Name of Jesus: Power to Pray for People and Places* will be an indispensable foundation for missions in urban areas and a powerful prayer life. I would strongly recommend this book to pastors, church leaders, and every member of the local church.

—**Suk Hee Han**, Communications director, Northern Asia-Pacific Division

Ron understands the great implications of *not* reaching people with the kingdom message we have been given. He draws telling conclusions that we are losing ground and cannot do what we have been called to do. Therefore, Ron begins at our starting point, our foundational issue, which is too often assumed and not practiced enough. The starting point to reach people? Our work of prayer. It is not a defensive act but an offensive one. This is how we break down the gates of hell. I highly recommend that we read this book, digest it, discuss it, but mostly let it move us to the kingdom work of praying for lost people.

—**Roger Walter**, Oregon church pastor and author of *Evangelism Intelligence: Why Adventist Churches Grow Differently*

In the Name of

Power to Pray for People and Places

JESUS

RON E. M. CLOUZET

Pacific Press®
Publishing Association

Nampa, Idaho | www.pacificpress.com

Cover design by Steve Lanto
Cover design resources from iStockphoto.com

The author assumes full responsibility for the accuracy of all facts and quotations as cited in this book.

Additional copies of this book are available for purchase by calling toll-free 1-800-765-6955 or by visiting adventistbookcenter.com.

Library of Congress Cataloging-in-Publication Data

Names: Clouzet, Ron E. M., 1956- author.
Title: In the name of Jesus : power to pray for people and places / Ron E. M. Clouzet.
Description: Nampa, Idaho : Pacific Press Publishing Association, [2020] |
    Summary: "Instruction and rationale to pray for specific people and groups of people in
    various places"— Provided by publisher.
Identifiers: LCCN 2020035752 (print) | LCCN 2020035753 (ebook) | ISBN
    9780816366842 | ISBN 9780816366859 (kindle edition)
Subjects: LCSH: Prayer—Christianity. | Intercessory prayer. | Missions—Miscellanea. |
    General Conference of Seventh-Day Adventists—Doctrines.
Classification: LCC BV215 .C645 2020 (print) | LCC BV215 (ebook) |
    DDC 248.3/2—dc23
LC record available at https://lccn.loc.gov/2020035752
LC ebook record available at https://lccn.loc.gov/2020035753

September 2020

Dedication

To Christoffer Andrew, Alexander David, and Stefani Elizabeth, the subject and joy of my most heartfelt prayers.

Contents

Acknowledgments

M y deep thanks go to those who read the manuscript, especially those who made suggestions or noted needed corrections, including the ones who have endorsed the book, an excellent group of church leaders, pastors, and friends.

In addition, I would like to thank the administration of the Northern Asia-Pacific Division for allowing me time to write for the sake of the church. May this book be the greatest possible missional blessing to this challenging territory of the world.

Thanks also to the folks at Pacific Press for believing in the message of this book: Scott Cady, Dale Galusha, and Dan Ross, my editor. They have all been gracious and focused.

And thanks to my wife, Lisa, who endured many hours of reading and engaged in additional discussion with me over the contents of the book. She was my first editor, my loyal critic, and steady encourager.

I especially want to thank the Lord Jesus for His enduring forgiveness in the face of the many opportunities missed where I should have prayed to the Father instead of ignoring His source of power and the Holy Spirit, for gently encouraging me to write in spite of my most obvious limitations and persistent self-recrimination.

To God be the glory!

Introduction

When I started this book, it was meant to be a book on prayer walking. Then, COVID-19 came in 2020 and took the world hostage. When the coronavirus pandemic forced us to work from home for some time, the book changed. Even though the encouragement for Adventist churches to prayer walk remains a key objective, the book has become much more, deeper. I added chapters not planned before. More focus is made on the nature of the great controversy relative to prayer and corporate praying. More focus is also placed on intercession and practical steps for churches to become prayer-saturated churches.

Ian Bremmer, a well-known political scientist specializing in global politics, wrote not long ago that "the international order is unraveling." Global financial recession, migrant crises, unrest in Europe, an explosion of mass killings, nationalist trends (and he would no doubt add today the worldwide COVID-19 pandemic) have led to "geopolitical creative destruction . . . too loud to ignore."[1]

Bremmer is right. And what are we, Adventist believers, doing about that? In 1849, when Sabbatarian Adventists were perhaps only about a hundred members and living only in North America, God commissioned them to take the three angels' messages to *the whole world*! Some of them got together to pray over the first issue of *The Present Truth*. Ellen White remembered, "We knelt around the papers, and with humble hearts and many tears besought the Lord to let His blessing rest upon these printed messengers."[2] Did you catch that? "Humble hearts and many tears." Do we pray like this today? Do we believe God can change the world in spite of our meager resources and little power?

According to the Joshua Project, an organization providing data for Christian missions, there are about 17,424 distinct ethnic and cultural groups in the world, but 7,410 of them have not been reached with the gospel. That's 42.5 percent of the groups in the world! About 3.2 billion people in the world do not know Christ at all, let alone today's last-day message.[3] Clearly, we face a tremendous task, yet comparatively smaller than the one Adventist pioneers faced back in

1849. What did *they* do? They prayed with "many tears" for the world. That should always be the first step: prayer, earnest prayer.

By the time World War I was fought, firearms had become too fast and much more accurate than before. Soldiers could no longer face each other on the battlefield. Rapid-firing machine guns left them no option for survival except to dig trenches in the ground and take cover. The problem? Soldiers could be protected, but they could not go on the offensive. As soon as they did, they were overly exposed to the enemy. That stalled the war. Both armies would do nothing for days and even weeks but hide in the trenches, where human defecation and food supplies mingled with mud and misery. Soldiers were stuck. Then, one day, the British army invented the tank by engineering an armored car onto the chassis of a farm tractor. The tank turned the nature of the war from an almost purely defensive operation to one of offensive mobility.[4] The tank could go anywhere. It could pierce enemy lines. For the Christian, the tank is strategic prayer. It will go anywhere and pierce any and all enemy lines.

Using an analogy from the sport of baseball, we could say that prayer is reaching first base, without which it will be impossible to reach home. The church must engage in serious and organized global intercession *now*. Ellen White expressed her shock at so many Christians' lack of reaction to living in a world that is perishing at such an alarming rate:

> There is little enmity against Satan and his works, because there is so great ignorance concerning his power and malice, and the vast extent of his warfare against Christ and His church. Multitudes are deluded here. They do not know that their enemy is a mighty general who controls the minds of evil angels, and that with well-matured plans and skillful movements he is warring against Christ to prevent the salvation of souls. . . .
>
> . . . [Satan] is intruding his presence in every department of the household, in every street of our cities, in the churches, in the national councils, in the courts of justice, perplexing, deceiving, seducing, everywhere ruining the souls and bodies of men, women, and children, breaking up families, sowing hatred, emulation, strife, sedition, murder. And the Christian world seem to regard these things as though God had appointed them and they must exist.[5]

It is time to say enough is enough! We, the church, must line up behind our commander Jesus Christ and fight for the souls who can still be rescued from the world. We must pray, seriously, faithfully, and strategically so the kingdom of God may triumph over the kingdom of darkness. If not us, whom? If not now, when? "Everywhere there are hearts crying out for something which they have not. They long for a power that will give them mastery over sin, a power that will deliver them from the bondage of evil, a power that will give health and life and peace."[6]

This is a book on strategic praying. The first section is about what the Bible teaches regarding strategic prayer. The second part deals with practical strategies for prayer in the local church or Adventist institution. Since I currently serve in northern Asia, where the vast majority of people live in abject spiritual darkness, the need for prayer has become a real burden on my heart. But the entire world needs strategic prayer. "Prayer is the greatest resource of the church," urged Wesley Duewel. "It is not the only thing you must do, but it is the greatest thing you can do."[7]

Then, let's do it.

---

1. Ian Bremmer, "The Era of American Global Leadership Is Over. Here's What Comes Next," *Time,* December 19, 2016, http://time.com/4606071/american-global-leadership-is-over/. Bremmer is the author of *The J Curve: A New Way to Understand Why Nations Rise and Fall* (New York: Simon and Schuster, 2006); *Every Nation for Itself: Winners and Losers in a G-Zero World* (New York: Portfolio Penguin, 2012); and *Superpower: Three Choices for America's Role in the World* (London: UK Penguin, 2015).

2. Ellen G. White, *Life Sketches* (Washington, DC: Review and Herald®, 1915), 126. See also George R. Knight, *A Brief History of Seventh-day Adventists* (Hagerstown, MD: Review and Herald®, 1999), 56.

3. "Global Summary," Joshua Project, accessed May 1, 2020, https://joshuaproject.net/.

4. Stephen Kendrick and Alex Kendrick, *The Battle Plan for Prayer: From Basic Training to Targeted Strategies* (Nashville, TN: B&H, 2015), 15, 16.

5. Ellen G. White, *The Great Controversy* (Washington, DC: Review and Herald®, 1911), 507, 508.

6. Ellen G. White, *The Ministry of Healing* (Washington, DC: Review and Herald®, 1905), 143.

7. Carrol Johnson Shewmake, *When We Pray for Others: The Blessings of Intercessory Prayer* (Hagerstown, MD: Review and Herald®, 1995), 99.

PART I

Power Untapped

Prayer is the key to victory. Oh, yes, we know *Jesus* is the key to victory, of course (Philippians 4:13). And we know that faith is the key to victory (1 John 5:4). But we cannot know Jesus unless we communicate with Him by prayer, and we cannot experience the life of faith unless prayer is very real in our Christian life.

Most of us, however, pray little. And many pray without faith. In this section—the most important of the book—my attempt is to focus on some of what the Bible says about prayer with the hope to awaken in you a longing for prayer, especially corporate prayer. There is so much that could be said here! And I freely acknowledge that others, such as E. M. Bounds, Andrew Murray, and A. W. Tozer, have said it better than I could possibly say it here. I have many pages of notes, quotes, and stories that I do not include in this section; otherwise, it would be too long and cumbersome. But there is plenty to think about, to learn, and to discuss with like-minded friends. My prayer, for now, is simple: that God would show us what is possible in His name.

CHAPTER 1

The Need for a Strategic Revolution

A few years ago, I had the privilege of visiting the ancient city of Ephesus, in what is now Turkey. I was astonished by what I saw. Here was the magnificent Curetes Street, with public latrines and shrines to foreign gods; the Odeon, or concert hall that sat three thousand people; the facade of the famous Celsus Library, one of the largest in the ancient world; the lower *agora*, or marketplace; and the famous Great Theater, with capacity for twenty-five thousand people, where two thousand years ago the Ephesians chanted for hours in favor of the goddess Diana against the new God of heaven preached by the apostle Paul (Acts 19:23–34).

But what astonished me even more than this magnificent ancient archaeological site was reflecting on the amazingly successful ministry of Paul in such a large, cosmopolitan, Christless city, where the temple of Diana was considered one of the seven wonders of the ancient world. Ephesus was both "the most magnificent" and "the most corrupt" of the cities of Asia. It was a city reeking with spiritualism and demonic practices.[1] How did Paul do it? How did the apostle, in less than three years (Acts 19:8–10), turn one of the most influential cities in the world from paganism to Christianity? The Christians in Ephesus were legendary for their "first love" (Revelation 2:1–4), Jesus Christ. Ephesus became the center of operations for the last living apostle, John, and the church there, the most vibrant in the first century. Paul's achievement would be the equivalent of today's Tokyo (pop. 37 million) becoming mostly Christian through the ministry and presence of a few dozen missionaries!

One of the keys may be found in Paul's letter to the Ephesians, written from a Roman prison years after his time in Ephesus. After describing the components of the armor of God to be worn by the soldiers of Jesus (Ephesians 6:10–17), the apostle requested the Ephesian Christians to pray "for me," as he said, "that utterance may be given to me, that I may open my mouth boldly to make known the mystery of the gospel, for which I am an ambassador in chains" (verses 19, 20). Amazing! He did not ask his friends to pray for his release or for better treatment while in chains, but for power to witness while still in prison! And it worked. Ellen White says a number of the people from the household of Nero, the Roman emperor at the time, converted to Christianity because of Paul's witness.[2]

Paul was a man who prayed for doors of opportunity to open for the gospel (Colossians 4:2–4). He excused his delay to the city of Corinth with these words: "I will tarry at Ephesus. . . . For a great and effective door has opened to me, and there are many adversaries" (1 Corinthians 16:8, 9). Ephesus was ripe for a change, he thought, and with God, all things are possible, but it is not easy.

What Paul brought about in Ephesus was a revolution, and the revolution began and was sustained by prayer. And he also recognized that the enemies of God would fight to keep their city in darkness. Much prayer was needed.

The challenge today

As a denomination, we are working in 212 of 235 countries and areas of the world, and as of 2020, we number over 21 million members. Many thousands join the church each year because faithful laity, pastors, and leaders share their faith and are ready to bless others and because churches are still willing to open their doors to share the three angels' messages. However, more than 75 percent of our baptisms come from only four of the fifteen territories comprising our world church, and several divisions have seen consistent gain registering barely above zero. Yes, 0 percent, by comparison.[3] The truth is that despite progress—a narrowing ratio between population and church members that stands at 356 to 1 today[4]—we keep falling behind, statistically speaking.

Each year, approximately 137.7 million people are born, and 57.2 million people die.[5] That means there are 80.5 million *additional* people in the world every year. And of course, that number continues to increase. That figure is almost four times the entire membership of the Seventh-day Adventist Church today. According to church statistics, accounting for losses, between 2017 and 2018, church membership increased by only 687,432.[6] We praise God for each new member! But how does an increase of less than a million members compare with 80 million new people being added to the world each year?

Obviously, wonderful institutions, thousands of young people attending schools in our vast and recognized educational network system, efficient methods and resources for evangelism, and a global organization that is hard to match are not enough to make *substantive* progress. We make progress, yes, but nothing out of the ordinary. What is needed is a true revolution—a strategic revolution that may need to be as simple as it is efficient.[7]

What we need is to walk and pray together for God to open the hearts of the people in our cities. Worldwide, more people live in cities today than in the country or in small towns. In many of the populous Asian countries, more people have lived in cities now for decades.

Cities were never the invention of God. The first city builder was Cain after he killed his brother Abel and left the presence of God (Genesis 4:16, 17). Ancient cities were meant to be fortresses to protect citizens against their enemies. But today, cities are full of danger, corruption, and sin of every imaginable sort. Sodom and Gomorrah were two cities God was forced to destroy, their corruption being irreversible (Genesis 18:20, 21; 19:1–17). But the few inhabitants that escaped were saved by the prayerful intercession of Abraham (Genesis 18:22–33). Nineveh was a huge city that God saved because a reluctant evangelist interceded on God's behalf (Jonah 1–4).

Think of such cities as Mumbai, Shanghai, Berlin, or New York. Do the millions who live there need rescuing from the claws of Satan? Think of cities such as Buenos Aires, Sydney, Johannesburg, or Jakarta. Are those cities known as *Adventist* cities? Think of the cities of Tokyo, Cairo, Bangkok, and Hong Kong. Are all their citizens aware of the wonderful offer made by the Creator and Redeemer of the world? Think of cities such as Seoul, Nairobi, Rio de Janeiro, or Paris. Are the three angels' messages the flag that flies over these massive populations? The answer is . . . no. There are cities like Sao Paulo, Mexico City, and Manila that have hundreds and even thousands of Adventist churches within their borders, but even they would not be recognized as *Adventist* cities.

Take, for instance, the division where I serve, comprising the countries of China, Japan, North and South Korea, Taiwan, and Mongolia.[8] These six countries alone have a population of 1.6 billion people. Less than 4 percent are Christians, and less than 0.05 percent are Adventists! No wonder my division describes itself as "the most challenging division." Twenty-five of the fifty largest cities in the world are in this division. When Westerners visit China or Japan for the first time, they see a number of people in the subways or on the streets that they could not have imagined.

My point is this: the work to get the gospel to all the world—and most of the world lives in cities now—is incredibly challenging. If we continue as we have, working hard, creating resources to train and to share, establishing schools and hospitals and churches, and praying for God to bless our plans, we will never finish the work of evangelizing the world. Another six thousand years from now, we may still be here. What we do is simply not enough. But the Lord told us He will come when the gospel goes to all the world (Matthew 24:14).

Prayer is the strategy

Perhaps we need to think of prayer as being the strategy. We usually think of prayer in a supporting role to ministry, but when it comes to these large cities in the world, our first strategic step should be a prayer plan that works.

Prayer walking our cities may be the simplest of all strategies. Other strategies can also be implemented, as we will see. Generally, every Adventist knows how to walk and how to talk. Prayer walking is something everyone in the church can do: the youth with their friends after school, the young mothers staying home with their children, the retired people who walk for their health, or those who walk as part of their lunch break at work. Everyone can do this. Teams of three or four people can prayer walk the same area of town several times a week for about thirty minutes. They can pray aloud, as if talking with one another, or pray silently as they walk. They can pray for every person they see on the sidewalk, in the restaurants and shops, at the bus stops, and in the subway stations. They can pray for their neighbors and for those who live in the houses and apartments they see. "God, in the name of Jesus, we ask You to bless the woman waiting to cross the street who appears so sad and worn out. May Your Spirit reach her to give her hope today. May You direct her thoughts, somehow, to what things could be like in her life rather than what they may be right now. Find any excuse, Lord, to bless her and for her to be able to recognize that such blessing comes from above. Keep the enemy from taking further advantage of her today. In Jesus' wonderful name. Amen." It's that simple.

That was Hudson Taylor's strategy. Taylor spent fifty-one years as a missionary to China. He was the founder of the China Inland Mission, through which he brought over eight hundred additional missionaries to that great country, began 125 Christian schools, and led over eighteen thousand converts to Christ. He sacrificed much for China and prayed much for China. One time, he and some of his missionary colleagues were in Taiping on market day. His heart was "moved by the crowds that filled the streets for two or three miles, so that we could hardly walk," he remembered. And here comes the strategy: "I was constrained to retire to the city wall and cry to God to have mercy on the people, to open their hearts and give us an entrance among them."[9]

Overwhelmed by the numbers of people groping in darkness who desperately needed the Light of God, he prayed. He prayed for a door of entrance to their hearts. They didn't even know they were in darkness. But the Christian missionary did, and that's why he prayed. You see, Taylor saw that great multitude and couldn't know how to begin. Whom would he approach? What would he say? Where would he start? So he prayed for God to open the door. And a door opened *immediately*.

His next paragraph reads this way: "Without any seeking on our part, we were brought into touch with at least four anxious souls." Then, he tells about one of them: "A man found us out, I know not how, and followed me to our boat. I asked him in and inquired his name. 'My name is Dzing,' he replied. 'But the question which distresses me, and to which I find no answer, is—What am I to do with my sins? Our scholars tell us that there is no future state, but I find it hard to believe them. . . . Oh, sir, I lie on my bed and think. I sit alone in the daytime and think . . . but I cannot tell what is to be done about my sins. I am seventy-two years of age. I cannot expect to finish another decade. . . . Can you tell me what to do with my sins?' " Hudson Taylor replied, "I can indeed."[10]

The same thing that happened to Taylor can happen to us because people are still groping in darkness and because God still answers prayers of faith. Note three things here: (1) Taylor and his friends walked among the multitude and prayed for people they saw that day, praying for a door of entry to their hearts. (2) Four people *approached them* seeking light. (3) In the case of the older man named Dzing, his burden was twofold: what happens after death and what to do with one's sins.

Today's multitudes also wonder what will happen after death and what they must do to atone for their sins and mistakes. Their burden is the same as that of billions of others over thousands of years of human history. We must connect with these people. The problem is that we don't know who they are. We cannot go knocking from door to door, asking, "Do you know what happens after death or what to do with your sins?" The police would soon be after us for bothering people while displaying what many would label as religious fanaticism.

But God knows who they are. And He knows the first door of entry is the door of *our own* hearts. Are we willing to meet with them? Are we willing to befriend them? Are we willing to help answer their questions? Are we actually willing to pray for them? Pray, not once or twice or for a month, but consistently for them for a year or two or three, until that door opens? Once God knows we're willing, He can move those in the crowd longing for light to connect with you and me—the Seventh-day Adventist missionaries who cared enough to pray for them.

Ellen White wrote something we must keep uppermost in our minds: "*All over the world* men and women are looking wistfully to heaven. Prayers and tears and inquiries go up from souls longing for light, for grace, for the Holy Spirit. *Many are on the verge of the kingdom*, waiting only to be gathered in."[11] Think about this! All over the world, people are looking for light, and many of them are ready to be gathered to the Adventist Church!

Jesus knew the same thing. After a conversation He had with a Samaritan woman, leading her to accept Him as the Messiah, she brought a crowd from her city, Sychar, to listen to Jesus (John 4:5–30, 39–41). We must remember that the Jews at that time considered Samaritans backslidden Israelites. They viewed them as having forfeited their chance for salvation. They were considered worse, in fact, than pagans. That's why the disciples were shocked to see Jesus speaking with a Samaritan woman. At the end of that eventful day, Christ turned to His disciples to share a very profound truth we must also keep in mind: "Lift up your eyes and look at the fields, for they are already white for harvest!" (John 4:35).

Many more people are ready to respond to God than we can possibly imagine! And they are ready to respond *now*! When we talk of doing evangelism, we often say that very few are interested in our message. That's what *we* see, not what God sees. God sees an entire field ripe and ready to respond. Prayer will help them come out from the crowd.

Questions for Group Discussion and Personal Reflection

1. Do you think the Adventist Church will ever be able to reach the whole world with the gospel? Why, or why not?

2. Is it reasonable to call for a prayer "revolution" in the church? If so, how much of a "revolution" is needed?

3. How feasible do you think prayer walking is as a ministry plan for the Adventist Church? How about for your local church or Adventist institution?

4. What are your thoughts on Ellen White's statement that many people are "on the verge of the kingdom, waiting only to be gathered in"?

5. Do you really believe that, in your city or community, the fields "are already white for harvest," as Jesus said? What makes you think so, one way or the other?

---

1. Ellen G. White, *The Acts of the Apostles* (Washington, DC: Review and Herald®, 1911), 286.

2. See Ellen G. White, *The Story of Redemption* (Washington, DC: Review and Herald®, 1947), 315.

3. Those four divisions are East-Central Africa, with 27.49 percent of all accessions to the church from 2015 through 2018, Southern Africa-Indian Ocean (19.23 percent), South American (15.82 percent), and Inter-American (14.30 percent), for a total of 76.84 percent of total accessions to the church during said period. The ones struggling the most are the Middle East and

North Africa Union Mission (0.02 percent), the Trans-European (0.18 percent), Euro-Asia (0.18 percent), and Inter-European (0.27 percent) Divisions. The Northern Asia-Pacific Division (1.13 percent) is faring just slightly better. See *2019 Annual Statistical Report, New Series, vol. 1: Report of the General Conference of Seventh-day Adventists® 2018 Statistics*, page 4, table 3, accessed August 10, 2020, https://documents.adventistarchives.org/Statistics/ASR/ASR2019A.pdf.

4. See *2019 Annual Statistical Report*, 96.

5. See "World Population," Worldometer, https://www.worldometers.info/, accessed April 27, 2020.

6. See *2019 Annual Statistical Report*, page 4, table 4.

7. Of the real need of Adventism I wrote elsewhere, in *Adventism's Greatest Need: The Outpouring of the Holy Spirit* (Nampa, ID: Pacific Press®, 2011). We need the infilling of God's Spirit as we focus our attention on the goodness and grace of Jesus as our Savior and Lord. What I am speaking about in this book is a *strategic* revolution.

8. At the time of this writing, this was the composition of the Northern Asia-Pacific Division (NSD). Later, China became an attached field of the General Conference.

9. Howard Taylor and Geraldine Taylor, *Hudson Taylor's Spiritual Secret* (Peabody, MA: Hendrickson, 2008), 166.

10. Taylor and Taylor, 166.

11. White, *Acts of the Apostles*, 109; emphasis added.

CHAPTER 2

Walking Around Jericho's Walls

Skeptics say this never happened, but more recent archaeological evidence has shown correlations between the scientific data and the Bible story that tells of the fall of the walls of ancient Jericho.[1] A city falling to its enemies was a common occurrence in ancient times. So why do some people doubt this happened with Jericho? Because the fall of Jericho was the result of Israelites *walking* around the city for one week—no siege, no battle, no weapons. It sounds so implausible that no evidence will convince those who are intent on unbelief.

Yet, it happened. The massive walls of the wealthy city-fortress of the Canaanites fell flat as the people of God walked around it at the command of God on the seventh day of their walk (Joshua 6:3–5, 12–20). This was quite a miracle.

Israel was a nation that, for four hundred years, had been enslaved in Egypt. They had been brutalized and dehumanized for generations (Exodus 3:7). God took that nation of about two million people, opened the Red Sea for them, and led them through the wilderness for forty years, protecting them every step of the way. But now, God told them it was time to conquer Canaan—the Promised Land. However, the wicked inhabitants of Canaan were not going to leave simply because the God of Israel requested it. Israel's first challenge would be Canaan's premier fortress, the city of Jericho. To conquer such a fortified city full of seasoned soldiers, the attacking nation would need catapults and many other implements of war. They would also need generals and warriors that would know how to pierce through seemingly invulnerable sets of walls. Being victorious was very important for Joshua and Israel. If they failed, it would embolden their enemies. If they succeeded, it would weaken them.[2] But the Israelites were farmers and bricklayers! There were no soldiers! How could they take a city that even large, experienced armies would find very difficult to conquer?

All they had to do was walk and pray, just as God told them to. Prayer is not actually mentioned in the text of the book of Joshua, but Hebrews 11:30 reminds us: "By faith the walls of Jericho fell down." You cannot have faith unless you pray (Luke 18:1–8). They walked around the city while silently praying on the first day and then went home. They did the same on the second and third days and all that week. On the seventh day, they walked around the city seven times. Then, they shouted a shout of victory—*as if* the walls had just fallen down—and the massive walls came tumbling down (Joshua 6:12–20). Their shout was an act of faith. The result was that news of this amazing miracle under Joshua's leadership "spread throughout all the country" (verse 27).

Cities: Satan's strongholds

Why is this story relevant to a prayer-walking initiative? It is relevant because of what cities represent and what such a strategy can do to accomplish God's plans.

According to the United Nations Population Fund, 2008 was a landmark year in the history of the world. For the first time, the population of the world's cities surpassed that of the rural areas and small towns. In the twentieth century, the world's urban population grew from 220 million to 2.8 billion. It now stands at 3.3 billion, and it is expected to grow to 5 billion in just a few more years. In Africa and Asia, "the accumulated urban growth . . . during the whole span of history will be duplicated in a single generation." By 2030, those cities' populations will double that of 2000.[3]

In 2013, there was a five-day conference at the General Conference of Seventh-day Adventists dealing with the challenge of missions to the cities. The report recognized the challenge is not easy: "Mission to the cities may seem impossible. Yes, work in cities may seem difficult. Church members are busy, with little time to engage in mission. The population is full of people whose lives are often defined by dollar bills or Hollywood. The cost of mission workers, housing, property, and operations is far higher in cities than [in other] urban areas."[4] In most Third World cities, the majority of people are poor—many living in slums—and crime is part of daily life. In the Developed World, people living in cities are highly stressed; live in small, expensive quarters; battle traffic or public transportation each day; and live with insecurity. All of these factors affect Adventists living in cities.

The truth is that living in a large city is an ideal context for the devil to operate. Crime and poverty are, in his hands, great tools to denigrate and dehumanize people, leading souls to discouragement and despair. Stress and busyness keep people distracted from what God has to offer. Inappropriate entertainment establishments are all too common and accessible to both young and old alike. In cities, every form of evil and selfishness is expected. No one is shocked. Most are immune to human sympathy, and peer pressure to resist evil has little effect. Cities make people hard and distrustful of others. Ironically, where so many live close together physically, most live far apart from one another emotionally. The city is the perfect place for strangers to stay strangers. It is like a crowded elevator: full of people, but no one looks at another or cares about their lives.

Good or bad, that's where people live, and they are the people the church must reach. Many people who have experienced ministering in cities suggest that the key to reaching the city is found in the statement by Ellen White that speaks of mingling with people wanting their good, having compassion for them, meeting their needs, and gaining their confidence before encouraging them to follow Jesus.[5] In other words: compassion ministries. However, as wise as this counsel is, it calls for a long-term commitment, and it assumes people are available to encourage them to follow Jesus eventually. My experience in many countries—about seventy to date—has shown me that most Adventists do not do this, and of those who do, most don't know how to help people take the vital last step of trusting Jesus.

It may be that the weakness here is failing to do the basic work that precedes compassion ministries. And that work is the ministry of prayer for the Holy Spirit to awaken people to their need of God. There is a real war going on for the souls of men and women in the world. Satan and his allies understand that, so they prepare and act accordingly.[6] The church needs to understand it, as well.

The church at war

In Ephesians 6, the apostle Paul paints a picture of the warfare the church of God wages against the enemy of souls. We will analyze the text in more detail in a later chapter, but the point here is that the church is marching to take the city. What city? Satan and his imps have fortified themselves behind walls of lies, and have many deceived people now trapped inside. They cannot escape. The enemy is powerful: "For we do not wrestle against flesh and blood, but against principalities, against powers, against the rulers of the darkness of this age, against spiritual hosts of wickedness" (Ephesians: 6:12). We could call this city Hell, Satan's citadel. However, Jesus is our Commander, as we see in the book of Joshua (Joshua 5:14), and He expects the members of the church of God to march on until they breach the wall. He said, "On this rock [on Himself] I will build my church, and the gates of hell shall not prevail against it" (Matthew 16:18, ESV). That can only mean His church is marching against the gates of Hell, and His church will prevail against it!

This is a wonderful promise. The church, Christ's followers, will pierce through walls erected by principalities and powers of darkness, allowing them to rescue those trapped by Satan's lies and sophistries. But what of our weapons of warfare? What do we use to get through those walls? According to Paul, "the weapons of our warfare are not carnal but mighty in God for pulling down strongholds, casting down arguments and every high thing that exalts itself against the knowledge of God" (2 Corinthians 10:4, 5).

A stronghold is a fortification, a place made strong to defend something treasured. *Fortification* comes from two Latin words: *fortis*, meaning "strong," and *facere*, which means "to make." So, in the analogy of Paul, the stronghold is the place Satan makes strong. But those strongholds will fall because the weapons of our warfare are "mighty in God." Do we have any idea of the specific weapon Paul may be referring to? What is "mighty in God?" Back to Ephesians 6. The one weapon available against the enemy is "the sword of the Spirit, which is the word of God" (Ephesians 6:17).

You may wonder: what does the Word of God have to do with prayer and walking? Much in every way. The very next words after Ephesians 6:17 tell us to take the sword, "praying always with all prayer and supplication in the Spirit" (verse 18). Thus, the Word of God is the sword of the Spirit, and prayer is something we do in the Spirit. The link is obvious. The most effective way to pray is to claim the promises found in God's Word. This is what it means to pray in the Spirit, since the Holy Spirit is, actually, the author of God's Word (2 Peter 1:21).

A silly strategy?

Walking around an area in the city or the neighborhood while praying for the people you see and those behind closed doors may seem like a silly strategy. Why not just pray in the privacy of your home? Why not pray with others in the church for those who are in darkness? As we will see, prayer walking *sensitizes us* to people much more readily than praying for people we can't see. It connects us with the people! Walking and praying around the fortress of Jericho must have seemed like a very silly strategy to the Canaanites inside the walls and, perhaps, even to some Israelites doing the walking, but it worked. God keeps things simple for us, knowing that the power is not in the particular strategy used but in whether or not we will obey whatever He tells us to do.

The history of prayer walking is recent in the Christian church. It began in the mid-1980s among some churches in the United States. By the 1990s, it became a significant international ministry taken seriously by those involved, and a number of books were written about it over the next few years.[7] Groups of

Christian students have prayer walked for their schools. Christian businesspeople have prayer walked for their counterparts in the city. Mothers with small children have banded together and prayer walked their neighborhoods, and even older people have come out to prayer walk on behalf of the lost. It is so simple to pray while we walk together! But the devil will try his best to dissuade us that these things don't work, that they don't really make a difference.

But they do. For Israel, their first challenge in the land of Canaan was overcome in merely one week. This gave them the courage to keep moving forward with the rest of the territory.

A few years ago, my wife and I had speaking appointments in Bermuda, a small island country under the British flag, lying east of the coast of North America. Before we arrived, I had heard about Johnny Barnes, the best-known citizen of that country. After going up and down the entire island, I noticed only one monument dedicated to one individual, and it was not to the queen, it was to Johnny Barnes (1923–2016), still alive at the time. This man had made a profound difference in the entire population. Even tourists came from other countries to learn about Johnny Barnes. He was known as Mr. Happy Man. They even made a movie about him.

Johnny Barnes was a faithful Seventh-day Adventist.[8] He was baptized decades ago and began a daily habit of communing with God starting at about three o'clock in the morning. One morning, he was impressed to share with others in his island country the love he received daily from Jesus. So he went to the Crow Lane Roundabout, the busiest intersection on the island, and began wishing all drivers and passersby blessings. He shouted, "I love you! God loves you!" while waving and blowing kisses to them, with a smile. At first, drivers must have thought it very odd to see a man do that. What a strange sight! Look at that silly man on the intersection! But Johnny Barnes kept coming. He came day after day, week after week, year after year, for almost thirty years. He was always at the same spot, from five to ten o'clock in the morning, rain or shine.

During all those years, he was forced to miss only a few times due to ill health. When that happened, the radio stations were flooded with callers asking, "Where is Johnny?" One time, he took sick and was rushed to the hospital. When large corporations on the island learned of it, they fought with each other to take care of his hospital bill. He was too valuable a national asset to lose. I read online about a lady who was sick in bed but decided to go to work because that's the only way she could hear Johnny Barnes tell her that God loved her. Another day, a woman was driven by her husband to the hospital to deliver their first baby. When they came to the roundabout, Brother Johnny was looking in a different direction, and she missed his greetings. She made her husband turn around so she could hear Johnny Barnes wish her a blessing from God. When he did, she felt all would be OK with the baby.

The first words Johnny said to me when I visited him in that busy spot was, "You are a pastor, aren't you? You know, Pastor, Jesus is coming real soon!" Being himself connected with Jesus, he sought to connect the world with Him.

Johnny Barnes did not think of a silly strategy in order to reach his world. He wanted to reach others with love, even if the strategy was uncommon and unorthodox. And what a difference he has made! If you Google "Johnny Barnes," you will find scores of comments about lives changed because Johnny was at that crossroads morning by morning. The strategy was very simple, but he stuck to it. And God blessed.

Those who engage in faithful praying and prayer walking for our cities and our neighborhoods may also make a big difference—even if the strategy seems too simple and even silly.

Questions for Group Discussion or Personal Reflection

1. Imagine yourself being among the Israelites who walked around the fortress city of Jericho and seeing its massive walls fall down. What are your thoughts?

2. What challenges to know and respond to the gospel do people in your city or community face?

3. Are you surprised by the implication in Ephesians 6:10–20 and Matthew 16:18 that it is the church that is on the offensive to breach Satan's city of despair?

4. What do you think about Johnny Barnes's strategy to reach others?

5. How do you think prayer walking around your city or community might make a difference?

---

1. Some of the evidence I note here. First, carbon-14 samples taken from the destruction site are dated to about 1410 BC, agreeing with the time the Bible indicates Jericho fell. Second, it is clear the city was strongly fortified. Third, it was attacked in the springtime, after the harvest (Joshua 2:6; 3:15). Fourth, the siege was short, unlike most in ancient Near East warfare (Joshua 6:15, 20). Fifth, the walls of the city were leveled (verse 20), most likely by a God-induced

earthquake. Sixth, the city was completely burned (verse 24), as evidenced by a three-foot layer of ash. And seventh, after the destruction, Jericho was left unoccupied for centuries, as predicted by Joshua himself (verse 26; 1 Kings 16:34). These can be found in the notes made on Joshua 6 in the *Andrews Study Bible: New King James Version* (Berrien Springs, MI: Andrews University Press, 2010), 270. See also Orley Berg, *Treasures in the Sand: What Archaeology Tells Us About the Bible* (Boise, ID: Pacific Press®, 1993), 128, 129.

2. According to the Old Testament scholar Richard S. Hess, "The outcome of a leader's first 'campaign' was considered important in the Ancient Near East. . . . It was considered essential in establishing leadership." See his *Joshua: An Introduction and Commentary*, Tyndale Old Testament Commentaries (Downers' Grove, IL: InterVarsity, 1996), 136.

3. See United Nations Population Fund, *State of World Population 2007* (N.p.: UNFPA, 2007), 1, http://www.unfpa.org/sites/default/files/pub-pdf/695_filename_sowp2007_eng.pdf.

4. Michael L. Ryan and Jerry Page, *It's Time: Voices From the Front Line of Urban Mission*, ed. Bettina Krause (Silver Spring, MD: Missions to the Cities Committee, 2015), 9, 10.

5. Ellen G. White, *The Ministry of Healing* (Washington, DC: Review and Herald®, 1905), 143.

6. I am not advocating here what some Charismatic and Evangelical groups call prayer "to bind the demons" that control a city. The Bible doesn't give us that command. What is clear is that we must intercede for others in the clutches of the evil one, asking for the Holy Spirit to free them and help them see their need for Jesus as their Savior and Lord.

7. For example, Steve Hawthorne and Graham Kendrick, *Prayerwalking: Praying On-Site With Insight* (Orlando, FL: Creation House, 1993); C. Thomas Wright, *Taking Prayer to the Streets* (Alpharetta, GA: North American Mission Board, 1999); Rick Shepherd, *Prayer-Walking: What Is It? How Does It Work?* (Jacksonville, FL: Florida Baptist Convention, 2000); Randy Sprinkle, *Follow Me: Lessons for Becoming a Prayerwalker* (Birmingham: New Hope Publishers, 2001); and Dan Crawford and Calvin Miller, *Prayer Walking* (Chattanooga, TN: AMG Publishers, 2002). Some of these resources focused more exclusively on warfare prayer, such as Cindy Jacobs, *Possessing the Gates of the Enemy: A Training Manual for Militant Intercession* (Grand Rapids, MI: Chosen Books, 1991); Tom White, *Breaking Strongholds: How Spiritual Warfare Sets Captives Free* (Ann Arbor, MI: Vine Books, 1993); and Clinton E. Arnold, *3 Crucial Questions About Spiritual Warfare* (Grand Rapids, MI: Baker Academic, 1997). Again, we must be careful about our motives and scope as we pray for the lost. Not all these books mentioned express clear biblical theology, but in general, they should be helpful.

8. See *Wikipedia*, s.v. "Johnny Barnes," last modified June 30, 2020, https://en.wikipedia.org/wiki/Johnny_Barnes. The influential London *Telegraph* newspaper, in a 2001 story done about Barnes, said he was "a devoted Seventh-day Adventist." See also Sarah Lagan, " 'Mr. Happy' Barnes Dies at 93," *Royal Gazette*, July 11, 2016, http://www.royalgazette.com/news/article/20160711/mr-happy-barnes-dies-at-93, and "The Legacy of Johnny Barnes," Hope Heals, December 6, 2016, http://hope-heals.org/2016/12/06/the-legacy-of-johnny-barnes/.

CHAPTER 3

In the Name of Jesus

G reg Pruett, a long-time missionary and Bible translator in West Africa, tells the story of an unknown people group along the Niger River and how some missionaries found a way to share the gospel with them. The people had no Christians among them and no Bible in their language, and there were no prospects of missionaries being sent to their villages. They were so unknown that even their language name could not be found in any of the mission databases. Pruett learned that missionaries had ministered to that group in the 1940s, but their ministry had stopped long before when politics forced them out of the country. All that remained was a small church, now attended by different ethnic groups.

Not knowing how to begin, Pruett and his team decided their outreach strategy should be prayer. After one year of praying for God to open doors among this unknown people group, an African missionary showed up in town to show the film *Jesus*, the script of which is taken verbatim from the Gospel of Luke. Within two years, some from this unknown ethnic group began to attend the small church. Shortly after, a Korean missionary built a boarding school nearby to reach the same people. The small group of new Christians met opposition from the local Muslim majority but remained steadfast. Later, an organization called Pioneer Bible Translators sent a family to the village to translate the Scripture to the group's language. Today, there are Christians from this particular ethnic group in several villages. Pruett writes: "For two thousand years this people group remained virtually unaffected by the gospel and largely unknown to the church at large. Then everything changed—not because we came up with a brilliant strategy but because we made prayer *the* strategy."[1]

When you look closely at the words and deeds of Jesus in the Gospels, you can't help but marvel at His efforts to teach His disciples that the prayer of faith will move the hand of God.

Several prayer promises in the Bible, most of them made by Jesus, defy logic. Here is a table of them, in sequential order:

No.	Reference	Promise Summary	Speaker
1	Matthew 7:7–11; Luke 11:9–13	Ask, and you will receive, for everyone who asks receives.	Jesus
2	Matthew 18:19	If two of you agree on anything you ask, My Father will do it.	Jesus
3	Matthew 21:22; Mark 11:24	If you believe, you'll receive whatever you asked in prayer.	Jesus
4	John 14:13	I will do whatever you ask in My name for the Father's glory.	Jesus
5	John 14:14	If you ask for anything in My name, I will do it.	Jesus
6	John 15:7	If you abide in Me and My words abide in you, ask whatever you wish, and it will be granted you.	Jesus
7	John 15:16	I chose you to bear much fruit, and the Father will give you whatever you ask in My name.	Jesus
8	John 16:23, 24	If you ask the Father for anything in My name, He'll give it to you. Until now, you have asked for nothing in My name.	Jesus
9	1 John 3:21, 22	If we have confidence in God, whatever we ask, we'll receive from Him because we keep His commandments.	John
10	1 John 5:14, 15	If we ask according to His will, and we know God hears us, we have confidence we'll have the requests made to Him.	John

These are, without a doubt, astonishing promises—every one of them! They would be astonishing if some powerful general or a deeply respected spiritual leader were to have made them, but they're even more so when we realize the King of kings and the Creator of the universe made most of these promises. Because He does not lie—it is impossible for Him to do so (Hebrews 6:18; John 14:6)—we are left to either believe these promises at face value or discard them altogether.

Let's analyze these texts more closely. A careful reading reveals five components to these promises: authority, access, scope, conditions, and certainty. We will review the first two in this chapter and the rest in the following chapters.

Authority: In the name of Jesus

Half of the promises listed above were given in one night when Jesus met with His disciples to celebrate His last Passover on earth. In four of these, Jesus speaks about praying "in My name." Praying in the name of Jesus is praying based on His merits, His reputation, and with His authority. Jesus came to this world in His Father's name (John 5:43; 10:25) but returned to heaven as the representative of humanity before God (1 John 2:1; Hebrews 7:25). Jesus is the One who paid for the sin of the world on the cross to provide salvation for all (1 Timothy 2:1–4). He is the One who is loved by the Father even more so because He gave His life for us. He said, "For this reason the Father loves Me, because I lay down My life" (John 10:17).

When we approach God in prayer, we are to do so in the name of Jesus, rather than by our own merits (or demerits, actually). Coming to the Father in Jesus' name is what grants us an immediate audience with the God of the universe (Hebrews 4:15, 16). The name of Jesus is so powerful that the Jewish leaders expressly prohibited the apostles from ministering *in His name* (Acts 4:18; 5:40). They feared that uttering Jesus' name would radically change the situation! Praying in the name of Jesus is not a mere add-on at the end of a casual prayer. Praying in Jesus' name makes mountains move (Mark 11:22–24)! "In the name of Jesus" is an infallible phrase, a powerful weapon. Every time the enemy wants to influence, intrude, or invade, all that is needed is to tell him "in the name of Jesus" to leave, and it will happen.[2] Since the name *Jesus* comes from the Hebrew *Yeshua*, which means "salvation," praying in the name of Jesus means joining in God's mission to save humanity. We take responsibility to carry on that mission in His name.

A reference to the name of Jesus is a reference to His character of love and power. When Moses begged God to show him His glory, God responded: "I will make all My goodness pass before you, and I will proclaim *the name of the Lord* before you. I will be gracious to whom I will be gracious, and I will have compassion on whom I will have compassion" (Exodus 33:19; emphasis added). This is why theologian William Barclay says that "the test of prayer is: Can I make it in the name of Jesus?"[3] We would never pray for revenge against someone who offended us or to boost our pride or to appear superior to others. We instinctively know that this is not what God is like—that He would not approve of such requests. Praying in Jesus' name is praying according to His character, in other words, consistent with His way of thinking and acting. A prayer in *His* name is a prayer with inherent authority.

Imagine being in the ancient world while two nations are at war. One nation we will call "High." The other country we will call "Low." The king of High's son—let's say his name is John—is wounded and taken captive by his enemies in Low. A peasant from Low takes pity on Prince John and cares for his wounds at great risk to his own life. In the meantime, word reaches this peasant that his own son—Tom—has been taken captive by the soldiers from High while on the battlefield. The peasant longs to go to the enemy king and appeal for the life of his son, Tom. But he is only a peasant—a "nobody" in the court of a king—and furthermore, he is an enemy of the king of High! The man would never get past the first line of enemy soldiers. He stands no chance of success.

As the peasant cares for Prince John, the young man learns of his protector's plight. He asks for pen and paper and writes a letter to his father, the king of High. He seals the letter with his royal seal and sends the man to seek an audience with his father. Upon reaching the enemy line, the peasant displays the letter with Prince John's seal. The peasant, gathering courage, says, "I come in the name of the king's son—here is his seal." The enemy lets him pass. At every checkpoint, the same thing happens, and the peasant passes through High on the authority of the prince. Upon reaching the gates of the king's city, he again shows the son's seal and is let through. At last, the man reaches the innermost court of the king. As the peasant bows before the king, he gives him Prince John's letter. The king reads his own son's shaky penmanship and learns that the man before him has cared for the prince's life. The prince then requests in his letter that Tom, the peasant's son, be delivered back to him.

What do you think that the king—a father himself—will do? The king loves his son and happily grants his son's request on behalf of this stranger. It was his son who asked for the release of Tom, not just "a nobody" from the land of the enemy. In addition, the king now loves the man before him because it was he who saved the life of the prince.

This tale illustrates what it is like to pray in Jesus' name. Jesus—like the prince in the story—has done everything needed to secure our salvation. He is the One with supreme status before our Father God. Thus, it is on Jesus' authority—in other words—*in the name of the Son*, that we can boldly approach God—the King—to present our requests. God will surely hear them. They come endorsed by His own Son. Ellen White writes, "In Christ's name His followers are to stand before God [in prayer]. Through the value of the sacrifice made for them, they are of value in the Lord's sight. Because of the imputed righteousness of Christ they are accounted precious."[4] Prayer in the name of Jesus means we have access to the throne (Hebrews 4:15, 16).

Access: A friend of Jesus

In John 15:16, we read: "Whatever you ask the Father in My name He may give you." But there is a context to this verse. Jesus assured His disciples that He loved them as much as the Father loved them (verse 9). He then instructed them to "love one another" as He had loved them (verse 12). "Greater love has no one than this, than to lay down one's life for his friends," he added. "You are My friends if you do whatever I command you. No longer do I call you servants, for a servant does not know what his master is doing; but I have called you friends, for all things that I heard from My Father I have made known to you" (verses 13–15). The word translated "servants" is the Greek *douloi*, which literally means "slaves."

To be called a slave of the king was not a disgrace. Moses approvingly called himself the Lord's slave (Deuteronomy 34:5), and so did Joshua (Joshua 24:29). David did so, too, after becoming king (Psalm 89:20). And all the New Testament writers did the same: Paul called himself the *slave* of Jesus Christ (Romans 1:1; Titus 1:1), Peter did the same (2 Peter 1:1), and so did James (James 1:1), Jude, the brother of Jesus (Jude 1), and John the revelator (Revelation 1:1). The Bible characters happily saw themselves as God's *slaves*. But Jesus here said, "No longer do I call you servants [slaves], . . . but I have called you friends" (John 15:15).

When we come to God with our petitions, He doesn't view us as strangers, for we come in the name of Jesus, the Son of the King and our Friend. Ancient kings associated with a select group of people who were known to the court as "friends of the king." The king would often consult with them before consulting with his generals or his heads of state. These were people he trusted. They had access to the king at all times, even to his bedchamber early in the mornings. They had the ear of the king. Being a friend of the king had immense privileges.[5]

In the Bible, Abraham was called "the friend of God" (James 2:23). What I find interesting in relation to our topic is that Abraham was a first-rate intercessor, saving Lot and his daughters from the destruction of Sodom and Gomorrah (Genesis 18:16–32; 19:1–29). And God promised to give him the land—everywhere he had set his foot. God said to him: "Arise, *walk in the land* through its length and its width, for I give it to you" (Genesis 13:17; emphasis added).

We, through Jesus, are the friends of the King. We have His ear. He is eager to listen to us and grant us any favor that aligns with His Son's character. We have intimate access to God, in Jesus Christ! Despite this, we often pray as if we are strangers to God—as if He doesn't know who we are.

Even the early church was surprised when God answered prayer. When Peter was taken to jail and sentenced to die, the church in the house of Mary prayed earnestly for his deliverance. "The entire church engaged in fasting and prayer."[6] The execution was delayed until after Passover, and the believers could have found hope that their prayers were being heard. They continued praying the whole night before the day of the execution. Remember what happened? Peter was visited by an angel who unshackled him and led him past sixteen guards, unseen. Once free, Peter went to the very house church where the members were praying for him. The girl who saw him at the door announced Peter's arrival, but those who were praying did not believe her (Acts 12:1–16)! How is it that we continue to be similarly surprised when God answers our own prayers? We are friends of His Son, after all! Shouldn't we expect God to mercifully answer our prayers?

On the Day of Pentecost, three thousand were baptized in the name of Jesus (Acts 2:41). Days later, a paralytic was healed in the name of Jesus (Acts 3:6; 4:10). Paul became a champion of the gospel because he preached in the name of Jesus (Acts 9:26, 27). He cast out a demon from a woman used by Satan to derail his ministry and did it in the name of Jesus (Acts 16:16–18). Anointing for the sick should be made in the name of Jesus (James 5:13–15). At the end of time, when sin and sinners will be revealed before the universe, every knee, even that of His archenemy Satan, will bow at the name of Jesus (Philippians 2:9–11). And whoever will call on the name of Jesus will be saved (Romans 10:13)!

There is power—much, much power—in the name of Jesus!

Questions for Group Discussion or Personal Reflection

1. What are your thoughts when you see the prayer promises listed in the table in this chapter?

2. Do you have any insight or further thoughts about what it may mean to pray "in the name of Jesus"?

3. In what way does the story of Prince John and his letter on behalf of the peasant's captured son reveal something about God and His ways?

4. What does it mean to you that Jesus would call us His friends even though we would be happy to be known as His faithful servants (slaves)?

5. Discuss the implications of being "a friend of the King."

6. Why, do you think, was Abraham called God's friend?

---

1. Greg Pruett, *Extreme Prayer: The Impossible Prayers God Promises to Answer* (Carol Stream, IL: Tyndale Momentum, 2014), 15–19; emphasis in the original.

2. I should give credit for this thought to Bernard M. Lall, *Prayer: Heaven's Unlimited Power at Our Disposal* (Berrien Springs, MI: Geetanjali Publishers, 1987), 26.

3. William Barclay, *The Gospel of John*, vol. 2, The Daily Study Bible Series, rev. ed. (Philadelphia, PA: The Westminster Press, 1975), 165.

4. Ellen G. White, *The Desire of Ages* (Battle Creek, MI: Review and Herald®, 1898), 667.

5. Barclay, *Gospel of John*, vol. 2, 177, 178.

6. Ellen G. White, *The Acts of the Apostles* (Washington, DC: Review and Herald®, 1911), 144.

Chapter 4

Ask for Anything?

Asking in the name of Jesus involves a lot of power. As we submit our requests before Almighty God for Him to carry out, He graciously allows us to share in His power. I imagine asking in the name of Jesus as akin to the act of creation—yes, the creation of the universe. That supercharged Word of God who created billions of galaxies in an explosion of matter, atoms, energy, and light so long ago—that was done in the name of Jesus (Colossians 1:16). "By the word of the LORD the heavens were made. . . . For He spoke, and it was done; He commanded, and it stood fast" (Psalm 33:6, 9). That is the magnitude of power available to believers when we pray in His name.

In the previous chapter, we examined two components of what it means to pray in the name of Jesus—authority and access. In this chapter, we will study two more.

Scope: Ask for anything

Perhaps the aspect of Jesus' promises about prayer that we find most difficult to believe is the fact that He encourages us to ask for *anything*. Another unlikely word He uses is *whatever*, as in "whatever you ask in My name, that I will do. . . . If you ask anything in My name, I will do it" (John 14:13, 14). Or "I chose you and appointed you that you should go and bear fruit, and that your fruit should remain, that whatever you ask the Father in My name He may give you" (John 15:16). These are amazing promises.

When we ask for little, it is a sign that we believe our God is too small to help with anything bigger. Yet, according to Jesus, not even the sky is the limit. It is merely a reference point, as it were, on the way to how high we could go. The promises in John chapters 14 to 16 about the apparently infinite scope of our petitions to God are based on a statement Jesus made in the verse just before He mentioned prayer. He said: "Most assuredly, I say to you, he who believes in Me, the works that I do he will do also; and greater works than these he will do, because I go to My Father" (John 14:12). Jesus healed the sick, cast out demons, and raised the dead. We will do greater works than these?

Greater works. Greater in scope, since we're dealing with the prayers of the entire body of believers and not of just one Man. This was demonstrated by the early New Testament church. Peter and John healed a man disabled from birth (Acts 3:1–10). Paul cast out demons and healed the sick (Acts 16:16–18; 19:11, 12), and both Peter and Paul raised the dead, just like Jesus had (Acts 9:36–42; 20:7–12). "Through the hands of the apostles many signs and wonders were done among the people" (Acts 5:12). And not only through the apostles: "And Stephen, full of faith and power, did great wonders and signs among the people" (Acts 6:8). Likewise, "Philip went down to the city of Samaria and preached Christ to them. And the multitudes with one accord heeded the things spoken by Philip, hearing and seeing the miracles which he did. For unclean spirits, crying with a loud voice, came out of many who were possessed; and many who were paralyzed and lame were healed. And there was great joy in that city" (Acts 8:5–8). Greater works, indeed!

Recently, I came across a remarkable story of God's power through prayer. Bob Hunter was a government operative living in Washington, DC. He was a new Christian and was trying to understand some of the extravagant promises made by Jesus in the Bible. One day, he asked his friend Doug Coe,[1] "Doug, do you really believe what the Bible says about moving mountains when we pray?" His friend thought for a moment and answered, "Sure." He added that the statement needed to be taken in the context of everything else the Bible said about prayer, but that, yes, moving mountains was also what God could do in answer to prayer.

Bob decided he should pray about something big. He decided to pray for Africa. Doug suggested to maybe start with one country instead of a whole continent! So Bob chose Uganda. To encourage his new Christian friend, Doug made it even more interesting. He said: "I'll wager a bet with you. Pray forty-five days for Uganda—you can't miss a single day—and at the end of forty-five days, you'll be the judge of whether something significant has happened in the country. If something significant happens, you pay me five hundred dollars. But if you don't think anything big has happened in Uganda while you prayed for six weeks, you just tell me, and I'll give you five hundred dollars, no questions asked."

Bob accepted the terms and prayed every day: "God, help Africa. Help Uganda!" Remember, he was a new Christian. His prayers were simple but full of faith. As the story goes, on day thirty-two, he was attending a large dinner in Washington and sat next to an elderly woman. He found out she lived in Uganda and ran an orphanage there. Bob began asking her many questions about Uganda and her ministry. She finally asked him why he was so interested in Uganda, to which he responded, with some embarrassment, with the story of the Bible text and his friend's bet. The woman ended up inviting him to visit the orphanage, and he accepted.

Bob's heart was touched by the plight of the orphans in Uganda. When he returned home, he couldn't remove from his mind the need he saw for basic health care. He started making contacts with pharmaceutical companies and managed to coordinate the shipping of over a million dollars' worth of medical supplies to Uganda. The woman from the orphanage called to thank him and asked if he could come again for a special appreciation ceremony. In the meantime, the Ugandan president heard of the kind deed done for the orphanage, and he invited Bob to visit him. The president invited him for a ride around the city. Along the way, Bob noticed a stockyard full of men who appeared to be living in deplorable conditions. He was told they were political prisoners. Bob's reaction was spontaneous and from the heart: "That's a bad idea. You have to let them out. It's not right that human beings would have to live in those conditions."

A week after Bob Hunter returned home, he received another phone call, this time from the US State Department. They were thanking him on behalf of the United States government. The political prisoners he had seen a few days before were released, something the American government had urged Uganda to do for years, yet without success. Several months later, the Ugandan president asked Bob to go over and pray for him as he formed a new government. He wanted God's guidance in the process, and he wanted Bob to be there.[2]

Would that be considered something significant as an answer to prayer? I'd say yes! Influencing a nation's president and impacting the most powerful foreign ministry in the world is significant! I supposed Doug had no choice but to pay Bob the $500. This all happened because a man decided to pray for anything, no matter how big it was—a whole country—as if there was no limit to what God could do. Indeed, there was no limit to what God did do.

In the same way, there is no limit to what the church of God can accomplish by approaching Him in the name of Jesus. This means His promises regarding "anything" or "whatever" are not an invitation for indulgent prayers. We must pray according to *God's will* and with the intent of accomplishing *His purposes* on Earth. "The prayers of the disciples will be heard because the faithful petitioners belong to Christ, and, being united with him, offer only such prayers as are agreeable to him, the formal mention of his name proceeding from a real correspondence with him."[3]

Certainty: You will receive!

Another factor of Jesus' promises is the certainty we can have about receiving answers to our prayers. Read these promises again: "Ask, and it will be given to you; seek, and you will find; knock, and it will be opened to you. For everyone who asks receives, and he who seeks finds, and to him who knocks it will be opened" (Matthew 7:7, 8). Jesus assures us that *everyone* who asks—in faith, in accordance with His will—*will* receive! This promise is not reserved for the spiritually elite or the theologically profound; it is for *all* who will ask.

Every text in our list speaks of certainty. "Whatever you ask in My name, that I will do. . . . Anything . . . I will do it" (John 14:13, 14). "You will ask what you desire, and it shall be done for you" (John 15:7). "Whatever you ask the Father in My name He may give you" (verse 16). In other words, He's capable of giving it to you. "Ask, and you will receive, that your joy may be full" (John 16:24). None of these promises reveal any hesitation on the part of Jesus. He most certainly promises everything will be ours for the asking!

My personal favorite is this one: "Again I say to you that if two of you agree on earth concerning anything that they ask, *it will be done* for them by My Father in heaven. For where two or three are gathered together in My name, I am there in the midst of them" (Matthew 18:19, 20; emphasis added). Notice that Jesus starts by saying, "Again I say to you." Obviously, He had mentioned this before, but perhaps the promise was so amazing that His disciples had a hard time believing it. He needed to repeat His promise.

This next one defies belief: "Therefore I say to you, whatever things you ask when you pray, believe that you receive them, and you will have them" (Mark 11:24). Most people read this text and shake their heads, concluding this cannot possibly mean what it says. Some readers believe this is hyperbole, a way of saying something symbolically, but that we cannot take literally. However, when we look at the context of this statement, we realize Jesus is responding to the fact that He cursed a literal fig tree, and it actually withered! That is why He went on to say: "Have faith in God. For assuredly, I say to you, whoever says to this mountain, 'Be removed and be cast into the sea,' and does not doubt in his heart, but believes that those things he says will be done, he will have whatever he says" (verses 22, 23). Was Jesus speaking of an imaginary mountain? Many assume so. They think that Jesus must have been speaking of personal problems as "mountains" that needed to be removed. However, when He spoke those words, He was standing on a literal mountain, in Jerusalem, and was surrounded by other mountains!

Now, let's not forget that faith and praying for God's will with a surrendered heart are the conditions for receiving answers to such extravagant prayers. We will review those in the next chapter. But if those conditions are met, what Jesus is saying is that anything and everything is possible. Was it not possible for Joshua through prayer to stop the sun from setting until he finished the battle of the Lord (Joshua 10:12–14)? In terms of raw physics and astronomy, what Joshua prayed for was literally impossible to answer without causing a catastrophe on Earth and even in the entire solar system. Nevertheless, it happened, literally! The emphasis of Jesus in this text (Mark 11:24) is to believe—to count on the answer as soon as you make the petition. Live as having received the answer at the time the petition to God is offered! "Whatever gift He promises," writes Ellen White, "is in the promise itself. . . . As surely as the oak is in the acorn, so surely is the gift of God in His promise. If we receive the promise, we have the gift."[4]

We must remember two things when we consider claiming God's promises. The first one is that the context of these promises is that all have to do with the work of God in the world. These promises relate to the church's mission to reach a dying world. We cannot apply these wonderful promises for personal gain. For example, God is not likely to answer a prayer that says, "God, I wish You would put a stack of chewing gum packages around the corner for me to take home," unless that request has something to do with the fulfillment of the Great Commission! "He [Jesus] promised to answer certain kinds of prayers, including the ones that match His plans for the world."[5]

The second thing to remember is to pray *specific* prayers. When Jesus gave the model prayer, it was composed of specifics (Matthew 6:9–13). When He told His church what to pray for, He referred to specific things, such as prayer for those who persecute us (Matthew 5:43, 44), prayer to not fall into temptation (Mark 14:38), prayer to receive the Holy Spirit (Luke 11:9–13), or prayer for more laborers to be involved in God's mission (Matthew 9:36–38).

When it comes to the mission of God in the world, we in the church often pray general prayers. "Bless the missionaries," we say, or "May many come to know You," we pray. Praying general prayers may feel like the safe thing to do because no one can prove that the prayer was not answered! Somewhere in the world, some missionary was surely blessed, and some came to know Christ, but we have no idea who.

This kind of praying is not really thinking from God's perspective but from our own. Praying such general prayers hinders our own faith in God. We expect less and less from Him. And since the prayer is so general, we soon forget what we prayed, or worse, we don't bother to look for an answer. So instead of praying for evangelism to be done in our church, we should pray for fifty people to come out to our evangelistic training seminar or for fifteen people to make the decision to be baptized and become His disciples. Then we will know whether God is truly answering prayer.[6]

Questions for Group Discussion or Personal Reflection

1. Discuss the statement on the first page of this chapter that says, "When we ask for little, it is a sign that we believe our God is too small to help with anything bigger." How often do you think this is true?

2. What did you think about Bob's story of praying for Uganda?

3. Reflect on the seemingly preposterous promises by Jesus in John 14:13, 14; 15:7, 16; and Matthew 18:19, 20. What do you think about them?

4. Why did Joshua command, by the authority of God, the sun to stand still until the battle was completed?

5. What two things must we remember when we consider claiming God's promises?

---

1. Douglas Evans Coe is one of the key leaders of a Christian organization called The Fellowship. They network with politicians and other leaders to encourage Christian values in their lives and work. The Fellowship organizes the well-known annual National Prayer Breakfast event, which has been attended by many senators, congressional representatives, businesspeople, and every US president since Dwight Eisenhower. In 2005, Coe was named one of the twenty-five most influential Evangelicals in the United States by *Time* magazine. See Wikipedia, s.v. "Douglas Coe," last modified March 26, 2020, https://en.wikipedia.org/wiki/Douglas_Coe.

2. My account is based on Doug Nichols, "Uganda, a Bet, and a Prayer," Eternal Perspective Ministries, March 16, 1998, https://www.epm.org/resources/1998/Mar/16/uganda-bet-and-prayer/. Another version is found in John Ortberg's *If You Want to Walk on Water, You've Got to Get Out of the Boat* (Grand Rapids, MI: Zondervan, 2001), 91–93. In Ortberg's book, the country is Kenya. As it turned out, Bob Hunter established key relationships over the years with top leaders in Uganda, Kenya, and South Africa.

3. Daniel B. Stevick, *Jesus and His Own: A Commentary on John 13–17* (Grand Rapids, MI: William B. Eerdmans, 2011), 138.

4. Ellen G. White, *Education* (Washington, DC: Review and Herald®, 1903), 253.

5. Greg Pruett, *Extreme Prayer: The Impossible Prayers God Promises to Answer* (Carol Stream, IL: Tyndale Momentum, 2014), 24.

6. I'm indebted to Greg Pruett for some of these thoughts. See his *Extreme Prayer*, 71–74.

CHAPTER 5

Conditions for the "Anything" Prayer

G od governs the universe by the law of self-renouncing love.[1] When sin entered the world, it broke the symbiotic union humans had with God (Isaiah 59:2), turning them into self-centered beings. This triggered the plan the Godhead had devised "before the foundation of the world" (1 Peter 1:20)—the plan to send God's Son to live the perfect life Adam had failed to live and to die the second death that Adam and the rest of humanity had rightfully earned (Romans 6:23; Genesis 3:15). In the meantime, God's infinite love and wisdom created an avenue whereby we could come back to Him in spite of sin—a lifeline between Him and us: it's called prayer. But because we live in a war, a great conflict between good and evil, there are conditions to answered prayer; otherwise, Satan would accuse God of being capricious and discriminatory.

In this chapter, let's wrestle with some of the conditions articulated in God's prayer promises. Notice that seven of the ten marvelous promises in the table in the third chapter include the word *if*. First, "If you ask anything" (John 14:14). In other words, if we believe God can actually give us anything, no matter how difficult, unlikely, or impossible it seems, we must ask! Second, "if you ask for anything *in My name*" (John 16:23, 24; emphasis added), which is something we've already discussed. These two conditions are fairly obvious—the next few call for more intentional reflection.

Faith

The third condition for seeing these promises fulfilled is faith. Jesus said, "I say to you, whatever things you ask when you pray, believe that you receive them, and you will have them" (Mark 11:24). Prayer simply does not work without faith. Faithless prayer is not prayer that can reach God. Faithless prayers turn into complaints or petitions that find no Listener since the basic condition for prayer to connect with God is trust in Him. It would be like sending an email message to an address we already know does not exist. Lost in cyberspace, it may not even return to you. We don't want that to happen with our prayers. This is very clear in the Bible. "Without faith it is impossible to please Him, for *he who comes to God must believe* that He is, and that He is a rewarder of those who diligently seek Him" (Hebrews 11:6; emphasis added).

Andrew van der Bijl—known to many as Brother Andrew—was well-known in Christian circles a few years ago for leading a ministry that smuggled Bibles behind the Iron Curtain during the days of Soviet Communism. One time, several ministry teams were caught by the East German authorities, who confiscated thousands of Bibles. Brother Andrew couldn't understand why God would let them down like this when He had so consistently made it miraculously possible to get the Bibles through. He prayed and prayed for an answer, but the answer never came. Even though he stopped praying for an explanation, he still trusted that God would one day sort it all out for him. Many years later, only months after the Berlin Wall had fallen, he read in the newspaper that the East German secret police had been storing all the Russian Bibles they had taken from his ministry and had now shipped them to Christian churches in Russia! Twenty thousand Bibles were sent to Russia. Not one was lost.[2]

Faith needs to be faith in God whether or not we are able to see the results we expect; otherwise, it would be faith in *things*, not in *God*. Sometimes Christians pray broad, hesitant prayers because their faith is so fragile that it might dissolve if they learned a specific prayer was not answered as expected.

A well-known Bible scholar wrote not long ago: "We shouldn't go soft on that marvelous word *anything*. He said it, and He means it."[3] Yes, Jesus means what He says. And it is our immense privilege to actually believe it because we trust in Him! We will come back for more on this issue of faith and prayer in a future chapter.

Dependence

The fourth condition of prayer is dependence on God. In order to expect *anything* from Him, we must first depend on Him. Jesus said: "If you abide in Me, and My words abide in you, you will ask what you desire, and it shall be done for you" (John 15:7). Jesus was using the relationship between a vine and its branches as a metaphor. He is the Vine, and we are the branches. In order for branches to produce fruit, they are to be firmly attached—dependent—on the vine. And one way to do so is to take the words of God seriously. His words must dwell within our hearts. "The effective prayer which is addressed to God ultimately comes from God"[4]—that is, from His Word.

Years ago, I read about someone who repeated God's words back to Him with great effect. Her name was Corrie ten Boom, a Dutch woman who suffered greatly at the hands of the Nazis during World War II but who grew very strong in faith through the process. Sometimes, when serious difficulties surfaced in her postwar ministry, she would pray together with others of like heart. These remember her saying something like: "Lord! You must do something! There is no time to waste!" Then, she would tell God very specifically her petition as though speaking to a trusted friend. She held nothing back from God! Often, during these prayer sessions, she would take her Bible and find God's promises, which she read back to Him. Like a lawyer making her case before the judge, "she would lift her Bible into the air, point to the verse and say triumphantly, 'Here, Lord—read it Yourself!' "[5]

Does praying like Corrie ten Boom show lack of proper deference before Almighty God? On the contrary, her attitude of absolute confidence in God's promises showed how much she was willing to depend on Him. And that is what pleases God (Hebrews 11:6). This is not putting oneself above God. This is saying we want to follow Him, but we need Him to lead.

We must keep in mind, however, that dependence upon God also implies *persistence* before God. Ellen White made it clear that a condition for answered prayer is perseverance. It is necessary to grow in faith.[6] The need to pray persistently without obvious and quick answers is a blessing in disguise. If God were to answer like a candy machine—money in, candy out—we would give credit to our praying more than to our God. We would risk conceit and spiritual arrogance. Waiting on Him helps us with humility.[7] So, as we depend on God, we must also trust His timing.

According to His will

The fifth condition is closely connected with the fourth. God cannot grant our requests if they are against what He already knows to be detrimental to us. That would make Him a *bad* Father. He grants our requests when they are made according to His will for our good. The apostle John came to understand this well. He said: "If we ask anything according to His will, He hears us. And if we know that He hears us, whatever we ask, we know that we have the petitions that we have asked of Him" (1 John 5:14, 15). The reason we can be certain God hears our prayers and will answer them is that we pray for His stated will to be done. In the next chapter, we will explore this passage in much more detail.

Recently, I undertook a study of what the Bible expressly says is the will of God. I found at least fifteen clear statements about this. When I analyzed them,

I realized all the statements could be sorted into four major categories: God's will about our sanctification, God's will regarding choices as Christians, God's will about our salvation, and God's will regarding prayer![8] Yes, one entire category of the expressed will of God in the Bible is about our prayer life!

The apostle John wrote reassuringly about praying according to God's will: "Beloved, if our heart does not condemn us, we have confidence toward God. And whatever we ask we receive from Him, because we keep His commandments and do those things that are pleasing in His sight" (1 John 3:21, 22). He does not say whatever we ask we *might* receive from Him, but we *do* receive from Him! Why can John make such a sweeping statement? "Because we keep His commandments," he says, and because "our heart does not condemn us." In other words, if we consciously hold on to a sin we know goes against one of God's commandments, we will not pray with confidence before God. If we pray without confidence, we pray without faith. If we pray without faith, our prayers are useless. The reason is simple: our consciences remind us that there is a major barrier between God and us. It is called sin. It is like trying to love one's wife while having an affair with another woman. It won't work. Our guilt is ever with us. We are double-minded. This is why the psalmist declared: "If I regard iniquity in my heart, the Lord will not hear" (Psalm 66:18).

Unity

The last condition for obtaining *anything* in prayer and receiving *whatever* we ask is unity. The Lord said to the church, "Again I say to you that if two of you agree on earth concerning anything that they ask, it will be done for them by My Father in heaven. For where two or three are gathered together in My name, I am there in the midst of them" (Matthew 18:19, 20).

What a remarkable promise! And yet, the condition is clear: Pray together and pray in one accord. That was the challenge Jesus gave His disciples as He left this earth. He told them to stay in Jerusalem and to wait for the endowment of the Holy Spirit in order to carry out the Great Commission effectively (Luke 24:49; Acts 1:4, 8). As soon as Jesus went to heaven, His followers spent time in the temple (Luke 24:53) and "met together to present their requests to the Father in the name of Jesus. . . . In solemn awe they bowed in prayer, repeating the assurance, 'Whatsoever ye shall ask the Father in My name, He will give it you' . . . John 16:23."[9] And the Bible says, "These all continued with one accord in prayer and supplication, with the women and Mary the mother of Jesus, and with His brothers" (Acts 1:14).

It is hard to see how this group would naturally pray together. The men had sharp disagreements with one another only days before, during the Passover supper (Luke 22:24). There were male and female disciples, as well as members of the family of Jesus. The women usually prayed together but not with the men. And the brothers of Jesus had been hostile to Him and His disciples for Christ's entire ministry (John 7:2–5). They were not even mentioned among those gathered at the cross (John 19:25–27). So their conversion was very recent. How would these former critics be accepted in the circle of the disciples? And yet, there they all were, continuing "with one accord in prayer."

Getting along with one another is critical if we hope for God to answer our *anything* and *whatever* prayers. I believe this is one of the reasons God told us to pray *together*: so that we would have to deal with any differences that might separate us. "Divide and conquer" is an old military axiom that still works. And Satan has used that strategy to great effect against God's church. Paul told Timothy that his desire was to see "men pray everywhere, lifting up holy hands, *without wrath and doubting*" (1 Timothy 2:8; emphasis added). And Jesus, in the context of prayer, said that if we are not willing to forgive others, "neither will your Father forgive your trespasses" (Matthew 6:14, 15). As long as we're not united and remain unwilling to forgive one another, our *anything* and *whatever* requests will see minimal concrete answers. Greg Pruett said it well in a few words: "Jesus . . . explained that bitter grudges erect a major barrier to unified prayer. He taught that we should never stand at the altar of prayer under the shadow of broken relationships" (see Matthew 5:23, 24). "The static of ruined relationships hinders our prayers from being heard by God. If unified prayer attracts his pleasure like song, bearing a grudge strikes a sour note."[10]

Transformation by prayer

When I was a young pastor, I was transferred to an older, traditional church. The members liked each other, but somehow the church did not attract other people, and certainly, not young people. Some outsiders considered the members to be too exclusive—visitors were made to feel like outsiders. So the church was not growing. Since I didn't know what to do about the situation, I decided to focus on the three basics of the Christian life: the study of God's Word, prayer, and witnessing.

God's Word preached on Sabbath mornings began to attract younger people to the church. God became more real to them than before. Many professionals and middle-aged people also came. But the more people we had, the greater the potential for division. The older members of the congregation had a difficult time with all this new growth. One morning, I contacted all my elders and invited them to come to the church the following Monday and pray with me for the church and some struggling families. I would be there from five to seven o'clock in the morning. I thought maybe one or two might show up, but seven of the ten elders came. Praying together began to truly revolutionize the church. After a few weeks, we prayed twice a week, Mondays and Fridays. After a few more weeks, we prayed four days a week, and the deacons started coming. Then, some ladies joined us. After, maybe, three or four months, everyone in the church was invited to pray together each morning at five o'clock. Many of them came and kept coming.

The result was a revival in the church. Educated young professionals began to serve in the church and reach out to the community. They no longer offered the excuse of lack of time. Their priorities had changed. The church was full every Sabbath. We planned evangelistic outreach every year. Our elders visited all the members plus any regular visitors during a special visitation Sabbath every three months. Ministries in the church multiplied. Every six months or so, we organized a fasting and prayer weekend that lasted forty hours. What an impact that had on the congregation! Church attendance grew from one hundred to four hundred, and on some of those special prayer weekends, hundreds more participated. Giving went up so much that the tithe could have supported ten pastors. Offering for Church Expense was multiplied many times. Giving for evangelism rose fifty-two times! Small groups flourished. I remember meeting with the leaders of all the small groups every Tuesday night. We often prayed for one hour or more for people in the church. Our hearts were warmed by the Holy Spirit and by a genuine desire to advance the kingdom of God.

Almost two hundred people were baptized in less than five years. As the church grew, we planted a church in a bedroom community that today has 750 members. Even today, as I've traveled to different places, I have heard some who experienced the moving of the Spirit in those days say how much God used that praying church to change their lives.

"Greater works," Jesus said. We shall do greater works as we pray *together* in Jesus' name.

Questions for Group Discussion or Personal Reflection

1. Which of the four more detailed conditions to answering extravagant prayer requests, dealt with in this chapter, is the most difficult to meet? Why?

2. What do you think about Corrie ten Boom's approach to God in prayer?

3. Review the list from note 8 about God's will for us. Did any item surprise you or make an impression on you? Why or why not?

4. Comment on the author's description in the last part of the chapter about what happened in his church as a young pastor. How much do you think prayer had to do with those changes?

5. What will it take for something like what the author described happening in his church to happen in *your* local church?

1. Ellen G. White, *The Desire of Ages* (Battle Creek, MI: Review and Herald®, 1898), 20.

2. Brother Andrew with Susan DeVore Williams, *And God Changed His Mind . . . Because His People Dared to Ask* (Old Tappan, NJ: Chosen Books, 1990), 101.

3. Tom Wright, *John for Everyone: Part Two, Chapters 11–21* (London: SPCK, 2004), 64.

4. Daniel B. Stevick, *Jesus and His Own: A Commentary on John 13–17* (Grand Rapids, MI: William B. Eerdmans, 2011), 203.

5. The story is found in Brother Andrew and Susan DeVore Williams, *God Changed His Mind*, 88, 89.

6. Ellen G. White, *Steps to Christ* (Washington, DC: Review and Herald®, 1956), 97.

7. This point is also made by Greg Pruett, *Extreme Prayer: The Impossible Prayers God Promises to Answer* (Carol Stream, IL: Tyndale Momentum, 2014), 49.

8. Here is a more complete list of God's stated will for our lives: (1) to separate ourselves from intimacy with unbelievers (Ezra 10:11); (2) to be faithful stewards of God's given responsibilities (Luke 12:35–37, 42); (3) to have eternal life (John 6:40); (4) for all to repent (Acts 17:30); (5) to be baptized, for repentance, washing away our sins calling on the name of the Lord (Luke 7:30; Acts 22:14–16); (6) to redeem the time and be filled with the Spirit (Ephesians 5:15–19); (7) to be submissive to authority (Ephesians 6:6); (8) to abstain from sexual immorality (1 Thessalonians 4:3); (9) to rejoice always, pray without ceasing, and give thanks in everything (1 Thessalonians 5:16–18); (10) to offer prayers and supplications for all (1 Timothy 2:1–4); (11) to present our bodies as living sacrifices to God (Romans 12:1); (12) to put to silence the ignorance of foolish people by doing good (1 Peter 2:15); to no longer live in the flesh (1 Peter 4:2); (13) to be willing to suffer for Christ's sake (verse 19); and (14) to grant life to those whose sin is not yet unto death (1 John 5:14–16).

9. Ellen G. White, *The Acts of the Apostles* (Washington, DC: Review and Herald®, 1911), 35, 36.

10. Pruett, *Extreme Prayer*, 62.

CHAPTER 6

When God Hears

Many years ago, I had a prayer experience that left an indelible impression on me. I was the pastor of a fairly large and growing congregation when a godly sister in the church asked whether I had time to pray with her. It was right after the midweek prayer meeting service. Her burden was her two sons. If I remember correctly, one was twelve and the other fourteen, ready to face some of the most challenging years in a person's life.

The boys were good boys, but her fear was that successfully navigating the teen years would be a real challenge for them. She feared their love for Jesus might grow cold in view of the many temptations and distractions available to young men at that age. And so, we prayed. She prayed for a few minutes, then I prayed, then she'd pray again, and on we went. We had been praying for about forty minutes, claiming God's promises for guidance on behalf of her boys, when suddenly—I was praying at the time—she put her hand on my arm and gently said: "That's enough, Pastor. We don't need to pray anymore. I know now God has heard our prayers."

That was something I had never heard before, even though I had grown up in the church and had been a pastor for ten years by that time. Years later, I found that the Bible teaches such assurance. Let's look at it in 1 John 5.

Praying for the sinner

The apostle John wrote his first letter to the church while in his nineties. The first couple of generations of Christians had come and gone, and some strange ideas and doctrinal heresies were affecting the church. John wrote to remind Christians of the confidence they could have in the salvation that Jesus provided, of the allegiance of the Christian to God's commandments, and the confidence they could have of God's transformative work in them.[1] At the end of his first letter, he became very practical about sin (1 John 5:14–21). And he taught something very relevant to those who wish to know how to pray for the sinner.

Now this is the confidence that we have in Him, that if we ask anything according to His will, He hears us. And if we know that He hears us, whatever we ask, we know that we have the petitions that we have asked of Him.

If anyone sees his brother sinning a sin which does not lead to death, he will ask, and He will give him life for those who commit sin not leading to death. There is sin leading to death. I do not say that he should pray about that (verses 14–16).

The first two verses give the instruction, and the last verse the context. We are told to pray for those whose sin "does not lead to death" (verse 16). Don't all sins lead to eternal death? Doesn't Romans 6:23 say that "the wages of sin is death"? Yes, and no. Sins that are forgiven do not lead to death. Earlier in this same letter, John said: "If we confess our sins, He is faithful and just to forgive us our sins and to cleanse us from all unrighteousness" (1 John 1:9). And Jesus had said decades earlier that "every sin and blasphemy will be forgiven," but He added, "whoever speaks against the Holy Spirit . . . will not be forgiven" (Matthew 12:31, 32).

I met Roger Morneau some thirty years ago. He was a remarkable Seventh-day Adventist. At the age of twenty, he was a practicing Satanist, but through a series of gracious circumstances, God pulled him away from that pit of destruction.[2] The demons never forgave him and sought for years to end his life. He had many health problems, the chief of which was a diseased heart. Cardiologists hardly believed he was able to live with only 45 percent of his heart functioning properly. This heart situation caused Brother Morneau to need much rest. However, with more discretionary time at his disposal, he had the opportunity to develop a prayer ministry that involved praying for over two thousand people around the world. This was a man who believed in prayer.

Morneau wrote three powerful books on God's answers to his prayers. One of my favorite stories has to do with Henry. Henry was a thirty-two-year-old who, since age twenty, had apparently lost his mental faculties due to heavy drug use. The son of a faithful Adventist couple, he spent most days silently smoking and staring at a wall. Occasionally, he would violently strike his face, arms, or legs until he turned black and blue. At other times, he would explode into a livid rage, yelling that no one should speak to him. Obviously, this behavior was due to demon oppression. He let his hair grow to the middle of his back and allowed no one to touch it. Most of the time, he couldn't recognize his parents, and his speech was unintelligible. Medical science was unable to help. The parents were at a complete loss about how to help him.

One day, Henry's mother read one of Morneau's books and managed to locate him and connect with him by phone. She described the desperate situation of her son and pleaded for Morneau to help them pray for him. Morneau encouraged her and repeated some wonderful promises about God's ability to do the impossible. A few months later, Henry's speech became clearer, and he requested a haircut. A few months after that, he stopped smoking, and he did so overnight. His mind began to function better and better. However, the devil would not give up so easily.

One day, out of the blue, Henry became extremely violent and threatened to kill his father. His parents had to call the police and take their son to a mental institution. His mother was just heartbroken. She was devastated by what happened, especially after such good signs of improvement had taken place in Henry's life. She was ready to give up hope. What became clear to Morneau is that the forces of darkness would not give up Henry without a mighty struggle. But only days later, Henry woke up in that mental institution completely lucid and healthy, and he couldn't remember anything about the past twelve years of his life! He loved his parents. He visited old friends. He was a new man.[3]

Jesus said, "Every sin and blasphemy will be forgiven," and forgiveness brings healing (James 5:15, 16). God listened to the prayers of Brother Morneau and Henry's parents to forgive Henry's sins, even if he was unable to request it himself!

One thing that Morneau discovered, after many years of feeding on God's Word and the Spirit of Prophecy while praying for others, was the role of forgiveness and the Holy Spirit. Consistently, he prayed for others asking God to apply the merits of the shed blood of Christ for the forgiveness of their sins and for the power of the Holy Spirit to give people a new life.

Anything can be forgiven as long as it can be confessed (1 John 1:9). The problem is with this other sin against the Holy Spirit; that is, the persistent sin people engage in, which is not confessed and that the person does not want to give up. *That* sin, the sin against the Holy Spirit, will not be forgiven. Why? Because the person has turned deaf ears to the voice of the Spirit on that particular sin. God can no longer influence the person for good. It is not God who is unwilling to continue working with the sinner; it is that the sinner has for so long ignored the counsel of God that he has become immune to the Holy Spirit.

This dynamic is illustrated by what happened to me when we moved from a California church to teach at a university in the American south. We secured a temporary apartment near the school, but it was also close to a train crossing.

The first morning train crossed at five o'clock in the morning. In the United States, trains must blow their loud whistles as they approach a crossing. You can hear them from very far away. On our first night there, while all was quiet and I was asleep, suddenly, the train blew its whistle as it passed by at five o'clock. Being a very light sleeper, I immediately woke up, my heart racing, alarmed that something was going to run over our house! The next morning, the same thing happened. Not being used to that loud noise at that time, it shook me up every time. You may wonder how I ever got any sleep!

It only took a few days for my subconscious mind to get used to the train blowing its whistle at five in the morning. I realized there was nothing to worry about, that it was just a train passing by, and that I could keep on sleeping. In a week or so, I didn't hear the train anymore. Was that because the train stopped coming? The train kept crossing at the same time every morning. Was it because the conductor forgot to blow the whistle? The whistle never stopped blowing while I was asleep. What changed was my subconscious expectation. I told myself I didn't need to mind that sound, and eventually, I didn't hear it anymore.

That's how the sin against the Holy Spirit operates. If we are conscious of doing wrong but continue to do it, ignoring the whisper of the Spirit to stop or to give it up to God, eventually it leads to the sin against the Holy Spirit. The sin that leads to death—or the sin, literally, *that goes toward irreversible death*[4]—is the one we hold on to, no matter how many times the Spirit convicted us we should abandon it. This is like a man swimming in a lake while holding on to a very heavy rock, his unwillingness to let it go will eventually cause him to drown.

And how do we know whether the person we wish to pray for has already committed the sin against the Holy Spirit or not? (We are told not to pray for such a person since it is already too late.) We *don't* know! That's the point: God wants us to pray for every sinner, regardless of their circumstances, since we cannot possibly know whether that person is beyond redemption.

The key to effective prayer
That's the context for the promise found in 1 John 5:14, 15. Now, let's look at the rest of it. I believe verses 14 and 15 form what Bible scholars call a *chiasm*, a structure that shows inverted parallelism.[5] The first point in the statement corresponds with—or is parallel to—the last point in the statement. The second point mirrors the next to the last point in the statement, and so on. Eventually, the climax or the main point of a given statement is found in the center of the statement. This is illustrated below:

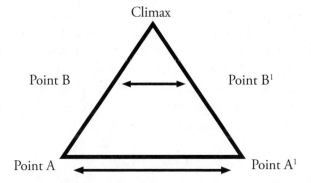

Read those two verses again. Do you see the parallelism between the first statement in verse 14 and the last in verse 15? First, "This is the confidence that we have in Him," and last, "we know that we have the petitions that we have asked of Him." So the first statement is about having confidence in God, and the last about knowing we have the petitions we made of God. Both statements are about having something. It looks like this:

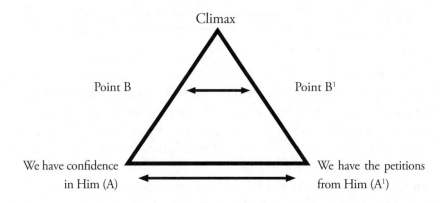

Now we'll see the next statement in verse 14 and its parallel in verse 15: "if we ask anything according to His will," and "if we know that He hears us." As you can see, these two statements are conditionals; they start with "if." The whole promise depends on these two conditions, whether we will pray according to God's will (in the context of praying for the sinner) and whether we know God has heard our prayer. The final statement, then, is the heart of this promise, and it's in the center of the statement. It simply reads: "He hears us." To "hear" means to be favorably disposed to hear, it means to hear in order to answer![6]

The apostle John wrote in very simple Greek because Hebrew was his mother tongue, not Greek. Greek was the *lingua franca* of the day, the language of government, education, business, and literature across the nations of the Roman Empire, much like English is the language today that most people learn to speak with foreigners around the world. But even though he wrote in Greek, he thought like a Jew. In Hebrew thought, the climax of an issue was always in the center, unlike in Western thought, which is always at the end.

The apostle John says, then, that *God's hearing us* is the key to our success praying for others. In our diagram, it looks like this:

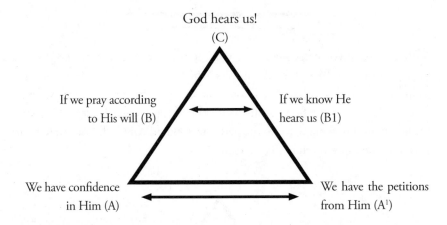

The first and last statements—that we have confidence in God and that we have the petitions we requested of Him—are so because of the marvelous power and grace of God. In other words, it is because of what God does that we have confidence in Him and we have the petitions we requested. The other two statements are up to us, the believer.[7] Have we prayed according to His will? It is always His will that people come to repentance, right? (2 Peter 3:9). Have we come to know for certain that He has heard our prayers?

When I came to understand this wonderful truth, that it is just as important to *know* that God hears our prayers as it is to *ask* according to His will, the prayer of my sister in the church so many years ago made sense. She had been praying for her sons, of course, all of their lives—and perhaps even more so when she was concerned for what was just ahead of them. But for some reason, she hadn't been absolutely certain God had heard her prayers, until that night. Think about it. If we continue asking the same thing from God *after* we are certain He has heard our prayer, those prayers are expressions of unbelief in Him, not expressions of faith. This would be the time to express thanksgiving to God for the certainty of answered prayer! If we're praying according to His will—and we know it's His will that all should repent and follow Him—we must keep praying, in faith, until we know for sure God has heard our prayer. Ellen White, speaking of teachers praying for students, said the teacher "should learn how to come to the Lord and plead with Him until he receives the assurance that his petitions are heard."[8]

We keep praying not because God is a reluctant giver but because we are reluctant to believe. When we choose to believe His mercy and His promises, we can be certain God has heard our prayers.

The prayer of faith will be answered

The servant of the Lord also had this to say about prayer:

> We must show a firm, undeviating trust in God. Often He delays to answer us in order to try our faith or test the genuineness of our desire. Having asked according to His word, we should believe His promise and press our petitions with a determination that will not be denied.
>
> God does not say, Ask once, and you shall receive. He bids us ask. Unwearyingly persist in prayer.[9]

Have you read the story of George Müller? Müller was a thief and a liar. He carried on an immoral life and constantly drank with friends. But one day, at the age of twenty, at a house meeting with other Christians, he understood why Jesus died on the cross for him and "was constrained to love Him in return." He went into ministry and pastored for a few years before he decided to live completely by faith in God. He renounced his church salary and simply prayed for God to supply all his needs.

Eventually, he began an orphanage in Bristol, England. Over seventy years of ministry, he helped care for ten thousand orphans, sponsored two hundred missionaries overseas, and paid hundreds of staff members without a sponsor or a foundation or any actual source of income. How did he raise today's equivalent of US$150 million without ever asking anyone for money? He proved God was faithful. He trusted Him implicitly for every need.

When he was thirty-nine, he began praying for five of his former partying friends to surrender to the love of Christ. He prayed every day for them. After eighteen months, the first one turned his life to Christ. He thanked God for this and continued to pray for the other four. After an additional five years, the second one became a Christian. He thanked God, and he continued to pray daily for the other three. After six more years, the third one turned to God. He thanked God again and continued to pray for the last two friends.

Decades went by, and those last two friends were not converted, even though Müller had prayed for them every day. Someone finally asked him about this. Did he still believe they would be converted? His response was, "I hope in God, I pray on, and look yet for the answer."[10]

Müller lived to be ninety-three. For fifty-four years, he had prayed daily for two of his friends. He was old now, and they were not converted. Yet, he was certain God had heard his prayers. Just before Müller died, the fourth one turned to God. And a few years later, the last one turned to God. What a joyful reunion Müller will have with these last two men when Jesus comes and raises the righteous to life!

God hears our prayers. And when God hears, He acts. Perhaps that's what the psalmist had in mind when he wrote:

I love the LORD, because He has heard
My voice and my supplications.
Because He has inclined His ear to me,
Therefore I will call upon Him as long as I live (Psalm 116:1, 2).

Questions for Group Discussion or Personal Reflection

1. What is your experience with having the certainty that God has heard your prayers?

2. Does your understanding of the unpardonable sin match what you read in this chapter? If not, how is it different?

3. What surprises you most about the story of Henry and his wonderful transformation?

4. What do you think about the idea that when God hears, it is because He intends to act?

5. Who are you praying for today that needs to come from darkness to light and from sinfulness to holiness?

6. What are some of your struggles when praying for a loved one for a long time without any apparent change?

1. See I. Howard Marshall, *The Epistles of John*, The New International Commentary on the New Testament (Grand Rapids, MI: Eerdmans, 1978), 2–8.

2. The fascinating story of Morneau's former life and marvelous conversion is found in Roger J. Morneau, *A Trip Into the Supernatural* (Hagerstown, MD: Review and Herald®, 1993).

3. Roger J. Morneau, *More Incredible Answers to Prayer* (Hagerstown, MD: Review and Herald®, 1993), 38–41.

4. In the original Greek, such sin is said to be *pros thanaton*, toward death, or whose end is death. This is why it can only be the sin against the Holy Spirit. That is, any sin that continues because we don't wish to give it up is the sin that resists the work of the Holy Spirit in our lives. See William Barclay, *The Letters of John and Jude*, The Daily Bible Study Series, rev. ed. (Philadelphia, PA: Westminster Press, 1976), 120, 121.

5. *Chiasm* comes from the New Testament Greek letter *xi*, in the shape of an X. The X represents the concept of inverted parallelism, where one end corresponds with the other end.

6. Marshall, *Epistles of John*, 244.

7. In his writings, three other times John has laid down conditions for answered prayer. In 1 John 3:22, he states that *obedience* is a condition. In the Gospel of John 15:7, he says that abiding, or *remaining in Jesus, and letting His words abide in us*, are conditions for answered prayer. And in John 14:14, *praying in His name*, as we have seen three chapters earlier, is a condition for answered prayer.

8. Ellen G. White, *Counsels to Parents, Teachers, and Students* (Washington, DC: Review and Herald®, 1913), 231.

9. Ellen G. White, *Christ's Object Lessons* (Washington, DC: Review and Herald®, 1941), 145.

10. See one of the best biographies on Müller, Roger Steer, *George Müller: Delighted in God* (Ross-shire, Great Britain: Christian Focus, 1997). His answer to the question about his two remaining friends, given at the age of seventy-five, is found on page 193.

CHAPTER 7

How to Really Pray

Melody Mason tells the story of an Adventist church in Vietnam that decided to pray for perfect strangers. Pastor Hahn, the lay pastor, led his members to fast and pray for an unreached village 150 miles (240 kilometers) away from their own. Some members had relatives there who did not know Christ. Shortly after they began praying, the aunt of one of the members, by the name of Yen, came to the town where the house church was, seeking medical care for her stomach cancer. Once there, she accepted the invitation to attend the house church. She began reading the Bible and eventually accepted Jesus as her Lord and Savior. However, her cancer got worse, and she was sent home to die.

The church continued to pray for Yen and her village. They had rejoiced at the relatively quick answer to their prayers, Yen being the first convert in that village for which they were praying. But the cruel irony was not missed on them that she would soon die. A month went by, and Yen's sister-in-law called Pastor Hahn, saying she was in her last hours. Pastor Hahn gathered the church for an emergency prayer session. They earnestly prayed while claiming Psalm 30 for her life. Their argument with God was, "If You let Yen die, who will praise Your name in this village?" There was no one else who claimed the blood of Christ in that village. After praying for two hours, they had the assurance that God had heard their prayers.

On the next day, they gathered again to pray for Yen. Pastor Hahn called to see how she was. She hadn't eaten or even sat up for two weeks. He learned that she was unconscious, barely breathing. Pastor Hahn told the caregiver that only God could save her now and gave her some instructions. She needed to get Yen's Bible, open it to Psalm 30, kneel down next to her, and read the words of the psalm, putting Yen's name in the verses. He told Yen's sister-in-law, "God is able to heal and restore her." Yen's relative said nothing. She was not a Christian and didn't know anything about what must have sounded to her like a Christian burial ritual!

Right after the phone call, however, Yen stopped breathing, and she died. Her relative began preparing her body for burial. She carefully wrapped her whole body in blankets. As she was doing this, she remembered she hadn't carried out Pastor Hahn's instructions. So she found Yen's Bible, looked up Psalm 30, and began reading the psalm placing Yen's name in it:

> "I cried out to You, O LORD;
> And to the LORD, I made supplication [for Yen]:
> 'What profit is there in [Yen's] blood,
> When [she goes] down to the pit?
> Will [her] dust praise You?
> Will it declare Your truth?
> Hear, O LORD, and have mercy on [Yen];
> LORD, be [her] helper!' " (Psalm 30:8–10).

Suddenly, while she was reading Psalm 30, Yen's relative noticed Yen's blankets moved. She stared in amazement and fear at what thirty minutes before had been the dead body of her beloved sister-in-law. Yen finally kicked the blankets off her and sat up, asking for something to eat. She had come back to life! Not only that, but she was also completely healed from her devastating cancer! This great miracle of resurrection by the simple and faith-filled prayers of people living 150 miles away made a profound impression on the people of this village. It wasn't long before more than fifty additional people joined the Seventh-day Adventist Church, establishing a new redemptive presence in that place.[1]

Prayer works. Prayer can no longer take a secondary place in the missionary plans of the church. Prayer must *be the strategy*. "We have to meet most powerful adversaries," wrote Ellen White, "and it rests with us to determine which shall win."[2] What did Pastor Hahn and his members do that is instructive to the rest of us? First, they set a God-sized goal. It was no small prayer to intercede for the population of a pagan city so far away from theirs. Second, their prayers were specific. To begin with, they prayed that people in that village would turn to the Lord, then, that Yen would turn to Jesus, and then, that she would be healed for the sake of the village. Third, they persisted in their prayers. They did not simply pray for a week, and when they saw no progress, give it all up. They kept on praying until God answered their prayers. Fourth, they prayed based on the promises of Scripture. They claimed the Bible as the source of their authority, in the name of Jesus, to have results. And last, they prayed with faith in God. They continued to pray for Yen after clear evidence that she would likely die. They sensed that God was answering their prayers and would not quit until they saw a favorable result. They believed Jesus *could* answer and that He *would* answer.

Do we know how to pray?

Most Adventists that I know of—and I have met thousands on every continent—pray little; and when they pray, they do so without living faith in our heavenly Father. And this group includes me![3] So we suffer from two deadly spiritual diseases: one is that we don't pray enough, allowing our spiritual life to slowly ebb away, and the other is that when we do pray, we seldom pray believing something will actually happen! In this narrow sense, we're worse than demons because at least demons are consciously aware of the mighty power of God to change the situation. That's why they "believe—and tremble!" (James 2:19).

Have you attended a typical Adventist midweek prayer meeting service lately? If you have, you belong to a very small minority in the church. Most Adventists seldom go to the prayer meeting, and most prayer meetings are *talking* meetings with a little prayer at the end. When we spend more time on prayer requests than on prayer, we have upended our priorities. Ellen White has warned that "cold and frozen prayers cast a chill" at prayer meetings, and that long prayers or speeches make the meeting unappealing. Prayer in public should be short and to the point unless the Spirit of God moves on someone in a special sense. She warns that many pray long prayers in public because they don't actually pray much at home, in private. "They hope to pray themselves into the favor of God."[4]

E. M. Bounds was a lawyer and a minister in the United States. He rose at four o'clock every morning to spend about three hours in private prayer. His books on prayer have become classics in the English language. "Much time spent with God is the secret to all successful praying," he wrote. "Our short prayers [in public] owe their point and efficiency to the long ones that preceded them."[5]

True, the secret of successful prayer is private prayer, but the secret to a successful church is *corporate* prayer. It is when we pray *together*, pressing before God His promises for the advancement of His work, that we can expect things to start changing. Ellen White had this to say about corporate prayer:

We are encouraged to pray for success, with the divine assurance that our prayers will be heard and answered. . . .

The promise is made on condition that the united prayers of the church are offered, and in answer to these prayers there may be expected *a power greater than that which comes in answer to private prayer.* The power given will be proportionate to the unity of the members and their love for God and for one another.[6]

Corporate prayer is not complicated. All we need to do is agree on a place and time to gather together and pray. And the prayers need to be audible for all to benefit from those who pray.[7] When the disciples met in the upper room to pray, they were "with one accord in prayer and supplication" (Acts 1:14). How would they know they were in agreement unless they heard each other pray? Obviously, they prayed audibly. These were not private prayers. Jesus said, "I say to you that if two of you agree on earth concerning anything that they ask, it will be done for them by My Father in heaven" (Matthew 18:19). For that verse to be true, those praying need to hear one another pray. Some are shy or lack experience praying in front of others. No one should feel forced to pray. However, we must remember that our prayers are as precious to God as the simple prayers of our small children are to us.

In my former church, we had a small room where we placed pillows on the floor to kneel and pray together. When I taught at Southern Adventist University, we prayed at noon each day with students and teachers in the chapel on the second floor of our building. At our division, we have been meeting voluntarily at noon every day for over two years now to pray for specific objectives, big objectives.[8] God's promise is that the power emanating from praying together will be greater than if we prayed alone.

Ellen White has written about how we should pray, in faith, for example, when we pray for the Holy Spirit. The early Adventist pioneers often referred to the Holy Spirit as "the gift" or "the blessing." This statement is lengthy but worth reading every word:

Shall not our half-hearted supplications be turned into petitions of intense desire for this great blessing [of the Holy Spirit]? We do not ask for enough of the good things God has promised. If we would reach up higher and expect more, our petitions would reveal the quickening influence that comes to every soul who asks with the full expectation of being heard and answered. The Lord is not glorified by the tame supplications which show that nothing is expected. He desires everyone who believes to approach the throne of grace with earnestness and assurance. Do we realise the magnitude of the work in which we are engaged? If we did, there would be more fervency in our prayers. Our entreaties would rise before God with convincing earnestness. We would plead for power as a hungry child pleads for bread. If we realised the greatness of the gift, if we desired the attainment of the blessing, our petitions would ascend with earnestness, importunity, urgency. It would be as if we were at the gate of heaven, soliciting entrance.

We should ask with an earnestness that will not be denied. The Lord has an intense desire that everyone should take advanced steps in absolute certainty, relying upon God. He is the light and life of all who seek Him. The measure which we receive of the holy influence of His Spirit is proportionate to the measure of our desire to receive, of our faith to grasp, and of our capacity to enjoy the great goodness of the blessing and to impart it to others.[9]

A few years ago, I read about a church north of the Arctic Circle, in Russia, where the members decided to pray together. Their winters were so cold and so long that most men who worked there lived alone, every few weeks visiting their families living in southern, more temperate climates. The Adventist church had twenty-two members, but as a result of attrition, the membership dwindled to eight: the pastor, his wife, and six other men. They recognized that they were going to become extinct unless something drastic were to happen.[10]

Since they really didn't know what to do, the men gathered together each morning to pray. They prayed for the Holy Spirit to fall on them; they prayed for the ability to lead others to Christ; they prayed for strength and zeal to do God's work. How did they make sure they remained focused and motivated? Each morning at six o'clock, they met for prayer at a fishing club, where people went ice fishing. They gathered around a fishing hole, knelt down together, and prayed for the Holy Spirit and for souls, claiming the promises of God. Then, they took their clothes off, broke the ice that had formed overnight in the fishing hole, and dunked themselves in the water, one by one!

This apparently strange behavior was for a reason. They knew that if they were expected to meet with others at the club each morning, they were more likely to do this consistently than praying alone at home. That would be too easy to ignore or forget. And getting in the water was their way of saying: "Lord, we are ready to baptize people any time You send them to us. We will not wait to go to work for You until after winter is over. We're ready now!"

And God honored their faith and commitment. Within just one year of their starting to pray like this, God brought eighty new people to the church! Imagine that, from eight to eighty, 1,000 percent growth! And over the next few years, that church planted five or six additional churches in other nearby villages. God answers corporate prayer!

Faith or failure

"Every failure on the part of the children of God is due to their lack of faith," said the servant of the Lord.[11] Every failure! So when I am impatient with my son or daughter, it is because I'm not really trusting God with them. I want to control something about their lives that seems out of control to me. Instead of turning to God to strengthen me and give me wisdom, I turn to my natural inclination. I don't need to exercise faith to do that. I just need to be myself. Or when I get discouraged because things are not going as well as they should at work, I'm not really trusting God either. Instead of holding on to the thought that God can provide solutions to our problems, I focus on the problems, which leads to more discouragement. Or when we fail in our church to boldly reach out to others because we think we don't have enough time or ability to do it, we also fail! The failure is not that we *weren't successful* in reaching out to others. The failure was in not trusting God with our time and abilities. If God's priority for our lives is to seek others for Him, we should trust that He will provide the means and the ways to do the job!

When God led the people of Israel to the Promised Land, Moses sent twelve spies to "see what the land is like: whether the people who dwell in it are strong or weak, few or many" (Numbers 13:18). God had already promised the Israelites He was *giving* them the land! He was not going to lead them through the desert, after so many miracles associated with their exodus, to either die in a foreign land or turn around and end up back in Egypt! So the conquest of the Promised Land was already an accomplished fact in the mind of God. All that was left was for Israel to claim that fact and act accordingly.

But instead of focusing on the wonderful advantages of the land God was giving them, most of the spies focused on the difficulties: the people are strong, the cities are fortified, giants live in the man-eating land (Numbers 13:28, 29, 32, 33). Caleb, on the other hand, focused on the promise of God: "Let us go up at once, and take possession" (verse 30). Were the Israelites strong enough to defeat Egypt, the largest empire on earth at the time? Of course not. But God gave them victory. Were they able to build ships and cross the Red Sea to escape their enemies? Of course not. But God made dry land *across the sea* so that Israel could cross to safety.

A matter of perspective

The difference between faith and failure is perspective. If we see our circumstances from our own perspective, we can't imagine the victory will be ours. At the time of Saul and David, all Israel was petrified with fear of the giant called Goliath. Who could possibly defeat him? He was too strong, too big, too experienced at warfare. But when a teenager by the name of David saw the situation, he didn't see it from his own perspective, like that of a lowly shepherd boy with no experience in battle. He saw the problem from God's perspective (1 Samuel 17:45–47). And God is always bigger than the biggest giants! Although David was forced to look up to the giant, he knew God was looking down on the giant. So he trusted in Him; he trusted God's perspective. He trusted that even if he didn't wear protective armor, God could defeat the giant. He trusted that God would guide his smooth rock to the place it should go. He trusted God to take the initiative and not simply wait to react to what the giant did. David lived by faith. And because he lived by faith, he was victorious.

Every world religion, outside of Christianity, is based on rituals, philosophies, and steps people take to feel accepted by the deity. Only Christianity is based on faith. Only Christians trust with all their heart a God who is real, yet whom they cannot see. That's not because they exercise blind faith but because they remember the words of God. God's promises become a greater reality than what they sense, see, or hear around them. No wonder the apostle Paul said, "Whatever is not from faith is sin" (Romans 14:23). I don't need to commit *sin* in order to sin. I only need to refrain from trusting God. What a great tragedy! Lack of trust in God is suicide in slow motion.

When my wife and I lived in Michigan, one of the coldest states in America during winter, I often had to shovel snow off my driveway before I could drive away in my car. One morning, there was close to three feet (about a meter) of snow to clear. That was a lot of hard work. In addition, it was very cold, and the sky overhead was gray. The reason I remember that day is because my wife took a picture of me slaving away with the snow shovel. But only hours later, I also took a picture, a very different picture. It showed a blue sky and warm sun over a blanket of endless, puffy, white clouds. You see, after I cleared the snow, I went to the airport to fly somewhere else. The plane went up and up until it broke through the clouds. Below the clouds, it was cold and gray. Above the clouds, it was sunny and pleasant. As Christians, we have a choice. The choice is to live according to the circumstances that surround us—cold and gray—or to live according to the promises God gives us—sunny and pleasant. We might live below the clouds, but we can imagine ourselves above the clouds. We don't need to believe in God to live miserable lives, full of discouragement. But we do need to believe in Him, *in His view of reality,* to have victory over our senses.

Are we listening to our feelings, or are we listening to God? Martyn Lloyd-Jones was a British preacher who understood this struggle. He said, "Have you realized that most of your unhappiness in life is due to the fact that you are listening to yourself instead of talking to yourself?"[12] His point was that we should not listen to our feelings but rather that we should tell ourselves to focus on God's facts! Believe His promises. Count on them. "When the enemy seeks to enshroud the soul with darkness," wrote Ellen White, "sing faith and talk faith, and you will find that you have sung and talked yourself into the light."[13] She once wrote to a leader in the church and recommended: "Let us talk faith and act faith, and we will have faith."[14]

As we look at the immense cities of the world, full of busy people who have no knowledge of the God of heaven, we can become discouraged by the enormity of the task. How can we reach these people? Not even billions of dollars and thousands of full-time workers could make much of a difference in a world that is so secular and bent on self-destruction. But we must not forget that God did not hesitate to give us the Great Commission, nor did He make a mistake. God does not regret giving us such an enormous task because He knows that the impossible for us is possible for Him (Luke 18:27). All we need to do is march on in faith, not thinking about what won't work, not looking at the task from our human perspective, but believing that, for God, our great challenges are like small change.

The exercise of faith

One of my favorite Jesus stories tells of what happened the morning after the extraordinary events on the Mount of Transfiguration (Matthew 17:14–21; Mark 9:14–29; Luke 9:37–43). As Jesus and three of His disciples came down the mountain, they were met by chaos. A man had brought his demon-possessed son to be healed. He was his only precious son (Luke 9:38). The nine disciples who had remained at the bottom of the mountain had tried to cast out the demon but failed miserably. Confused by the outcome and with their pride wounded, they became the easy target of the scribes, who accused them of being deceivers. The enormous crowd that had gathered at the foot of the mountain was prone to side with the scribes.[15] You can imagine the shouting and the blaming that went on. The disciples had had experience casting out demons, as commanded by Jesus (Matthew 10:1, 8), but something didn't work as expected that day.

When the father finally appealed to Jesus, the Lord did not cast out the demon right away. That was surprising, as Jesus always cast out demons "with a word" (Matthew 8:16), not allowing them to say much or draw attention to their world of darkness. But not this time. This time, Jesus asked that the boy be brought closer, and He allowed the demon to display his power, making the boy contort and foam at the mouth (Mark 9:20). And then, as if to prolong the misery, Jesus asked the father how long had this situation been going on! It seems strange that Jesus would need to know this fact before He could cast out the demon. But Jesus saw a bigger problem that morning than the actual demon, and He dealt carefully with it.

As the father recounted the painful story of the suffering inflicted by the demon upon his son, he finally burst out: "If you can do anything, have compassion on us and help us" (verse 22). Jesus' response is worth pondering: "If you can!"[16] "All things are possible to him who believes" (verse 23). In other words, *Are you seriously asking Me if I can do anything? Of course, I can! All things are possible for the one who believes!* Then, the father immediately "cried out and said with tears, 'Lord, I believe; help my unbelief!' " (verse 24). The father wasn't quite sure, yet he believed Jesus could help with a problem that had grown so large in his life over the course of many years. But he couldn't help notice that Jesus actually believed *He* could. So he was willing to concede that Jesus, at least, believed He could do something about it!

The story ends well. The demon is cast out, and the father is relieved. But when the nine disciples cornered Jesus later, they wondered why they could not cast out the demon. His answer? "This kind does not go out except by prayer and fasting" (Matthew 17:21). Wow! Was Jesus saying this case of demon possession was so severe that nothing less than prayer *with fasting* was needed? Check the story again. There is no Bible evidence that Jesus fasted before He expelled the demon. Were the disciples to have fasted before trying to cast it out? And how does that fit with the habit of Jesus casting out demons without delay?

When Jesus said "this kind," He was not referring to the kind of demon. *He was referring to the kind of unbelief!* This is clearly confirmed by reading the account in Matthew 17. There, Jesus is quoted, saying the reason they failed was "the littleness of your faith" (Matthew 17:20, NASB). Jesus' first reaction when He saw the despairing father, the anxious disciples, the accusing scribes, and the careless multitude was "O faithless generation, how long shall I be with you?" (Mark 9:19). The reason He kept stalling before casting out the demon was that He was waiting to see any hint of faith in Him from anybody in that entire crowd!

The father finally caught on, and he chose to believe. Think about this: When you analyze the story in Mark 9, you discover four progressive prayers. The first one is implied. That's when the nine disciples attempted to cast out the demon. We could summarize their request as "God, help them!" They prayed to God to help both father and son. The second one is alluded to in verse 17, when the father approached Jesus, in effect, saying, "God, help him!" That is, help my son. The next prayer is found in verse 22. The father cries in despair: "God, help us!" And the last prayer is a wrenching plea: "God, help me!" That is, help my unbelief! That's the prayer Jesus was waiting to answer all along. Help them, help him, help us, help me—*help my unbelief!* Do you see the progression? The demon was not the problem for Jesus; the lack of faith was the problem. To act on their behalf, He needed someone to actually believe He could do this. Once the father gingerly relied on Jesus to do what only God could do, the demon was cast out.

For decades now, I have found encouragement in this wonderful statement by Ellen White: "Nothing is apparently more helpless, yet really more invincible, than the soul that feels its nothingness and relies wholly on the merits of the Saviour. By prayer, by the study of His word, by faith in His abiding presence, the weakest of human beings may live in contact with the living Christ, and He will hold them by a hand that will never let go."[17]

The demon that must be exorcised is our lack of faith. When we live by faith, everything is possible for God through and for us. Praying together for our neighbors, our community, and our city, with the conviction that God will hear our prayers and respond accordingly, will not only sensitize us to the needs of people and increase our faith in God but will also move mountains. It will give us a wonderful opportunity to see the miracles of God. And our own demons will be exorcised when our faith in God, as God, is exercised.

Questions for Group Discussion or Personal Reflection

1. Think about the opening story of the house church praying for un-believers and for Yen's recovery. Would your church, or the Adventist institution where you serve, be ready to pray like that?

2. Reflect on the statement, "The secret of successful prayer is private prayer, but the secret to a successful church is *corporate* prayer." What do you think about that?

3. Read the long citation by Ellen White again. What will it take for us to pray like that?

4. Ellen White said that "every failure on the part of the children of God is due to their lack of faith." Ponder over two or three recent failures in your life—we all have them. Is what Mrs. White said true in your case?

5. When the author writes about victory being a matter of perspective (e.g., David facing Goliath from God's perspective, not from his), what are the implications for our daily lives?

6. What does the story of the demon-possessed boy tell you about Jesus and about us?

---

1. Melody Mason, *Daring to Ask for More: Divine Keys for Answered Prayer* (Nampa, ID: Pacific Press®, 2014), 178–180.

2. Ellen G. White, *Testimonies for the Church*, vol. 7 (Mountain View, CA: Pacific Press®, 1948), 213.

3. Apparently, I am not the only one who has experienced this. This is what Ellen White noticed: "I have frequently seen that the children of the Lord neglect prayer, especially secret prayer, altogether too much; that many do not exercise that faith which it is their privilege and duty to exercise, often waiting for that feeling which faith alone can bring. Feeling is not faith; the two are distinct. Faith is ours to exercise, but joyful feeling and the blessing are God's to give." Ellen G. White, *Christian Experience and Teachings of Ellen G. White* (Washington, DC: Review and Herald®, 1922), 126.

4. Ellen G. White, *Testimonies for the Church*, vol. 2 (Mountain View, CA: Pacific Press®, 1948), 577–582.

5. E. M. Bounds, *The Complete Works of E. M. Bounds on Prayer* (Grand Rapids, MI: Baker, 1990), 460.

6. Ellen G. White, *Manuscript Releases*, vol. 9 (Hagerstown, MD: Review and Herald®, 1990), 303; emphasis added.

7. Since I've lived in Asia, I've noticed most of our members are used to praying together, yet *individually*. They are in the same room but pray silently, on their own. That is not the evidence of corporate prayer we find in the Bible or the Spirit of Prophecy. When Peter and John were released from prison, they went to pray with their brothers and sisters, and the context is clear that they prayed aloud (Acts 4:24–31). The prayers of David were published for people to read and sing them (Psalm 72:20). Ellen White and the early pioneers spent precious time praying together. This was following the Methodist practice of praying aloud (half of the early Adventist pioneers came from Methodism), around the circle, one after the other. In Ellen White's writings, corporate prayer is never silent, individual prayer.

8. At the Northern Asia-Pacific Division we have been praying strategically. Some of our strategic requests to God: (1) Open North Korea to the gospel. (2) Reduce government restrictions in China. (3) Revitalize the church in Japan. (4) Strengthen pastors in Mongolia. (5) Reach out to the majority ethnic group in Taiwan. (6) Renew member commitment in South Korea. (7)

Impact the largest cities in the division. (8) Establish more Seventh-day Adventist schools. (9) Become a people filled with the Spirit of the Lord.

9. Ellen G. White, "Ask and It Shall Be Given You," *Bible Echo*, August 5, 1901, 4.

10. I told this story in a previous book I wrote, *Adventism's Greatest Need: The Outpouring of the Holy Spirit* (Nampa, ID: Pacific Press®, 2011), 35, 36.

11. Ellen G. White, *Patriarchs and Prophets* (Battle Creek, MI: Review and Herald®, 1890), 657.

12. D. Martyn Lloyd-Jones, *Spiritual Depression: Its Causes and Cures* (London: Harper-Collins, 1998), 20.

13. Ellen G. White, *Counsels to Parents, Teachers and Students* (Washington, DC: Review and Herald®, 1913), 234; emphasis added.

14. Ellen G. White, *Manuscript Releases*, vol. 7 (Hagerstown, MD: Review and Herald®, 1990), 403.

15. See Ellen G. White, *The Desire of Ages* (Battle Creek, MI: Review and Herald®, 1898), 427.

16. Some manuscripts say "If you can believe," but others "If you can!" such as the well-respected one published in the *Nestle-Aland Greek New Testament*, 27th ed., and in the *United Bible Societies' Greek New Testament*, 4th ed.

17. Ellen G. White, *The Ministry of Healing* (Washington, DC: Review and Herald®, 1905), 182.

CHAPTER 8

Prayer and the Great Controversy

One of the strangest stories from Roger Morneau's prayer ministry (see chapter 6) took place when a dedicated Seventh-day Adventist woman he called Norma told him about the constant harassment of evil angels in her life. Norma heard windows and doors opening and closing during the night. She heard footsteps going up and down the stairs in her home. She often felt a dense blackness hovering around her, oppressing her spirit. Sometimes, while in bed, she was shaken violently in the middle of the night. When these things happened, she cried out to Jesus, and the harassment stopped.

What may be more difficult to understand is why this would happen to a committed follower of Jesus. Morneau kept asking questions and figured out that the harassment might be associated with Norma's exposure to a blind woman she cared for, for a while. The harassment was strongest when Norma had been in that woman's house. When Morneau found out Norma still had a gift that the blind woman had given her, he told her to get rid of it immediately. He writes, "A principle of spirit behavior [is] that they have access to a person if that individual keeps certain objects associated with them" in their possession. Morneau had experienced something similar. For six months after he left Satanism, demons kept harassing him until he threw away some books on spirit worship he still had in his possession.[1]

The great conflict between good and evil is real, very real. And unless we understand the parameters of the conflict, we will not know how best to pray for others. Let's go to the beginning of the conflict and seek to understand the legal issues associated with prayer and good versus evil.

The beginning of the problem

Before the earth was created, there was a war in heaven. This was an ideological war between God and Satan, or "Michael and . . . the dragon," in the words of John (Revelation 12:7–9).[2] The war could not be a war in the traditional sense—weapons and soldiers—because who could begin to think of

74

fighting an all-powerful God? There would be no contest. This was a war—a legal war—of ideas, and Lucifer, as became evident, had a weak case and lost. The war in heaven must have gone on for some time; it was not a mere battle; it was a *war*.

What was the war about? Both Isaiah and Ezekiel fill in the blanks. Isaiah says that Lucifer, later known as Satan, or the dragon, wanted to exalt his throne—his position—above the stars, or the angels of God,[3] and that he aspired to be like God Himself (Isaiah 14:12–14). Ezekiel reveals that Lucifer was once "the anointed cherub who covers," that is, one of the two cherub angels next to the throne of God, as represented on the ark of the covenant (Exodus 25:10–20). The prophet also writes that Lucifer was "perfect . . . till iniquity was found" in him. His heart became proud because of his beauty and splendor (Ezekiel 28:12–15, 17). Since Lucifer became *proud*, his aspiration to be like God was not altruistic, it was not like wanting to reflect God's *character* but more like wanting to take God's *place*. Luke reveals that Satan wanted to be worshiped (Luke 4:1, 2, 5–7).

How could Lucifer dare think of such a thing? He was the creation of God (Ezekiel 28:15), like the rest of us. He was not divine. Lucifer was a mighty angel, ranking highest in heaven. We are told the war was between him and *Michael*. Michael, the Hebrew *mika'el*, means "Who is like God?" as a question or a challenge. The Bible makes clear that the One who is "like God" is the Son of God (John 5:18),[4] but Lucifer wanted *His* position and status. In Lucifer's mind, the Son of God became his enemy. In order to depose the Son and take His place, he had to attack His character, His integrity, His law. So he began to spread lies about the Son. Ezekiel 28:16 says, "By the abundance of your *trading* you became filled with violence within, and you sinned" (emphasis added). What does that mean? The word translated as "trading" is the Hebrew *rekulla*, which means "trading in goods or words, slander."[5] Lucifer began to slander the name of the Son. I can only imagine him casually conversing with other angels in heaven, saying something like, *Have you heard that someone here is not pleased with God's way of running things?* That would be both true and deception, which makes it an even more powerful lie. It would be true that someone in heaven was unhappy—he himself, though not revealed—but behind the veneer of sincere concern would be the evil intention of sowing seeds of doubt, a lie.

The nature of love and freedom
Some people, at this point, usually begin to think that the right thing for God

to have done is to have destroyed such a sly, conniving creature. He was upsetting heaven and the entire cosmos with his unfounded speculations. Others even conclude that since God did not prevent evil, He must be responsible for it. However, theologian Richard Rice is correct when he writes that "God is responsible for the *possibility* of evil, but not for the *actuality* of evil."[6]

The fundamental law God uses to run the universe is the law of self-renouncing love.[7] "God is love" (1 John 4:8), and God's creatures were made to follow God, worship God, and honor God because they *love* God. They *choose* to love God. They choose Him over themselves in the same way He chooses sinners over *Himself*, as demonstrated at the cross. Being free moral agents and having the freedom to love implies God's creation also has the freedom *not* to love. Lucifer chose not to love by focusing on self. Destroying Lucifer at that point would have caused a huge and devastating misunderstanding because angels had never been exposed to some of the concepts Lucifer was espousing, and they didn't know those selfish thoughts were evil. All they had ever known was perfect self-sacrificial love, so they would have assumed Lucifer was operating under the same parameters. If God had used unilateral force to destroy Lucifer and his angels—his followers—it would have come as a shock to unfallen beings, and fear would have crept in, making many wonder whether Lucifer might have a point, after all.

A third of the angels were deceived and agreed with Lucifer that intelligent, holy beings like angels did not need God's law for governance. So they were cast to the earth (Revelation 12:4).[8] Many years later, Jesus would declare that the devil "was a murderer from the beginning" (John 8:44). Murder is also the result of slander since it is killing someone's reputation. Jesus added that Satan "does not stand in the truth, because there is no truth in him. When he speaks a lie, he speaks from his own resources, for he is a liar and the father of it" (verse 44).

So sure was God that His law of self-renouncing love would conquer any sort of evil that He cast the devil down to the very planet that He planned to make the home for a new set of beings created "in His image" (Genesis 1:26, 27).[9] This was a special creation. When Adam and Eve were created, God warned them about Satan, which literally means "the adversary." He told them to stay away from the tree of the knowledge of good and evil (Genesis 2:16, 17) because He had limited Satan's presence to that tree. If they were to eat from its fruit, they would die.

This, of course, was a test. Would Adam and Eve trust the Word of God over their curiosity or inclination? In time, Eve wandered by the tree, quite casually, and Satan was ready to pounce. In the form of a beautiful serpent, he spoke to her, casting doubt on God's commandment: "Has God indeed said" such and so (Genesis 3:1)? In other words, *Do you really believe what God said?* Eve must have been quite taken by the fact that an animal could speak and reason with her, but she tried setting the record straight (verses 2, 3) since Satan had slightly misquoted God. Satan distorted God's word again by saying, "You will not surely die" (verse 4). This was a legalistic response. It was true that they would not know physical death immediately, but they would know *spiritual* death instantly! After Satan went on to paint a picture of a higher level of existence that could be achieved by eating the fruit, "she took of its fruit and ate. She also gave to her husband with her, and he ate. Then the eyes of both of them were opened, and they knew that they were naked" (verses 5–7). Satan had tempted them with the intriguing idea of being like God (verse 6), just as he had aspired to be while he was in heaven (Isaiah 14:14). However, they found they were nothing *without* God. They saw their true naked condition apart from Him.

I can only imagine the scene: Angels of God, always ready to assist when the human family is faced with any predicament, surrounding the tree, being held back from crying out, "Get away from him! He will ensnare you!" More than one of them would have sacrificed themselves to save Eve or Adam from the Fall, but the angels had to honor Adam's and Eve's God-given free will. They followed the serpent's suggestions of their own accord, and, as Ellen White has said, "angels cannot then protect those who are disregarding one of the divine precepts."[10] No one forced Adam and Eve to disregard God's words. They were clearly warned. Eve "disbelieved the words of God, and this was what led to her fall."[11]

Adam and Eve discovered that instead of experiencing a higher level of existence, their connection with God was most definitely broken. Their natural tendency to run toward God at the sound or sight of His presence turned into fleeing from Him and hiding (Genesis 3:8). Something very bad had taken place, and they knew it. Their freedom was used for selfish purposes, and they were now more predisposed to hear the beguiling serpent's words than the sure Word of God.

Lessons from Job
The incident in the middle of the garden made Satan "the ruler of this world" (John 14:30). He now had the legal right to present himself in heaven as the representative of human beings. The reason was simple: they followed *him* instead of God. Satan must have felt exultant. He must have felt justified in his reasoning that complete obedience to the laws of God was folly, an impossibility.

Hadn't he, as well as scores of other angels, and now the human family, been unable to do it?

The story of Job gives more breadth to this issue. Written by Moses during his days as a shepherd,[12] the story, along with the book of Genesis, became the first and only portion of Scripture available to the Israelites on their journey to Canaan. The book of suffering and the book of origins. How appropriate as foundations for living in this world. We find that, at the time of Job, the devil still had access to heaven as the representative of the world he conquered (Job 1:6, 7; 2:1, 2).[13] Satan was convinced he could make everyone on earth follow his worldview and disregard the Lord. So he was very bold. Biblical scholar Sigve Tonstad notes the similarity between Satan "walking up and down" the earth (Job 1:7; 2:2) and his former walking "up and down" in the midst of stones when he was the covering cherub (Ezekiel 28:14).[14] He thinks he owns the place. And God does not contradict him.

God points to His servant Job as one who is blameless, who fears God and shuns evil. Satan protests that Job's motives are suspect—Job is faithful to God because God blesses him (Job 1:8–10). Then, he challenges God in front of the entire heavenly assembly: "Stretch out Your hand and touch all that he has, and he will surely curse You to Your face!" (verse 11). God ignores the insolence because He is concerned about the cosmic impact of the challenge. And it would be fair to add that some in that heavenly council may have wondered whether Satan did not have a point.

Well, we know the story. Satan is given enormous latitude to cause suffering and pain to God's servant Job. Conventional wisdom dictated that he must be suffering because of some great sin in his life. But the entire book of Job is to disprove the doctrine of retribution, that God unilaterally punishes the sinful and blesses the faithful. The issues are much more complex. The story proves that Job maintains his integrity and does not curse God, as Satan predicted, even though Job believes, wrongly, that all his pain is caused *by God* (Job 2:10; 3:23; 6:4; 7:20; 9:22; 10:7, 16, 17; 13:24; 16:9–13; 17:6; 19:6, 8–11; 31:23)! Though Job is beside himself with grief because he does not understand why God would want to treat him this way, he knows God well enough to believe He is not making a mistake. Then, God Himself, at the end of the story, says that Job had spoken what is right about Him, unlike Job's miserable comforters (Job 42:7).

But now comes the biggest surprise: The Lord tells Job's three friends, "Take for yourselves seven bulls and seven rams, go to My servant Job, and offer up for yourselves a burnt offering; and My servant Job shall pray for you. For I will accept him, lest I deal with you according to your folly" (verse 8). Burnt offerings were sacrificed as a ransom for sin. The sacrifices substituted the death of the sinner. They legally "paid" for the sinner (Hebrews 9:22). It is fascinating to see that God entrusts the work of intercession to Job and that He will hear Job's prayer on behalf of his foolish friends. Why? Because Job has proven he trusts in God under any and all circumstances. "The effective, fervent prayer of a righteous man avails much" (James 5:16). But then, again, this is not the first time Job interceded on behalf of others through prayer. His ten children liked partying and drinking, not something a God-fearing father would wish his offspring to practice. But he loved his children, and he trusted in God's promises. So every time his children partied, "he would rise early in the morning and offer burnt offerings according to the number of them all. For Job said, 'It may be that my sons have sinned and cursed God in their hearts.' Thus Job did regularly" (Job 1:5), individually for each of his children.[15]

Cosmic rules of engagement

People are often surprised by the seeming latitude God grants Satan, the adversary, to harass human beings. If he is as fearsome an enemy as demonstrated by what he did to Job and his family, why would God give him so much freedom to do harm? To some, it looks as if God is nicer to His enemy than to His faithful servant Job! We certainly would not act this way, we muse. True, we would not, because we cannot see the big picture that God constantly keeps in view.

So what is the big picture? The problem of sin is not only an individual problem; it is a universal problem. And even God is under scrutiny. That is why the apostle Paul says God must demonstrate that He is *both* "just and the justifier of the one who has faith in Jesus" (Romans 3:26). And David associated God's forgiveness for sinners with His legal right to do so: "That You may be found just when You speak," he wrote, "and blameless when You judge" (Psalm 51:1–4).

My sin actually impacts a myriad of other factors in this cosmic conflict. And God's plan to solve this problem reaches much farther than what I can perceive. Let's say I have a habit of being lazy. As a man with a family, such a habit would not only be lamented by my wife but also become more obvious to our children as they get older. To one, it may prompt her to be more industrious, more responsible, in part as a subconscious negative reaction to avoid as much as possible Dad's bad example. To another, it may encourage him to *indulge* in laziness, justifying his behavior: "If Dad does it, why not me?" This, in turn, impacts the children's lives and work; even the persons they may end up marrying; and of course, in turn, their own children—and we could add here, impacts other family members, friends, and even coworkers. Sin is a cancer that grows unabated, contaminating more and more people unless there is a supernatural intervention to stop it. And since this world is the theater of the cosmos (1 Corinthians 4:9),[16] God is very keen on dealing with sin in such a way that once gone, it will be gone forever.

The first two chapters of Job give us a hint about how God has arranged for this. Theologian John Peckham, in his excellent book on the subject, *Theodicy of Love*, calls this arrangement "rules of engagement." In today's warfare, there are typically rules of engagement that control the use and degree of force, specifying circumstances and limitations for engaging in combat. For example, one of the rules would be not to attack the enemy's hospital ship. That would be off-limits in a war. The various Geneva convention treatises of the twentieth-century have stipulated that "the wounded and sick must not be murdered, tortured, exterminated or exposed to biological experiments," and that prisoners of war would only be "required to give their name, rank, birth date, and serial number when captured" and be given "suitable housing and adequate amounts of food."[17] Dozens of countries are signatories to these rules.

Since the cosmic controversy is between good and evil, both parties have come to an agreement on how to conduct this before the onlooking universe. Remember, Lucifer's capability for deception extends to unfallen beings across the universe. At first, they were not able to see what became so obvious to God from the start. That's the reason for the pact.

"Biblical evidence indicates that there are rules of engagement in the cosmic conflict such that both parties know the limits within which they might operate toward settling this conflict," writes Peckham. In addition, these rules appear to be covenantal, that is, "they exist as part of a bilateral agreement between parties that effectively limits the action of both and that neither party can unilaterally change."[18] In practical terms, God is limited in His power to rescue or prevent harm, and Satan is limited in his power to abuse people. These "dynamic" limitations can be broken, of course (which is also envisioned by both parties). If someone chooses to spend time with practices, people, or evil clearly known to be the territory of Satan (Ouija boards and seances, for example), Satan can take further advantage of them. If someone prays, submitting and trusting in God, appealing to His power on the basis of God's victory at the cross, God is given greater control over the situation, to help and to heal.

If this is a new idea for you, it may sound surprising, even far-fetched. God making a treaty with the devil? It is important to recognize this is not a treaty between two equal parties. It is a treaty—rules of engagement—much like the ones seen among nations in the Old Testament. The conquering or more powerful nation would make a treaty with the conquered or weaker nation. The powerful pledged not to ignore it, and the weaker nation worked within its stipulated guidelines.

We are not privy to these cosmic rules of engagement, but the Bible provides sufficient hints about the idea. When Christ was tempted in the wilderness, one of the offers Satan made to Christ, in exchange for worship, was to give Him back all the kingdoms of the world. Why could he offer that? Because, as he said, "this has been delivered to me, and I give it to whomever I wish. Therefore, if You will worship before me, all will be Yours" (Luke 4:6, 7). Jesus never disputed the veracity of that statement. All He said was that worship belongs to God only (verse 8). Adam and Eve had been given dominion over the earth (Genesis 1:26, 28), which they promptly relinquished once they surrendered their wills to Satan. Three times Jesus Himself acknowledged Satan as "the prince of this world" (John 12:31; 14:30; 16:11). At one point, the apostle Paul revealed to the church in Thessalonica that he and his associates had wanted to come to them a number of times, but that "Satan hindered" them (1 Thessalonians 2:17, 18). All this implies that God's power and access to the world are limited, for the time being. His ontological power—His sheer ability to do what He wants—is not limited, but His *moral* power is limited. He can function only within the parameters agreed to in this great conflict.

Here is another example. Jesus and His disciples went to Gadara, on the eastern side of the Sea of Galilee. There they met two demon-possessed men. So many demons had taken over these men that they called themselves "Legion," a military unit of up to six thousand soldiers. When they saw Jesus, they instantly recognized the Son of God, "and suddenly they cried out, saying, 'What have we to do with You, Jesus, You Son of God? Have You come here to torment us *before the time?*' " (Matthew 8:29; emphasis added; see also Mark 5:7). This incident reveals that there are agreed-to time parameters before the final judgment of evil angels (2 Peter 2:4; Jude 6). God has pledged not to destroy them until *that time* has arrived. That time will arrive at the end of the millennium, as indicated in Revelation 20, and not at the time Jesus walked the earth as a Man.

Prayer impacts the rules of engagement

Even though we are not told the specifics of the cosmic rules of engagement, we are told two extremely important things about them: things about faith and prayer. Faith and prayer are key components of this engagement. If people pray in faith, God's parameters expand, and His ability to intercede in the lives of others increases! He has legal, moral rights to restrict the influence of the evil one for the benefit of those who are prayed for in faith! How can this be so?

Jesus Himself gives an example. On the night of His betrayal, while Christ and His disciples were in the upper room, He said to Peter, "Simon, Simon! Indeed, Satan has *asked for you*, that he may sift you as wheat. *But I have prayed for you*, that your faith should not fail; and when you have returned to *Me*, strengthen your brethren" (Luke 22:31, 32; emphasis added). Notice, Satan requested *permission* to shake up Peter, to test him, much like he had with Job centuries before. Peter was a leading disciple of Jesus, and he had declared in front of all others his allegiance to the Lord even to the point of being willing to die for Jesus (John 13:37). Both Satan and Jesus knew Peter better than he knew himself. Anticipating his weaknesses, Satan tempted Peter to be boastful before others, to fall asleep in the garden instead of praying for the Master and themselves (Mark 14:32, 33, 37, 38), and finally, to deny the Savior before the lowest in society (John 18:15–18, 25–27). Peter failed, and he failed miserably at the most critical times. But Jesus had prayed in faith for Peter, and Peter recovered. He repented of his great sin and went on to humbly pastor the flock of Christ, and he became willing to sacrifice even life itself for the Master (John 21:15–19).

Who knows how much lower Peter could have gone had Jesus not prayed for him! Who knows what depths of discouragement and depression could have shut the fervent disciple away from Christ and from ministry for the rest of his life had Jesus not prayed for him! No other disciple that we know of prayed for Peter that night. But that was not the issue because the objective of Satan was to *use* Peter to the detriment of Christ's ministry of salvation. If he could get Peter, a leading disciple of Jesus, to apostatize, he could boast that God's promises and government were just as bad as he's been saying they are since the war in heaven. The intercessor that made a difference that day was Jesus.

Faith and prayer are key in the battle between good and evil. On the days we don't pray, the enemy advances. But on the days we do, Christ is armed with legal, moral rights to tell the adversary: "Thus far shall you go and no further." Such was the experience of Israel over its enemies when Moses prayed when his arms were not too tired to pray (Exodus 17:10, 11).

When we don't pray, when we don't go to God in faith, the activity of God is constricted, just like all world economies were diminished due to the recent COVID-19 pandemic. God's *ability* to do is not abated, but the *moral reason* for doing it is not supported. If God were to act unilaterally simply because He can, the devil would then say: "Why are You trying to help these people? They're not asking You to help them. They are distracted by what I'm giving them to do. They don't really believe in You as much as they say they do. You said you would deal with integrity. Integrity demands that You refrain from aiding people who don't seem too concerned that You do." So while God remains all-powerful, ontologically, in terms of His nature, there may be things He cannot morally do that He would otherwise want to do.

On His second visit to Nazareth, after He began His public ministry, Jesus again made an impression on the residents as He spoke in the synagogue. These were His people, His family. He grew up in that city. There must have been people present for whom He made furniture in His carpenter's shop. He must have desired to bless them as much as Capernaum, Bethsaida, and other Galilean towns had been blessed. But it was not possible: "He could do no mighty work there, except that He laid His hands on a few sick people and healed them." How tragic! Why? Mark says: "He marveled because of their unbelief" (Mark 6:1–6).

Unbelief is a much greater impediment to the Lord's mighty work among His people than any disasters, disagreements, or disease that the devil is capable of throwing at us. The story of the demon-possessed boy we explored in a previous chapter makes the same point (Matthew 17:20; Mark 9:23, 24). The greatest "demon" to exorcise is a lack of faith.

"The same compassionate Saviour lives today, and He is as willing to listen to the prayer of faith as when He walked visibly among men. The natural cooperates with the supernatural. It is a part of God's plan *to grant us, in answer to the prayer of faith, that which He would not bestow did we not thus ask*."[19]

Ask, ask, *ask*! Jesus needs you to ask. He needs all of us in the church to ask. The more of us that ask, in faith, the more freely He can move within the stipulated parameters for waging the great conflict.

Questions for Group Discussion or Personal Reflection

1. What was Lucifer's issue with God that led him to fight Him?

2. Why did God not destroy Lucifer and his followers when they rebelled?

3. Why couldn't God's angels help Eve avoid eating the fruit?

4. On what grounds dare Satan show up in heaven as earth's representative?

5. Comment on Job's intercession for both his children and his friends. Why would God hear Job for them?

6. What do you think about the idea that God and Satan are limited in what they can do by a cosmic set of "rules of engagement"?

7. Can you cite biblical evidence pointing to such "rules of engagement"?

8. How does intercessory prayer impact such "rules of engagement"?

---

1. Roger J. Morneau, *More Incredible Answers to Prayer* (Hagerstown, MD: Review and Herald®, 1993), 59–63.

2. The identity of the dragon is easy to spot; the Bible says the dragon was "the old serpent and Satan" (Rev. 12:9). The identity of Michael is a bit more challenging. See note 4.

3. In the Bible, "stars" often symbolize angels (Judges 5:20; Job 38:7; Isaiah 14:13; Revelation 1:20).

4. "Michael" appears five times in the Bible, each time in the context of conflict, or warfare. In Daniel 10:13, He is identified as "one of the chief princes." In Daniel 10:21, Daniel is told by the heavenly being that Michael is "your prince." In Daniel 12:1, Michael is "the great prince." In Jude 9, He is identified as "the archangel," or chief over the angels. In Daniel 9:25, the Messiah is identified as "the prince." And in 1 Thessalonians 4:16 "the Lord Himself shall descend . . . with the voice of an archangel . . . and the dead in Christ will rise first." Jesus said that "the dead will hear the voice of the Son of God" (John 5:25). So according to Jesus and Paul, Michael, the archangel, is the Son of God. And according to the prophet Daniel, Michael is the Messiah. Evidently, prior to the Incarnation, the Son of God identified with His creatures the angels and was known as Michael: Who is like God!

5. The Hebrew verb *rakal* literally means to "go about, from one to another [for trade or gossip]." See Richard M. Davidson, "Ezekiel 28:11–19 and the Rise of the Cosmic Conflict" in *The Great Controversy and the End of Evil*, ed. Gerhard Pfandl (Silver Spring, MD: Biblical Research Institute, 2015), 68.

6. Richard Rice, *Suffering and the Search for Meaning: Contemporary Responses to the Problem of Pain* (Downers Grove, IL: IVP Academic, 2014), 47; emphasis in the original.

7. "It will be seen that the glory shining in the face of Jesus is the glory of self-sacrificing love. In the light from Calvary it will be seen that *the law of self-renouncing love is the law of life for earth and heaven*; that the love which 'seeketh not her own' has its source in the heart of God; and that in the meek and lowly One is manifested the character of Him who dwelleth in the light which no man can approach unto." Ellen G. White, *The Desire of Ages* (Battle Creek, MI: Review and Herald®, 1898), 20; emphasis added.

8. "He began to insinuate doubts concerning the laws that governed heavenly beings, intimating that though laws might be necessary for the inhabitants of the worlds, angels, being more exalted, needed no such restraint, for their own wisdom was a sufficient guide." Ellen G. White, *Patriarchs and Prophets* (Battle Creek, MI: Review and Herald®, 1890), 37. The best piece of writing on this topic is the first chapter of *Patriarchs and Prophets*, entitled "Why Was Sin Permitted?" Every page in that chapter is full of wisdom and clearly shows how this controversy began and why.

9. "God's choice of precisely this devil-ridden location for the creation of the earth and of humanity may seem shocking. But, in fact, it contains a lesson with far-reaching implications. Paradoxically, God's salvation reveals itself in the very place that rejected Him—the world created out of darkness and the void." Jacques B. Doukhan, *Secrets of Revelation: The Apocalypse Through Hebrew Eyes* (Hagerstown, MD: Review and Herald®, 2002), 110.

10. White, *Patriarchs and Prophets*, 256.

11. White, 55. She also adds: "In the judgment men will not be condemned because they conscientiously believed a lie, but because they did not believe the truth, because they neglected the opportunity of learning what is truth." White, 55.

12. Ellen G. White wrote, "During this time [while being a shepherd in Midian], under the inspiration of the Holy Spirit, he wrote the book of Genesis and also the book of Job." "Moses," *Signs of the Times*, February 19, 1880, 1.

13. It was not until the resurrection of Jesus that the devil was finally forbidden access to heaven. That is what Jesus anticipated when, only a few days before the cross, He said: "I saw Satan fall like lightning from heaven" (Luke 10:18). All heavenly beings were convinced now that the Son was right and that the devil lied.

14. Sigve K. Tonstad, *God of Sense and Traditions of Non-Sense* (Eugene, OR: Wipf & Stock, 2016), 246.

15. Ellen White says that Job "offered sacrifices for them individually." See *The Seventh-day Adventist Bible Commentary*, vol. 3 (Washington, DC: Review and Herald®, 1954), 1140.

16. The full words of Paul are: "For I think that God has displayed us, the apostles, last, as men condemned to death; for we have been made a spectacle to the world, both to angels and to men." The word "spectacle" is the Greek word *theatron*, from which we get the English word *theater*. And the word translated "world" is the original Greek word *kosmos*, or cosmos.

17. See "Geneva Convention," History.com, last updated August 21, 2018, https://www.history.com/topics/world-war-ii/geneva-convention.

18. John C. Peckham, *Theodicy of Love: Cosmic Conflict and the Problem of Evil* (Grand Rapids, MI: Baker Academic, 2018), 107.

19. Ellen G. White, *The Great Controversy* (Washington, DC: Review and Herald®, 1911), 525; emphasis added.

CHAPTER 9

Satan's Strongholds Will Fall

When we consider the enormous task ahead of us, most of us feel like turning away, already defeated. How can great, godless cities such as Tokyo, Beijing, Kolkata, and New York be won to the gospel? It's impossible, we say. I've been to these cities. In each of them, we have a few Adventist churches, but what are they compared to the millions and millions of secular people who don't seem to have a smidgen of interest in what we have to offer?

We forget that much can be achieved by one person with conviction. Have you read the story of Horatius at the bridge? The last king of Rome, before it became a republic, was Tarquin the Proud. He was a cruel, selfish despot, and eventually, in the late sixth century BC, the people of Rome deposed him and sent him away in exile. Tarquin, however, made a treaty with the Etruscan army to attack Rome so he could regain the city. The Romans did not expect the Etruscans to attack them, so they were not prepared for an invasion. The first to see the enemy on their way to Rome were peasants and farmers outside the city. They immediately ran to seek refuge behind the walls of Rome. Rome was strategically built behind the Tiber River, accessible by one bridge.

The large enemy force inspired fear in the Roman soldiers, who also ran toward the bridge to get behind the walls. Horatius, a junior officer in the Roman army, realized that if the enemy took the bridge, they would take Rome. Standing at the start of the bridge, he began fighting off every enemy soldier that dared try to cross the bridge. Two senior officers joined him, and he called on the rest to destroy the bridge behind them. The three took a lot of punishment, but they held their ground. Two eventually retreated due to their wounds. But not Horatius. He seemed like a man possessed, determined to defend the bridge at all costs. Once the bridge collapsed, he dove into the Tiber waters and managed to swim to safety. The Etruscan army viewed the defense of the city by one man as an omen that the gods would not be with them. And to the great anger of Tarquin the Proud, they retreated and went home. Severely wounded, Horatius became a hero for generations of Romans. They never again allowed themselves to be ruled by a king.[1]

One person of conviction can make a real difference for many people and for years to come. God has always looked for persons of conviction, willing to appeal to God for others until there is an answer. When no one is found, God is deeply disappointed (Isaiah 59:16; 63:5). At the time of Ezekiel, God groaned about the sins of Jerusalem. Her prophets were corrupt, murdering, and stealing (Ezekiel 22:25). Her priests made no distinction between the common and the holy, profaning the Sabbath (verse 26). Her city officials were like wolves, destroying lives for dishonest gain (verse 27). And her prophets gave false visions and lied (verse 28). "So I sought for a man among them," said God, "who would . . . stand in the gap before Me on behalf of the land, that I should not destroy it; but I found no one" (verse 30).

Are we willing to stand in the gap? Moses was willing. When the Amalekites came unexpectedly to destroy the people of Israel in the desert, Moses told Joshua to confront them while he went up a mountain to pray for victory. As long as he prayed, a victory for Israel seemed possible. When he stopped praying, the enemy would get the upper hand (Exodus 17:8–13). Prayer was the cause of victory that day.

And prayer will be the cause of victory in our cities and neighborhoods if we practice it with faith in God. "For the weapons of our warfare are not carnal but mighty in God for pulling down strongholds, casting down arguments and every high thing that exalts itself against the knowledge of God, bringing every thought into captivity to the obedience of Christ" (2 Corinthians 10:4, 5).

Taking cities for God

In Ephesians 6, we see, in contrast to the story of Horatius, an offensive rather than a defensive strategy. Let me explain. Ephesians 6:10–20 shows that the followers of Jesus need to wear "the whole armor of God." We are told to wear the belt of truth, the breastplate of righteousness, the shield of faith, the helmet of salvation, and the sword of the Spirit because the enemy consists of "principalities, . . . powers, . . . rulers of the darkness of this age, . . . spiritual hosts of wickedness in the heavenly places" (verse 12). We're also told to put on, or tie on, the sandals of "the preparation of the gospel of peace" (verse 15). Some have thought this should be translated "the equipment" of the gospel of peace since all the other items mentioned are part of the equipment of the armor, but the correct translation is "preparation."[2] What does that mean, exactly?

It is interesting to note that most commentaries simply do not address that issue, but Ellen White does. There are sixteen direct references in her writings to Ephesians 6:15, "the preparation of the gospel of peace." Two things become clear. One, "preparation" has to do with the understanding and application of grace and Christlikeness in our witnessing work. And two, this work must move forward. She views this verse in the context of a marching disciple seeking the lost.[3] In the view of Ellen White, the picture given by the apostle Paul is not one of an army in retreat, merely defending itself from the forces of darkness. Rather, the army of God is on the offensive, ready to take enemy territory.

The Roman soldiers that guarded Paul in prison when he wrote this letter wore the Roman caligae, a leather sandal they strapped halfway up their calves, which had iron hobnails at the bottom, for better traction. In hand-to-hand combat, they had to stand their ground. If they slipped or fell, the enemy would wound or kill them. Being able to stand without falling despite enemy blows was vital for them.

Although most of the armor of God is meant to protect oneself from "the fiery darts of the wicked one" (verse 16), Paul points to two items in the armor with either offensive or forward-moving implications: the sword of the Spirit—God's Word, the Bible—and the shoes that carry the gospel of peace.[4] The association between good news and feet (where shoes go) is seen in the Old Testament. In Isaiah 61:1, there is a prophecy about the Messiah who would "preach good tidings to the poor" while being "sent . . . to heal the brokenhearted." And in Isaiah 52:7, we find the picture of an ancient battle and a messenger sent back to the city to share how their armies are faring. If they are being overtaken, the crown is in danger, but if they are overcoming, the king is still in charge:

> How beautiful upon the mountains
> Are the feet of him who brings good news,
> Who proclaims peace,
> Who brings glad tidings of good things,
> Who proclaims salvation,
> Who says to Zion,
> "Your God reigns!"

Good news, then, is associated with a proactive action, that of sharing what God has done or is doing for us. However, three times Paul tells us "to stand," or "to stand firm" (Ephesians 6:11, 13, 14). Why is that?

There are only two possible battle scenarios that Paul could have had in mind: either two armies facing each other in a field or valley or one army sieging a city. In this last scenario, the greater danger for those sieging a city has to do with "fiery arrows." Archers on the wall can easily shoot arrows to inflict great loss to an oncoming army. This is why Paul tells us to stand. Taking the shield of faith, we must crouch behind our shields when those arrows come flying by. And come, they will. That's the devil's only strategy (verse 16). If we were to turn around and run, we would surely be struck in the back and risk destruction. Paul is saying, "Plant your gospel feet on solid ground, take your shield of faith for protection, and withstand the force of the devil's arrows upon your shield. Stand your ground!" As soon as a set of fiery darts is passed, the Lord's army is to keep moving forward toward the city, walking with the shoes of the gospel of peace.

You may wonder: *What city is this?* Years before Paul wrote to the Ephesians, Jesus said, "I will build My church, and the gates of Hades shall not prevail against it" (Matthew 16:18). That word *Hades* is made up of two Greek words that mean "unseen" or "underworld," a reference to death or the grave. The context here is eternal death. So Jesus said that His church will be victorious over the gates of death.

Now we can see more clearly what Paul had in mind. In Ephesians 6:10–20, Paul is making a rallying speech, much like generals or kings would make to the troops before engaging in battle. He admonishes the church of God to be fully clad with the armor of God and march forward with the good news of peace, and the sword of the Word, to breach the walls or the gates of Satan's citadel. The enemy has captured many souls by deception and discouragement and has placed them behind his prison walls. We, the church, under the command and leadership of Jesus, must march on to set them free! Clinton Arnold is perhaps the best-known New Testament scholar on spiritual warfare. He maintains that "spiritual warfare is both resistance and proclamation." The church stands in the armor of God, but she also marches forward as she announces to the world the good news of Jesus. " 'The Word of God and the work of the Spirit are the tools in the hands of the church to step out in defiance of Satan and rob his domain.' "[5]

This is God's call for the church. There are thousands all around us who wish to be set free. If only they knew how to get out. "My brethren and sisters, there are souls in your neighborhood who, if they were judiciously labored for, would be converted. . . . The fields are ripe for the work that all can do whose souls are prepared by living the Word."[6]

Major changes can take place
We may think that praying around our neighborhood with our team or around

a designated part of the city will not do much in the war against the forces of darkness. What can it do? Remember that we cannot see what God and the angels can see. Praying for those we see on the street, in our neighborhood, in the stores, in the subways, will give God a *legal standing* to check the power of the devil. Satan's right to harass and deceive people is based largely on people's ignorance. As long as they don't know whom to go to for help, they are more vulnerable. But when you and I pray for people, Jesus can point to us intercessors as the reason why He is now entitled to move on their behalf and to curb the influence of evil.

We could do great things for God if we only took Him at His word and set out to "walk around the walls" as Israel did around Jericho. "The Lord is disappointed when His people place a low estimate upon themselves. . . . He has a use for them, and He is well pleased when they make the very highest demands upon Him, that they may glorify His name. They may expect large things if they have faith in His promises."[7] God's first desire is to work through His last-day remnant people, but He will work through any who are willing enough to trust in Him.

Rees Howells was a British pastor who followed Jesus very closely. He had learned to trust God with all his needs and aspirations. His prayer life was legendary in England and Wales, even while he was still alive. As the head of a Bible college, Howells had always prayed for the gospel to go to the entire world. In the 1920s, the Nazi leaders in Germany began a military buildup. Europe became concerned that once again, Germany would be intent on world conquest. By 1925, a series of treaties were signed in Locarno, Italy, between Italy, England, France, Belgium, and Germany. The treaties made England and Italy guarantors if the treaty between the other three was broken. The intent was to check Germany's ambitions. However, the Nazi military machinery kept building over the years, and Hitler's increasing nationalistic rhetoric made many in Europe very nervous.

On December 26, 1934, Rees Howells woke up with a tremendous burden to intercede for the nations, asking God to avert an expected war for the sake of the gospel. On January 1, 1935, the school he led dedicated itself to what they called "The Every Creature Vision." They knew a war in Europe would greatly hinder the gospel. "Prevail against Hitler" was the message of the Holy Spirit to them.

> They became responsible to intercede for countries and nations, as well as for individual missionaries and societies. . . .
>
> Their prayers became strategic.[8]

No doubt, many other Christians in Europe were also praying for God to intercede in geopolitical affairs, but were they praying strategically for entire countries, believing their prayers could actually change the course of history? Germany eventually occupied the Rhineland, a stretch of country that had been under the control of Allied forces since the Treaty of Versailles in 1919. Howells prayed and fasted for three weeks. In the sixth century BC, the prophet Daniel also prayed and fasted for three weeks, asking God to intercede for His people in the face of enemy control by the Medes and Persians, and God answered his prayers (Daniel 10:1–14). The struggle between Europe and Germany went on for two more years. In 1938, Hitler annexed Austria and planned to take over the Sudetenland, a part of the Czech Republic populated by ethnic Germans.

Now Europe was truly on the verge of war. Hitler had confided to some close to him that he was guided by a voice that told him which decisions to make and that he obeyed that voice, for it never failed him.[9] England was the only country capable of engaging Germany in the case of a war, but they were not quite prepared for it. Hitler was convinced England was not ready to defend Czechoslovakia and thought he should start the war in October 1938! In the meantime, Howells kept praying: "Lord, bend Hitler!"

On September 17, 1938, the press announced peace talks would take place between England, Germany, France, and Italy in Munich, scheduled for September 29. The college immediately went to pray. On the 30th, the Munich Pact was signed, allowing Germany to retain the areas invaded, but avoiding war for the time being.

You may wonder if prayer really worked. After all, World War II did take place. Yes, it did, but it was delayed an entire year. Between September of 1938 and September of 1939, England built up its military considerably, preparing for war. If that hadn't happened, the Nazis' advance in Europe would have had much greater consequences, consequences that may still be with us today. God listened to the intercession of Rees Howells and the students and staff of the college. After the war started, the college made direct and self-sacrificial intercession for the evacuation of Dunkirk—which allowed thousands of trapped Allied soldiers in France to escape alive—and for defeat in the German invasion of Russia—which proved the beginning of the end of the Nazi war machine.[10]

The point is clear: when we gather together to faithfully intercede on behalf of cities, peoples, *and* nations, God will hear that prayer for the sake of His mission priorities, to reach a world in darkness.

Are you willing to be part of an intercessory team?

Questions for Group Discussion or Personal Reflection

1. When you think about Horatius's story and God's plea: "I sought for a man among them, . . . who would . . . stand in the gap . . . but I found no one," how does that make you feel?

2. Do you believe you have put on the full armor of God? What evidence could you offer that this is so?

3. What do you think about the notion of the Adventist Church being on the offensive, seeking to rescue people captured by Satan through his lies?

4. What do you think about the story of Rees Howells and his Bible school praying for God to confront Hitler? Does it sound a bit extreme to you?

5. Is it really possible for everyday people—church members—to pray for entire countries and expect geopolitical changes to take place? How does one get to that point?

---

1. This story can be found in many sources. One of them is Wikipedia, s.v. "Horatius Cocles," last modified June 6, 2020, https://en.wikipedia.org/wiki/Horatius_Cocles.

2. See Harold W. Hoehner, *Ephesians: An Exegetical Commentary* (Grand Rapids, MI: Baker Academic, 2002), 842, 843.

3. See, for example, statements in the following writings: *Colporteur Ministry* (Mountain View, CA: Pacific Press®, 1953), 90; *Evangelism* (Washington, DC: Review and Herald®, 1946), 114, 174, 564, 639; *Gospel Workers* (Washington, DC: Review and Herald®, 1915), 305; *Testimonies for the Church*, vol. 8 (Mountain View, CA: Pacific Press®, 1948), 211, 212; *Testimonies for the Church*, vol. 9 (Mountain View, CA: Pacific Press®, 1948), 48; *Welfare Ministry* (Tacoma Park, MD: Review and Herald®, 1952), 100; *The Publishing Ministry* (Hagerstown, MD: Review and Herald®, 1983), 306; *Reflecting Christ* (Hagerstown, MD: Review and Herald®, 1985), 240; and *The Retirement Years* (Hagerstown, MD: Review and Herald®, 1990), 37.

4. See John B. Polhill, *Paul and His Letters* (Nashville, TN: Broadman and Holman, 1999), 373, 374; and Eckhard J. Schnabel, *Paul the Missionary: Realities, Strategies and Methods* (Downers Grove, IL: IVP Academic, 2008), 148, 149. Some scholars, such as Hoehner, in *Ephesians*, disagree, asserting the entire picture of the armor of God is exclusively for defensive purposes. We will see how this is a limited view, according to the text.

5. William F. Cook III and Chuck Lawless, *Spiritual Warfare in the Storyline of Scripture: A Biblical, Theological, and Practical Approach* (Nashville, TN: B&H Academic, 2019), 255.

6. White, *Evangelism*, 114.

7. Ellen G. White, *The Desire of Ages* (Battle Creek, MI: Review and Herald®, 1898), 668.

8. This fascinating story is recounted by Norman Grubb in *Rees Howells: Intercessor* (Fort

Washington, PA: Christian Literature Crusade, 1980), 207.

9. The British Ambassador to Germany had inside information about Hitler signing an agreement, that in principle, he would never have signed: "Hitler felt irritated with himself [for signing the Munich Pact]. A section of his followers were always egging him on to fight England while [England] was militarily unprepared. They reproached him for having accepted the Munich settlement and thus having missed the most favourable opportunity. . . . His Voice had told him that . . . there could be no more propitious moment for a [war] than that October; and for once he had been obliged to disregard that Voice and listen to counsels of prudence. . . . For the first time, he had been compelled to listen to contrary opinion, and his own faith in his Voice and his people's confidence in his judgment were [. . .] shaken. . . . [To British Prime Minister Neville Chamberlain, he said later, with some bitterness:] 'You are the only man [. . .] to whom I have ever made a concession.' " Grubb, *Rees Howells*, 210.

10. Grubb, 231–240, 247–250.

PART II

Power at Work

Even though I have been praying for decades and have led and taught on prayer for years, I'm by no means a prayer strategy expert. I'm not sure such expertise even exists. So what I say in the following chapters about prayer walking or about other prayer strategies is somewhat tentative; it is shared with a degree of hesitation.

What works well in some churches and cultures may not work well in others. And churches, as well as cultures, differ considerably, even in the context of the unifying message of the Seventh-day Adventist Church. So consider these chapters as suggestions, more to stimulate your own thinking and creativity about what to do in your case than prescribing a sure recipe for success. For success, reread the previous chapters, where the principles are outlined.

God will guide us and give us success as we earnestly seek His leadership in our lives and our communities. The important thing is to engage—to pray with faith and the determination to keep doing it until we see God answer. The deed is more important than the method.

CHAPTER 10

What Is Prayer Walking, and Why Do It?

Prayer walking is praying either alone or with others, focusing on the people and places where you walk. Key differences between prayer walking and praying for people in your home or in the church is that you don't just imagine the people you pray for or risk forgetting who they are. You pray for people you see or for people you understand live or work by the places you see.[1]

Praying for people you don't see takes more concentration and self-discipline, and it is easier to become distracted from those objectives. Seeing the prayer target tends to help the person praying to focus more, to pay attention to details about the person's life or struggles, even if you don't yet know that person personally. Prayer walking can actually sensitize you—make you more compassionate toward strangers in your world. It helps people understand better the enormous task of God to save an entire world from sin and death.

Praying walking alone

Praying while we walk by ourselves is good because it brings us closer to the heart of God. Remember reading about Paul in Athens? The Bible says, "His spirit was provoked within him when he saw that the city was given over to idols" (Acts 17:16). Paul was waiting for Silas and Timothy, who were doing post evangelistic work in Berea, assimilating new believers into the church (verses 14, 15).[2] While waiting, the apostle must have walked and prayed and walked some more. And seeing all the people there who didn't know the God of heaven must have made him wonder how God would reach such an idolatrous, intellectual city as Athens. That's why "his spirit was stirred" within him for this city.

My wife and I now live in a suburb of the city of Seoul, in South Korea. We live only about twenty-five miles (forty kilometers) from the border with North Korea. Keep in mind that, technically, both countries are still in a state of war and that the North Korean government rather frequently tests ballistic missiles, making South Korea nervous about their northern neighbors.

This city is the second-most populous city in the world, with some twenty-three million people living in the metro area.[3] Even though over a quarter of the country's population claims Christianity—by far the largest percentage of any country in Asia except for the Philippines—most people are burdened with the cares of life and work and have little or no time to know God. Many live without lasting hope. The rate of suicide is among the highest in the world, higher even than Japan's.

We've met several people with whom we're developing a friendship, and we pray for them to come out of darkness into the light of God in their lives. And we pray for our neighbors. When I'm home, I prayer walk our neighborhood two or three times a week. We live in an apartment on the fourteenth floor of building number 203, and there are nine more apartment buildings like ours in our complex. I have estimated 2,182 people live in those ten buildings. There may be more. These are our closest neighbors.

The night I wrote this chapter, for example, I had gone by building 202, and a boy of about seven or eight was looking out the window from his seventh-floor apartment. So I prayed, "Lord, bless that little boy. Bless his father and mother. Give them the wisdom to raise him. Somehow, lead that boy to know You, to trust You, and eventually to love You above anything else in the world. And may he become a tool in Your hands to lead members of his family and others to You." At the entrances of building 205 and building 206 were delivery guys, waiting in vain for people to open the door. My prayer for them was: "Father, please send Your Holy Spirit to these men. They work hard for little pay, and their work is dangerous, driving small motorcycles in heavy traffic all around the city. Please flood them with Your peace. Somehow, keep in check the normal frustrations related to their work—may the devil not take advantage of them. May they sense that Someone knows them and is interested in them."

Every time I walked past building 210, I prayed for our pastor and his family. That's where they used to live. Currently, in that building live two teenage brothers who often are out listening to music and living apparently carefree lives. I pray for them too. Across from building 207 is a small mom-and-pop convenience store, like so many that are run by older Koreans who make up the working poor in this country. My prayer for the man watching television—not many customers come to his store—was: "Dear God, send Your angels to be with this man. Awaken in him a desire for something higher and better than mere earthly survival. Put him in contact with a customer or a neighbor or a friend who can share the joy of knowing You. And may he be found by You and follow You. Please, Lord, provide for his needs."

In front of building 208, there was a young woman taking out the trash: "Dear Lord," I prayed, "may this lady sense that Someone in heaven is looking out after her. May You awaken a desire in her heart to learn about You, perhaps by visiting that Christian church she can see across the street from her building. Please, provide a friend for her that can be the instrument of the Holy Spirit on her behalf."

When I first started prayer walking my neighborhood, on the first day, I asked God for a sign that it was the will of God for me. I asked God that I may have meaningful contact with somebody, as the result of prayer walking that day. Now, you must understand that I not only look like a foreigner but that I also cannot speak Korean. What sort of meaningful contact may I have with anybody without speaking the language! Well, God, as it is His custom, answered my prayer, and this is one reason I love Him, as the psalmist says (Psalm 116:1, 2). My heart was full of the love of God when, going from building 209 to 208, I saw two older women struggling mightily to reach for some ripened persimmons off a tree by the walkway. The women were quite advanced in years and rather short in stature. One of them tried getting the persimmons with her cane but with no success. I immediately saw the situation and walked up to them, reaching several branches and pulling them down for them to get the fruit. It was my joy and my privilege to do so. And you should have seen the joy in their faces and how they expressed their deep sense of gratitude for this tall stranger who came to help them. Well, that was a meaningful contact, even if no words were exchanged between us. God confirmed my request.

I must confess that I often include other people while I prayer walk, people who are not from my neighborhood. I pray for my grown children in the United States, for challenging situations facing our division, or even for myself. For as I walk and pray for others, I become more aware of my need to love others as God loves me.

Prayer walking together

So we can prayer walk by ourselves either in our neighborhood or close to our workplace, for example, thinking and praying for those we see. For most, this would ensure that we actually pray for others besides our closest loved ones, when we may often forget to do so in the privacy of our homes. But prayer walking alone still takes second place to praying together. (Praying alone should mostly take place in private, alone with God.) Praying together is something Jesus told the New Testament believers to do.

Ellen White wrote several pages describing in some detail what took place in the upper room during the ten days between Christ's ascension and the Day of Pentecost.[4] Jesus' followers focused on what Jesus had taught them during the previous three years. They reviewed His words to them about His death and resurrection. They came into close fellowship with one another. They sang and praised God together. And they determined to boldly share with others what God had done for the world. This group praying together was almost the same group who, only a few days before, was divided and dispirited (Luke 22:23, 24). Praying together brought them closer together.

Ellen White urged a simple foundational strategy for reaching the cities:

The Lord has presented before me the work that must be done in our cities. The believers in these cities can work for God in the neighborhood of their homes. They are to work quietly and in humility, carrying with them wherever they go the atmosphere of heaven. . . .

Why do not believers feel a deeper, more earnest concern for those who are out of Christ? Why do not two or three meet together and plead with God for the salvation of some special one, and then for still another? . . .

The formation of small companies as a basis of Christian effort has been presented to me by One who cannot err. . . . If in one place there are only two or three who know the truth, let them form themselves into a band of workers. Let them keep their bond of union unbroken, pressing together in love and unity, encouraging one another to advance, each gaining courage and strength from the assistance of the others.[5]

Get together with others in your neighborhood, she says, and pray together for them, and stay united, and reach out to them. It is not complicated. If this is the counsel from "One who cannot err," we will certainly be successful.

And yet, how hard it is for the children of men to get together to pray! In perhaps one of the largest studies ever conducted about character and culture, Americans were found to be the quintessential individualistic society. Many live as if they don't need anyone else.[6] Even though this is more typical of the West, in general, it is surprisingly so in the East as well. I can see that now that I have lived here for four years. In technological societies, such as Japan, even though family ties and community are very important, a very large percentage of the population lives alone, including over a third of the people living in Tokyo, the largest city in the world. In modern society, we've accustomed ourselves to be self-sufficient. The technological advancements of the last fifty years have made us even more so. But Christians must be willing to buck the trend. The simple key to success is praying *together!* And praying together means praying *audibly together* (not all at once, of course), not praying individually, silently, while in the same room. If we are willing to take the time and make the sacrifice to do so for the sake of a dying world, God will certainly reward our effort and obedience.

What prayer walking is *not* about

It is important at this juncture to say a word about what this ministry is *not* about. Some in the prayer-walking movement associate it with spiritual warfare and fighting territorial spirits. They see prayer walking as a means to bind the evil spirits that may dominate a city or an establishment in the community. Several books have been written from this point of view.[7] But this is not the best approach for a prayer-walking ministry.

It is true that the Bible hints at territorial spirits, as alluded to in chapter 8. Jesus spoke of Satan as "the ruler of this world" (John 12:31), and in the book of Daniel, we read about a supernatural evil power labeled "the prince of the kingdom of Persia" (Daniel 10:13) and a second one called "the prince of Greece" (verse 20).[8] Also, Paul wrote that our struggle is not "against flesh and blood, but against principalities, against powers, against the rulers of the darkness of this age, against spiritual hosts of wickedness in the heavenly places" (Ephesians 6:12). Some Bible interpreters see a four-level hierarchy of evil angels in this text.

The counsel of God is not to fight directly *against* these evil spirits as if we were able to conquer demons. The counsel is to put on the armor of God and follow the Leader, Jesus Christ, who is the One able to fight against them successfully. "Fight the good fight of faith," says the apostle Paul (1 Timothy 6:12), and hold on to Christ (John 15:4, 5). Daniel's story is instructive in this regard. When the angel Gabriel was not able to withstand the power of "the prince of Persia," he called on Michael, the Son of God, to do the job (Daniel 10:12, 13). Nowhere do we see Daniel the prophet engaging in direct warfare with the devil or any of his imps. Even Gabriel needed assistance.

It is also true that Jesus gave His followers authority to cast out demons in His name (Matthew 10:8; Mark 3:15; Luke 9:1). And there is evidence that sometimes, at least, they were successful (Luke 10:17), although at other times they were not (Mark 9:15–18). But we must not forget that casting out demons is not the ultimate evidence that God is working through us. Listen carefully to the words of Jesus: "Not everyone who says to Me, 'Lord, Lord,' shall enter the kingdom of heaven, but he who does the will of My Father in heaven. Many will say to Me in that day, 'Lord, Lord, have we not prophesied in Your name, *cast out demons in Your name*, and done many wonders in Your name?' And then

I will declare to them, 'I never knew you; depart from Me, you who practice lawlessness!' " (Matthew 7:21–23; emphasis added).

The casting out of demons is not something Christians should initiate. It is something they can respond to when challenged by the forces of darkness. That was Christ's own methodology. He never sought out demon-possessed cases to cleanse. He simply freed those who were captive by demons when they came to Him for help.

The need for allies

In the work of soul saving, God needs allies. He can do the job alone, but He has chosen to make us partakers of His grace to the world (2 Corinthians 5:20). God limits His reach and power so that we may have a part in this process. This is deep, indeed!

Listen to this thought-provoking promise:

> Worldly wisdom teaches that prayer is not essential. Men of science claim that there can be no real answer to prayer; that this would be a violation of law, a miracle, and that miracles have no existence. . . . They represent God as bound by His own laws. . . . [But Christ] is as willing to listen to the prayer of faith [today] as when He walked visibly among men. The natural cooperates with the supernatural. *It is a part of God's plan to grant us, in answer to the prayer of faith, that which He would not bestow did we not thus ask.*[9]

This is a remarkable promise. Within His sovereign will, God allows enough flexibility that our intercession, our petitions, can actually change the course of events. Remember Rees Howells and his college? If no one had bothered to pray to God against the start of World War II, perhaps the war would have started a whole year earlier, and the aftermath of the war may have carried even greater and more terrible consequences. If God didn't need allies, why would He bother to listen to the petition of any of His children on behalf of others? And yet, time and again, we find in the Bible that people do ask God to intercede. God Himself urges the idea on those whose hearts are pure. Didn't He linger before Abraham to give him a chance to plead on behalf of Sodom and Gomorrah (Genesis 18:17–22)?[10] Didn't God allow Moses to beg for His mercy on behalf of wayward Israel in spite of initial rebuffs (Exodus 32:11, 12)? Didn't He tell Eliphaz to ask Job to intercede for him and his friends so they could live (Job 42:7, 8)? God needs allies to work on behalf of the lost, and you and I can be among those allied with Jesus for the benefit and blessing of others.

Some years ago, I read the story of a man who, after an evening of Bible study with friends, gained a new concept of prayer—one that included God speaking back to the petitioner.[11] He wondered whether God would still speak to people as He did in Bible times. It was about ten o'clock when the young man started driving home after the Bible study, and he began to pray, "God, if You still speak to people, speak to me, I will listen. I will do my best to obey."

Moments later, he had a strange impression to stop and buy a carton of milk. He shook his head and said out loud, "God, is that You?" He didn't get a reply and continued on toward home. But again, the thought came: *Buy a carton of milk.*

After some resistance, the young man decided to stop and buy the milk, just in case it was God who was putting this thought in his mind. But since he didn't know what to do with it, he kept driving home.

As he passed Seventh Street, he again felt the urge: *Turn down that street.* He thought that would be crazy and drove on past the intersection. But the impression persisted. So he turned back and headed down Seventh Street. He drove several blocks when suddenly, he felt as though he should stop. He pulled over to the curb and looked around. He was in a semicommercial area of town. It wasn't the safest part of town. The businesses were closed, and most of the houses looked dark, suggesting that people were already in bed.

But then, a clear thought came into his mind again: *Go and give the milk to the people in the house across the street.* The young man looked at the house. He saw no lights through the windows. It looked as though either the people were gone or they were already asleep. He started to open his car door but then sat back. "Lord, this is insane," he complained; "those people are asleep, and if I wake them up, they are going to be upset, and I will look stupid." But again, he felt that he should go and take the milk to them.

Finally, he walked across the street and rang the bell. He could hear some noise inside.

A man's voice yelled out, "Who is it? What do you want?"

The door opened before the young man could get away. The man was standing there in his jeans and a T-shirt. He looked like he just got out of bed. "Yes, what is it?" he said impatiently.

The young man thrust the carton of milk toward him: "Here, I brought this for you."

The man in the house immediately took the milk and rushed down a hallway. Then, the young man saw a woman come out toward the kitchen carrying the milk. The man was following her, holding a baby crying disconsolately. By now, the man—quite clearly the father of the baby—had tears streaming down his face.

He explained: "We were just praying to God for help. We had some big bills this month, and we ran out of money. We didn't even have the cash to get milk for our baby. I was asking God to show me how to get some milk."

His wife yelled out from the kitchen, "I prayed to God to send an angel with some milk. Are you an angel?"

Are you an angel?

God needs allies. What if that young man that night had not been willing to pray? What if he hadn't been willing to listen to God and trust Him? That baby and those parents needed help that night, and God found an ally in the city to bring the help they needed.

God needs allies today. The world needs intercessors.

Questions for Group Discussion or Personal Reflection

1. Define what prayer walking is and why anyone should bother to do it.

2. Reflect on the difference between praying *together* and praying alone. Why, when a group prays silently, individually, can it not be said they are praying *together*?

3. How does Ellen White describe her foundational strategy for reaching the city?

4. What should be avoided when engaging in a prayer walking ministry?

5. Does God actually need allies on this earth? Can He not get the job of outreach done without us? And if He can, why doesn't He?

----

1. J. Chris Schofield defined prayer walking as multipronged: (1) walking and praying, (2) a lifestyle of unceasing prayer, (3) intentional prayer for the Great Commission, (4) spiritual warfare prayer, and (5) vision-oriented prayer. See J. Chris Schofield, "Prayerwalking Made Simple," accessed August 12, 2020, http://web.kybaptist.org/web/doc/prayerwalkingbooklet.pdf.

2. See Ellen G. White, *The Acts of the Apostles* (Washington, DC: Review and Herald®, 1911), 233.

3. The United Nations figures listed in Appendix B show Seoul's population at about 10 million. But there are several cities of between 1.5 and 3 million each that are attached to the metro area, making the entire urban agglomeration about 23 million people.

4. See White, *Acts of the Apostles*, 35–38.

5. Ellen G. White, "The Work of Soul Saving," *Advent Review and Sabbath Herald*, August 12, 1902, 8.

6. Robert N. Bellah, Richard Madsen, William M. Sullivan, Ann Swindler, and Steven M Tipton, *Habits of the Heart: Individualism and Commitment in American Life* (Berkeley, CA: University of California Press, 1996).

7. For example, C. Peter Wagner, *Engaging the Enemy: How to Fight and Defeat Territorial Spirits* (Grand Rapids, MI: Baker, 1991); C. Peter Wagner, ed., *Territorial Spirits: Practical Strategies for How to Crush the Enemy Through Spiritual Warfare* (Shippensburg, PA: Destiny Image, 2012); Cindy Jacobs, *Possessing the Gates of the Enemy: A Training Manual for Militant Intercession*, 4th ed. (Bloomington, MN: Chosen Books, 2018); and John Dawson, *Taking Our Cities for God: How to Break Spiritual Strongholds*, rev. ed. (Lake Mary, FL: Charisma House, 2001). Although some of the approaches and biblical understanding in these books are objectionable, by no means all of it is. There are some very valuable insights in them as well. Readers are advised to keep very close to the content and tone of Scripture. For relevant warning, check William F. Cook III and Chuck Lawless, *Spiritual Warfare in the Storyline of Scripture: A Biblical, Theological, and Practical Approach* (Nashville, TN: B&H Academic, 2019), 279–282.

8. It would be easy to assume that this prince of Persia is Cambyses, the son of Cyrus, king of Persia at the time of Daniel's story. However, it wouldn't make sense that the highest angel in heaven, Gabriel, would not be able to withstand an earthly ruler such as Cambyses. The story shows that Gabriel needed help to oppose this "prince of Persia" and received help from Michael, a name for the Son of God (see Daniel 10:13).

9. Ellen G. White, *The Great Controversy* (Washington, DC: Review and Herald®, 1911), 525; emphasis added.

10. The Hebrew text in Genesis 18:22 is translated: "Then the men turned away from there and went toward Sodom, but Abraham still stood before the Lord." However, there is a problem with that. It implies that Abraham is the one blocking or stopping God's exit—standing before the Lord—when, in every respect, Abraham had demonstrated and would continue to demonstrate deference to the God "of all the earth" (verse 25). "There is good cause to reverse the roles," writes Old Testament scholar Derek Kidner. He suggests it should read "but the Lord still stood before Abraham," giving the reasons why (Derek Kidner, *Genesis: An Introduction and Commentary*, Tyndale Old Testament Commentaries [Downers Grove, IL: InterVarsity, 1967], 133). Adventist Old Testament scholars seem to agree, suggesting the way it is currently translated was a "scribal correction" to avoid the appearance of irreverence on the part of Abraham. The reasons given are a bit technical for a book of this nature, but they are sound. See Jacques B. Doukhan, *Genesis*, Seventh-day Adventist International Bible Commentary (Nampa, ID: Pacific Press®, 2016), 248.

11. One source for the story is "A Young Man's Story," http://www.gmu.edu/org/mnu/test1.html. GMU is short for George Mason University, the largest research university in the state of Virginia, USA.

CHAPTER 11

Forming the Teams

The first thing a successful prayer-ministry team needs is a vision for what's possible. Get together as a local church or Adventist institution, and take the time to read the first section of this book, along with the discussion questions at the end of each chapter. Think about these things and pray over what you're learning. You may also want to read some of the Bible promises listed in Appendix A of this book and talk and pray about them.

Once you catch a vision for what is possible, take time to pray over the entire project. Pray for the areas in town you're planning to prayer walk. Pray for the church, pray for each other, and pray for the Holy Spirit to guide in the formation of the teams and the prayer plan in general.

Getting organized

How do you form the prayer-walking teams? In some settings, it may be appropriate to simply divide the number of available volunteers into groups with members who know each other well. For example, if twenty people are willing to engage in this ministry, you may want to form five groups of four people, each of which would have men and women, and perhaps people of different ages. However, that generally calls for a rather mature overall group, one clearly committed to the plan.

In most cases, it might be easier to simply group people naturally. That is, let the people in the group select which teams they'd like to belong to. This allows for a more comfortable process. When faced with something new, people tend to want to do it with people they know. This relieves some of the stress of the new adventure. What is important to remember is to have *some balance*. If you see that out of twenty people, one group has eight people, and six groups have only two people each, you may want to appeal to at least a couple of those from the group of eight to become part of another group.

In some more group-oriented cultures, the pastor or top leader may use a portion of the Sabbath morning service or an extended worship time (in the case of institutions) to divide and assign willing participants into teams. In some Latin American cultures, that Sabbath can be made into a big deal. Anticipate creating many teams that involve the entire active church membership.

You may have groups of only two people, but if one of them gets sick or can't make it one day, it will become too easy simply not to go out and pray that day. For that reason, a group of *three* people is better, just in case one person cannot go. This is especially so for groups made up of working people or people with family responsibilities. Remember Solomon's wisdom: "Though one may be overpowered by another, two can withstand him. And a threefold cord is not quickly broken" (Ecclesiastes 4:12).

There are three categories of people that can easily become prayer walkers. One or more groups can be made up of *young people*. Teens have a natural predisposition to engage in social activities with their friends. Why not have three, four, or even five young people form a prayer-walking group? Groups of teens will influence other teens to form additional teams. They could choose to prayer walk their territory right after school is over, before reaching their home, for example.

Another natural group category would be *young mothers* who work at home. If they have babies or young children, they could agree to join with one or two others on prayer walks while the children nap in their baby strollers.

And the other natural category would be *retired people* who have extra discretionary time.[1]

Retired people and prayer teams

One key advantage of a group of *retired people* prayer walking is their greater time flexibility. Another is the fact that older people tend to be more aware of the benefits of walking for their health. A third advantage is that, because of their life experience, they can truly understand the great need to intercede on behalf of others. Few can intercede with the maturity and confidence in God as those with long experience in the things of God. Sometimes we bemoan the fact that our congregations are aging. However, a congregation with a lot of older people has a distinct *advantage* in the area of prayer intercession. *Older people can often commit to prayer walking every day, or at least several times a week, and should believe God will answer their prayers.*

Consider the wonderful story of how God answered the prayers of an older woman who lived in north London in the late 1800s.

Dwight L. Moody was a well-known minister in the city of Chicago, in the United States, when a terrible fire destroyed a very large section of the city, including his church. After dealing with that tragedy and getting the funds to rebuild the church, Moody went to England for a needed rest. One of his objectives was to keep a low profile and to listen to some other preachers, such as Charles Spurgeon and George Müller.

At one of the services he attended in London, however, he was recognized by another minister, who asked him to preach in his church the next Sunday morning and evening. Moody accepted. He preached to a large crowd of people in the morning, but the church seemed completely dead to spiritual things. His preaching had no power. "It seemed the hardest thing I ever did," he testified. Moody regretted having accepted the evening preaching commitment. But when the evening service came, something began to happen midway through his sermon. The cold attitude of the listeners changed radically: "the windows of heaven" opened, he said. Suddenly, people appeared interested, even eager to respond to the Spirit of God. So, at the end of his message, Moody, an experienced evangelist, invited those who wished to commit all to Christ to indicate so by rising to their feet. Hundreds stood up. He hardly expected this response. Thinking they must have misunderstood, he asked them to sit down again and announced a follow-up meeting for those who truly wanted to commit all to Christ.

A huge crowd stayed for the after meeting. Even the pastor couldn't account for this development. Moody repeated the invitation, carefully outlining the thorough commitment to Christ he was speaking about. Again, the entire group, close to five hundred people, rose to their feet. Moody told the local pastor he needed to follow this up, and an announcement was made for meetings every evening for the rest of the week. Moody left in the morning for Ireland, as planned.

As soon as he reached Dublin, Moody received a cablegram from the church pastor that read: "Come back at once. Church packed." Moody returned to London and preached every night for the next ten nights. It led to four hundred baptisms of new Christians just in that church! This major revival that began in that church and community spread all over London, with many churches experiencing similar revivals.

It was two years before Moody learned what caused this great transformation. How could that church go from being so spiritually cold to being so responsive to God in such a short time? He learned that there were two older sisters in that church who lived in the same house, but one of them was bedridden. She had been very active for God for years, but now that she could no longer walk, she became depressed. One day, however, while praying, she realized her job for God now was to pray, to intercede for others. Every day she prayed for her church, claiming God's promises. The church was asleep, unresponsive, Laodicean. Every Sunday, when her sister returned from church services, she asked her how the church was, and who had preached, hoping to see any indication of change. The answer was always the same, discouraging. But when she asked about it on the Sunday that Moody preached, her sister said, "A Mr. Moody, from Chicago, preached today."

Instantly, her sister turned pale as death and said, "I know what that means. There is something coming to the old church. Don't bring me any dinner. I must spend this afternoon in prayer!"[2]

Several years before, this dear sister had read an article by Dwight Moody in a religious newspaper called *The Watchman*. She was impressed to pray that God would bring this man all the way from America to preach in her church! Well, God led Moody to London, to her church. And that evening, things changed in the church, midway through the evening service. And they changed in the city, and in Mr. Moody's ministry, because one older person who could no longer work decided to storm heaven on behalf of her church until the situation was changed. Prayer changes things. Just like others who pray, claiming the promises of God, older people can also make a profound difference in the world.

Team commitment

Becoming comfortable with your team will not take long. The first few times going out together to pray will be exciting and new, and that will be a sufficient motivation to keep going. It is after praying for a few weeks that some uneasiness may surface. This may be because one of the team members prays so quietly that the rest of the team cannot hear his or her prayer. Or it may happen because one person talks too much, or because another tends to always be late to their prayer-walking appointments and the rest have to wait.

Satan will exploit our weak traits of character or annoying habits and use them against us. His first step is always discouragement, then doubt, then despondency.[3] Prayer teams must anticipate this and be ready for it. The enemy would like nothing more than for us to quit interceding for our neighbors and communities. He and his fellow demons know the power of prayer. "Even the demons believe—and tremble!" (James 2:19). You must not let this happen. One good way to help is by making a pledge or drawing up a contract together.

The second time the team meets to prayer walk, they should settle on a group leader. And, more important, they should consider taking a few minutes to write a brief statement of commitment—a group contract or covenant—and sign it.

The contract would articulate its mission and objectives and would indicate their time commitment to do this ministry. Here is a sample:

Our Pledge to Prayer Walk for People
This is our pledge in the name of Jesus and for His sake:

We, _____ (names of team members), pledge to prayer walk on behalf of _____ (name of community, neighborhood, or section of the city). Others who join our team will do so with the same understanding.

We commit to do this because we believe Jesus has many people in this community that could respond to Him and the Adventist message (John 4:35; Acts 18:9, 10). We take the example of Moses, who prayed through until God's mission was accomplished (Exodus 17:10–13).

We pledge to prayer walk every _____ and _____ (indicate days of the week), unless the weather makes it unsafe to do so. In that case, we pledge to meet somewhere to pray together or pray on the phone together. We consider our prayer-walking days and times very important and will honor this commitment to the best of our abilities.

We pledge to attend regular prayer and report meetings with other prayer-walking teams to share with others and hear from others what God is doing in our midst.

We will pray for the people we see and those we cannot see, and as we learn more about them, we will pray increasingly specific prayers on their behalf.

We pledge to acquaint ourselves with God's promises regarding prayer and then commit some of those promises to memory.

We commit ourselves to prayer walk our designated territory until _____ (indicate a date, preferably for one year or more but at least for six months from the time the team begins praying). At that time, we will evaluate what God would have us do next, whether to continue or change plans.

We expect God to open doors of opportunity as we continue to pray (Colossians 4:2–4), and will seek to be ready when those opportunities arise. We will be ready to pray *with* people, pray for whatever they request, and offer them literature or other help that may lead and help them in their search for God.

_____   _____

_____   _____

(signatures)

_____   _____

(place)   (date)

On the day you write and sign the pledge or team contract, you may also want to choose a recorder or a scribe. This person will be one of the team members who will be responsible for keeping notes and reports relevant to the ministry. The notes can become the source of stories to share with the other teams or with the church or institution. Sharing with others what God is doing strengthens our faith in Him. Ellen White said, "If we have tasted and seen that the Lord is good we shall have something to tell."[4]

Here are some things to note or record:

- Specific people's characteristics and behavior. These would be people whom the team sees most often who catch the attention of the team. This will help begin focused prayer for them.
- Particular enemy strongholds that need to come down by the grace and power of God. For example, a bar in the neighborhood, a house known for drug dealing, a home where there is domestic abuse, or a CEO or company that is known to abuse their power or take advantage of people.
- People the team knows who are searching for God, are struggling with life, or might be ready to respond to the Holy Spirit.
- Any open doors, such as people asking the team questions or when an opportunity to give literature or have prayer with someone takes place.

When a team first gathers to pray before they go on their prayer walk, they can include some of these incidents and keep pressing heaven for clearer and clearer evidence of God at work.

The prayer teams list

Appendix B has a list of all the metropolitan areas in the world with a population of one million or more. The list totals 1,780,113,000 people in 548 cities, which is almost a quarter of the entire world's population as of 2018! That number is no doubt higher today. The list also includes the United Nations' population estimates for 2030. In the list, there is a column where I included the *minimum* number of teams that should prayer walk in each city. However, the *minimum ideal* should be ten times that number! Instead of one prayer team for every 100,000 people, it should be for one team for every 10,000 people. So you may add a zero next to each of those team numbers.

Now, I know this may seem overwhelming: the largest city in the world would require a minimum ideal of 3,750 prayer teams! That is barely under the entire active membership of the Adventist Church in that city today. A "small" city of one million would require 100 prayer teams. But think about the enormous encouragement prayer teams would get from knowing they are a part of such a massive mobilization to intercede for the lost.

In 2020, the General Conference of Seventh-day Adventists launched the *I Will Go* mission initiative worldwide. The principal objectives were to "revive the concept of worldwide mission and sacrifice for mission as a way of life," to "strengthen and diversify Adventist outreach in large cities," and to "make developing resources for mission to non-Christian religions and belief systems a high priority."[5] Systematic prayer walking for the lost in our cities and communities fits very well into these objectives.

Conference and mission leaders, churches, and families need to make plans and start covering their cities with prayer, even if the conditions are far from ideal. It is only one team per 10,000 people. The more teams, the better. Do something about it *now—in the name of Jesus!*

Questions for Group Discussion or Personal Reflection

1. How would it work best to form prayer-walking teams in your local church or Adventist institution?

2. What groups of people does the author consider should be able to easily become prayer-walking teams? Are there other groups in your church or institution that could also get involved?

3. What did you think about the older woman in London whose prayers

God answered, bringing a major revival to her church?

4. Why would it be wise to draw up a pledge as teams get together to prayer walk?

5. What would be the point of keeping a report of significant things happening while carrying on a prayer-walking ministry?

6. How many *minimal ideal* prayer teams should be praying for the place where you live? Are you ready to become part of a prayer-walking team?

---

1. There are a number of ways to get organized for prayer walking a city or community. In this chapter, I'm trying to keep things simple. However, a sound alternative would be to check Barbara Lardinais, "Prayer Walking," Hannah's Cupboard, https://hannahscupboard.com /prayer-walking/.

2. The first time I read the story it was from a book by S. D. Gordon, *Quiet Talks on Prayer* (Uhrichsville, OH: Barbour, 1984). The story can also be found at Jerry Falwell, "Ye Have Not Because Ye Ask Not," Little Flock Fellowship Church, February 19, 2000, http://lffc.org/id23 .html.

3. See Ellen G. White, "The Love of God," *Signs of the Times*, April 15, 1889, 2.

4. Ellen G. White, *Steps to Christ* (Washington, DC: Review and Herald®, 1956), 78.

5. See the I Will Go website at https://IWillGo2020.org.

CHAPTER 12

Prayer Walking the Streets

Praying while walking is a wonderful way to spend time with God and connect with other people. Even though you may end up not talking with anyone on the streets while you do this, you know you've connected with them by joining with God's Spirit in His work for souls. Somehow, there is a feeling that you're really on God's side and that you're contributing to His mission of outreach to a dying world.

Let's say that you are part of a church or Adventist institution, and you have the teams selected, and the places where to pray have been decided. Next, you get ready to start your prayer-walking outreach ministry. What are the steps to a successful ministry? There are three. Taking cues from the popular game called American football, the three steps are the huddle, the play, and the celebration. Let me explain.

The huddle

It would be ideal to launch this ministry with all the teams starting in the same week—at least most of them. That is the time when they will *huddle*. In American football, when a team has the ball, before they execute the play, they huddle—they gather together in a circle for a few moments—to determine the next play and how to execute it.

Let's imagine the following scenario, depending on how many participate in a given setting:

Adventist Church or Institution			
Team Composition	Days to Pray	Place to Walk	Team Name[1]/ Leader
1 Retirees	Sundays, Wednesdays, Fridays, Sabbaths	Neighborhood and park	Morning Strollers/ Joe

114

2 Work colleagues	Mondays, Thursdays, Sabbaths	Business center, bus terminal, shopping center	Our Business Is Prayer/Kim
3 Young mothers	Tuesdays, Thursdays, Sabbaths	Neighborhood	Walking Moms/ Lea
4 Young people	Mondays, Wednesdays, Sabbaths	City section near the school or the mall	Hanging Out With Jesus/ Patrick
5 Church friends	Sundays, Tuesdays, Thursdays, Sabbaths	Strategic area in the city	Warriors for Souls/Silvia

It would be best to prayer walk at least two days a week plus Sabbaths. Some teams may be able to do it three or even more days a week, but all the teams should plan to do it also on Sabbaths, if possible. God gives extra blessings on the Sabbath.[2]

When a church or an Adventist institution is ready to launch this initiative, their first day to prayer walk should be on Sabbath afternoon, although there might be some exceptions.[3] All the teams should plan to eat lunch together after the Sabbath morning service or eat together at the meal the church may have planned for that Sabbath. Afterward, all the teams should gather, led by the church pastor or institutional leader, whichever applies.

For this initial launching Sabbath, plan to spend a total of two to three hours together. The first thing the group should do is sing a few songs that focus on faith and mission. Reaching out to those in darkness is what this is all about. Then, the pastor or institutional leader should welcome everyone and pray, asking for the Holy Spirit to be present and for the love of God to take over their hearts. Only as we perceive God's love for us are we are capable of loving others.[4] It would then be good to review the teams and the locations where each of them will prayer walk. Make sure you show those locations on a map, perhaps a satellite image of each area, so all the groups know where others will be ministering.

After that brief but important review, it is time to go over some of the promises of God (see Appendix A), and maybe even pray those promises. Share with one another how God will be with each of them! Here are a few examples:

"Then Jesus went about all the cities and villages, teaching in their synagogues, preaching the gospel of the kingdom, and healing every sickness and every disease among the people. But when He saw the multitudes, He was moved with compassion for them, because they were weary and were scattered, like sheep having no shepherd. He then said to His disciples, 'The harvest truly is plentiful, but the laborers are few. Therefore pray the Lord of the harvest to send out laborers into His harvest' " (Matthew 9:35–38). This promise focuses on the compassion Jesus felt for the multitudes and His prayer that workers would be willing to reach out to the lost.

Notice, Jesus did not ask us to pray for more members to join the church, but for more people to be willing to work with Him to gather those who might be ready to join Him! So a follow-up prayer can be something like this:

> Dear God, thank You for showing us that You have a great deal of compassion for the nameless crowds we see in our cities and communities every day. Thank You that the thousands who ride the subway lines and take buses to work, and the untold numbers who drive the streets and highways, are not simply a mass of people to You, but they are souls for whom You died. You paid a very high price for each of them, and each is precious in Your eyes. Please, give each of us a measure of Your compassion in our own hearts as we see the multitudes today. Please, don't allow us to think they are merely a part of the city landscape, an unfocused background too easy to ignore. Give us hearts like Yours, oh, Lord, to sense a great deal of love and compassion for each person we see today. Dear Father, thank You for allowing us the privilege to fulfill, in a small measure, the answer to Your Son's own prayer two thousand years ago, asking for more laborers to go into the field. Today, we count ourselves among those laborers of Jesus, and we are willing and ready to go into God's field to seek and save that which was lost.

In a parallel text, Luke puts the words of Jesus this way: "The harvest truly is great, but the laborers are few; therefore pray the Lord of the harvest to send out laborers into His harvest" (Luke 10:2). My good friend Dr. Derek Morris wrote an excellent little book based on this text. And he made the point that the Greek verb translated "to send out" that is found in the original New Testament really means "to throw out." In other words, Jesus asked His disciples to pray a very bold prayer, not a puny prayer.[5] This is a radical prayer of great courage. There is so much to be done!

One, two, or even more Bible promises should include those texts having to do with the far-reaching "anything" and "whatever" prayers Jesus urged us to claim in His name. For instance, my favorite promise, even if it is challenging to envision: "Therefore I say to you, whatever things you ask when you pray, believe that you receive them, and you will have them" (Mark 11:24). And then, you can pray:

Oh, Lord, God of all heavens, You told your disciples that if they believed in You, they could pray for anything, and those things would happen. What a far-reaching promise! How gracious and generous You are, dear Father, to make such a sweeping promise and put that in the hands of fallen people like us! We know that when we ask for doors of entrance into the lives of the people we'll see this afternoon, that it is definitely Your will. For it is Your will that "all men would be saved" (1 Timothy 2:1, 3, 4). When You gave this promise, You illustrated it by stating that mountains could be moved out of their places and by showing that a tree can dry up overnight. These are miraculous developments, hard to fathom, and yet, You stand behind them! So we ask, Lord, that You move the mountains that keep people from seeing Your love and Your power at work on their behalf. We pray that situations in people's lives can also change overnight to reflect Your glory and Your purposes for their lives. We believe You can do these things, dear Father, because Jesus did these things and empowered His followers to do the same.

Another promise that can be claimed before going out to walk is this one: "If you abide in Me, and My words abide in you, you will ask what you desire, and it shall be done for you" (John 15:7). You can pray:

Dear God, we have read several of the wonderful promises You made to us, Your disciples. We believe Your words. We believe these amazing promises are applicable to us today. Thank You in advance for answering our prayers on behalf of the lost. Thank You for opening doors of entrance in the lives of the people we will be praying for this afternoon. We may not see those doors open today, but we know You will open those doors as surely as we know we are breathing and kneeling at this moment. Help us to continually remember Your promises, and live by them, as we engage in the search for those who stumble in darkness with hopes of finding the Light.

After taking some time to read and claim some promises and pray over them, you may finish praying for protection and for wisdom for each team, and then announce the time to return. For future gatherings, you will not need to spend as much time before walking as for this first get together.

It is important not to overdo the length of time spent prayer walking the first few times. Later, as a team feels more comfortable doing this ministry, it may choose to lengthen the time. They might become more sensitive to the leading of the Holy Spirit to do so. The first attempt at prayer walking should not last more than thirty minutes. In fact, for some groups—groups of youth or groups less enthusiastic about it than others—twenty minutes may be enough. Once a predetermined time to return and share their experiences is announced, the teams can begin the prayer walk.

The play

Now, it is time to execute "the play." That is, the teams are off to do their prayer work—the work they've been praying and planning for. Believe it or not, thirty minutes go by very quickly. So every precaution should be taken to make sure each team gets to its prayer destination without delay. Delays are often used by the enemy of souls to discourage and distract God's workers. *Each team leader should always keep this in mind.*

Let us imagine two teams. Team A prays along a busy avenue in the heart of the city, and Team B prays around a bedroom community near where they live. How do they pray?

Let's say that Team A is composed of four young professionals. Perhaps they are two couples, or a couple and two single young adults, or some other combination. Team A drives or rides the subway a short distance from the church or "huddle" location to where they will prayer walk. People are walking by them in both directions. Some are lost in their own thoughts. Some have their earbuds on, either listening to music or seeking to distance themselves from the world that surrounds them. There are many single people walking: some are middle-aged business people, well dressed, and apparently consumed by their concerns. Some are older people, walking more slowly, more gingerly, looking to the ground more than at what's ahead. Some are young people, usually two or three at a time, laughing or chatting loudly together. Some are mother-daughter sets, going shopping, or walking to the bus stop. How do you pray for them?

To begin with, don't be afraid of praying out loud. There are two clear benefits to this. One is that it makes it easier to stay focused on your prayer. Praying silently while you walk is all right, especially—and necessarily—if you are alone.

But it will demand much greater concentration, and it is not advisable unless you already have a lot of experience doing this. The second benefit is that the other team members profit from hearing you pray. Something you say may trigger a helpful thought in their minds or inspire their own praying as they, too, focus on the person you're praying for.

What you must learn is to not pray like the stereotypical religious leader when praying during the divine service: a lot of lofty words that say nothing to the heart. *Pray naturally, as if you were carrying on a conversation with your friends.* The only difference is that you're actually directing your words to the God of heaven. Obviously, then, you must pray with your eyes open. That's important so that you don't run into people or light posts! Do not try to pray with your eyes closed. It will take only a few times of doing this before you feel perfectly comfortable praying with your eyes open. And this is one reason why praying aloud helps. If you try to pray silently while keeping your eyes open, it will be too easy to get distracted. But if you pray aloud, it will help you stay focused. And remember, praying aloud is unlikely to bother any passer-by. Why? Because they'll automatically think you're simply talking with your friend. You are! You're talking with your Friend Jesus!

Back to Team A. Their walk brings them to a busy intercession. It will take from 90 to 120 seconds before the light turns green for them to cross. Typically, a number of people will gather right across the intercession from them. They may see a mother with a young daughter. How do they pray?

Dear Father, You see that young mother across the street. She's with her daughter, most likely, and has a great and happy burden in her hands. Please, Father, bless this mother. May Your Holy Spirit guide her mind, her words, and her actions as she seeks to raise her daughter in the best way that she knows. Give her stamina on weary days and wisdom on frustrating days. Give her patience when the child irritates her, and somehow show her how to love the young soul. Our Father, we also pray for this little girl. She has her whole life ahead of her. We don't know if she's growing up in a home that knows and treasures You, but regardless of her upbringing, we pray for the mighty power of the Holy Spirit to steer this little girl to know You and to honor You with her life. Protect her from harm. Give her opportunities to learn about You. Guide her with Your Spirit. In the name of Jesus, we pray. Amen.

Team A may reach a park and see many people there. Some children are playing, some couples are cuddling, and some older people are sitting on a bench, watching the birds in the sky and the dogs at play. Spotting the lonely can awaken in us a great deal of compassion. And when we see older people sitting alone, this should give us immediate reason to pray.

> Dear heavenly Father, there is an older man on that bench, feeding pigeons. He is apparently all alone in the world. We don't know if he has a family, and if he does, whether they have any time for him. We want to hold him up before You today. His days on this earth are waning. Won't You reach out to him? Won't You do some extraordinary thing to convey to this son of Yours that the God of the universe loves him and has died for his sins? Won't You, oh, Lord, bring to him someone he respects, someone he will listen to, that could share with him the wonders of Your love? His days are limited, Lord. Work on his behalf today, tomorrow, and the next day. For we know that You love this man, and his name is inscribed in the palms of Your hands. In the name of Jesus, we pray. Amen.

When we pray for the people we see, even though we may not know them, it allows the Spirit of God to do something in our hearts to love the world. Praying for strangers, as well as for friends, may turn out to be an unexpected blessing to *us*. And it certainly will be a blessing for them. We must keep in mind how hard the enemy works to confuse and deceive people so he can keep them in darkness. A Satanist priest once shared with Roger Morneau that demons flash "thought images" into people's minds to influence them in a particular direction.[6] Ellen White would seem to agree. "You have a diseased imagination," she told one Brother C, in 1868. "Gloomy pictures loom up before you; dark unbelief has enclosed you. By talking on the side of unbelief you have grown darker and darker; you take satisfaction in dwelling upon unpleasant themes." She recommended him to "talk hopefully; cheerfully," in order to rebuff Satan from controlling his thoughts.[7]

What about Team B? Let's assume prayer-walking Team B is a group of retirees. They choose to walk near their home. They recognize a number of the people they see because they are neighbors. In some cases, they know them personally. How do they pray for them?

Team B walks in a more quiet area, an area that does not have as many people as a busy city avenue full of cars, trucks, and buses. Near our apartment, there are several promenades well used by the people living in our community. They are walking paths that allow people to go here and there without having to walk next to noisy streets. Those are excellent sites for older people to walk and pray. Let's say they see a young couple ahead of them, holding hands. They might pray:

Dear Lord, we want to pray for the couple ahead of us. We don't know their names, but You do. You knew them even before they were conceived by their parents. We don't know their struggles, but You do. You know their weaknesses and in what ways the enemy of souls can take advantage of them. We pray today for the power and love of Jesus to surround this young couple, for the Spirit of God to guide them to make good decisions. We pray that You open a door of opportunity for them to get to know You, to discover who the God of heaven is, and to fall in love with You. Cover them with Your grace. Forgive their sins. Lead them to You. Bring about someone in their lives who can share who You are with them. Thank You for the privilege to pray for them, for we know You hear our prayer. In Jesus' name, amen.

Since Team B prayer walks in the community where they live, it is likely they will run into someone they have met before. Let's assume that happens, that they see on their walk a female neighbor who lives two buildings across from theirs. They may know her name—let's say it is Mary—but not much more about her. This is a great opportunity to cordially greet her unless it is clear that she is in a hurry and your greeting would be a bothersome interruption. After you greet her, normally, people will exchange information, such as where they are headed or what they are doing. If Mary shares that information, listen carefully to what she says because that will be your basis for praying for her. If she mentions family, pay attention to what Mary says about them, including names and places. If she mentions hardship, take mental notes. If she asks where the team is headed or what you are doing there, feel free to share that you come out every Monday, Wednesday, and Sabbath (let's say), to pray for the people in your community. This will probably come as a surprise to Mary. If she is intrigued and asks for more details, be happy to share with her, but keep it brief. Just remember that this encounter is not about you—it is about *her*. All the while you speak with her, pray silently in your mind that you may be a blessing to her and for God to guide your mind and your tongue for her sake. If appropriate, offer to have a short prayer with her. If you perceive she'd be open to it, hold her hand. If she is OK with your praying for her, share how it will go, so she knows what to expect. For example,

We are going to talk with the God of heaven about you, Mary, for a moment. There is nothing to fear. We will not do anything that embarrasses you or anyone else. We will simply close our eyes and talk with Jesus for a minute or two. You can close your eyes if you'd like—it might help you concentrate—or you might want to keep them open. Either way, are you ready?

Dear heavenly Father, it is a joy for us to see Mary today. It is good to hear that she is in good health and that she enjoys her family. Dear Lord, please be with Mary's two granddaughters that she mentioned today. May You bless their parents. May Your loving and peaceful Spirit abide in their home. Guide the girls in their studies and in their associations with their friends. And Lord, please be with Mary in any difficulty she faces in her life. May You give her wisdom and peace to face her challenges. We pray this in the name of Jesus, our Savior. Amen.

If Mary is not a Christian, or even if she is from a Catholic or Orthodox background, what will surprise her is this type of prayer. Non-Christians and even many Christians are not used to praying to God as if talking to a friend. This will be an important seed planted in her mind, ready to bear fruit at the right time.

The celebration

The teams had their huddle, they engaged in the play, and now it's time to celebrate. The ideal plan would be for various teams from the same church or institution to get together, at least on Sabbaths, to celebrate their outreach that afternoon. They simply agree to be back at the church or institution at a certain time for a few more minutes together. Sometimes it's not possible, but when it is possible, each of the teams participating would greatly benefit from a brief gathering.

Once all the teams are back, the pastor or leader invites each of the team recorders to share some team experiences from that afternoon. The stories should be kept short and to the point unless there is a remarkable incident to share. And if there is nothing special to share, there is no need to share. Don't feel compelled to do it just to say something. Maybe next time.

Here is an example of what happened with a church in Taiwan that took this ministry seriously.

In southern Taiwan, there is an Adventist church in Mao Lin. The community dubbed them "the Butterfly Church" because of the large butterflies sculpted at the church's front facade. A couple of years ago, they decided to start prayer walking. Rather than having several teams, ten to fifteen church members committed to prayer walking together every morning at six o'clock! They prayed audibly for the community as they walked. At times, along with a guitar, they would stop and praise God in song together. With some neighbors, they offered prayer. It is important to realize that Taiwan is a deeply Buddhist country. This is not a Christian-friendly environment. But God honored their efforts. The Adventist members who engaged in this ministry believed God would touch hearts.

God did touch hearts. After they had been prayer walking for six months, twenty-five new people joined the church! Of course, not every new convert was a direct result of the prayer-walking ministry, but God used it to move in the hearts of more people than expected. If we pray consistently for some who won't respond, God will apply those prayers on behalf of those whom He knows *will* respond.

So here it is. The plan is simple, and the execution of the plan should not present major difficulties. The prayers mentioned in this chapter are only examples. Each person should pray as they are moved by the Holy Spirit. And as the teams go out time and again, consecrating time and effort to the cause of Christ, more creativity can be incorporated into their ministry. Persistence will be a major key to their success. People need to simply incorporate prayer walking into their weekly routine. If they move out in faith, God will reward the time invested on behalf of others.

Questions for Group Discussion or Personal Reflection

1. Why should prayer-walking teams "huddle"?

2. Which of the various prayer promises in this book (Appendix A) is your favorite? Why?

3. Imagine you are part of a prayer-walking team. What do you envision happening as you go out to prayer walk for others?

4. Were you surprised to learn that demons can flash "image thoughts" into people's minds, thus leading them to gloom and misery? What do you think about that?

5. If Jesus were to ask you to get involved in this type of prayer ministry,

what objections would you have, and how do you think Jesus would respond to them?

6. What would be the chief benefit of getting all the prayer-walking teams together for a few minutes on Sabbath after they finish?

---

1. These team monikers are only suggestive, of course. If a church or institution has several prayer-walking teams, it might be interesting to find a distinctive label for each. The nicknames should be chosen by each specific team, not by the entire group of teams.

2. See Ellen G. White, *The Desire of Ages* (Battle Creek, MI: Review and Herald®, 1898), 288.

3. For some Adventist institutions, such as a hospital or a publishing house, Sabbath may not be the best day to start, unless the workers all live in a community close to each other. If they don't, Monday may be the best day for them to begin.

4. This is what the servant of the Lord has said about this: "Love is the basis of godliness. Whatever the profession, no man has pure love to God unless he has unselfish love for his brother. But we can never come into possession of this spirit by *trying* to love others. What is needed is the love of Christ in the heart. When self is merged in Christ, love springs forth spontaneously. The completeness of Christian character is attained when the impulse to help and bless others springs constantly from within—when the sunshine of heaven fills the heart and is revealed in the countenance." Ellen G. White, *Christ's Object Lessons* (Battle Creek, MI: Review and Herald®, 1900), 384; emphasis in the original.

5. Derek J. Morris, *The Radical Prayer* (Hagerstown, MD: Review and Herald®, 2008), 43–46. His wife, Bodil, even put the words of the text to music, sung and recorded by Trilogy.

6. Roger J. Morneau, *More Incredible Answers to Prayer* (Hagerstown, MD: Review and Herald®, 1993), 45, 65, 81. Morneau referred to this sobering fact several times in his books, such as in *When You Need Incredible Answers to Prayer* (Hagerstown, MD: Review and Herald®, 1995), 70.

7. Ellen G. White, *Testimonies for the Church*, vol. 1 (Mountain View, CA: Pacific Press®, 1948), 699. See also *The Great Controversy* (Washington, DC: Review and Herald®, 1911), 516, 517. She wrote, "Satan can most readily control the minds of those who are unconscious of his influence."

CHAPTER 13

Prayer Warriors and Intercessors

T he largest single congregation in the world is in Korea. The Yoido Full Gospel Church (YFGC) has about 560,000 members. A part of the Assemblies of God denomination, it holds seven services each Sunday and has tens of thousands of active cell groups throughout Seoul. The church was founded and led for fifty years by Pastor Yonggi Cho, a bright and charismatic leader. Even though the church strongly models lay empowerment at every level of ministry, the top leader has retained enormous influence over the years regarding the character and nature of the church.[1]

One day, an Adventist doctoral student by the name of Craig Dossman interviewed Dr. Cho, asking him the secret of his church's phenomenal growth. The legendary pastor walked over to his shelf and pulled out two books written by Ellen White: *Christian Service* and *Gospel Workers.*[2]

There is no doubt that much of what characterizes the YFGC is clearly endorsed by Ellen White: small groups for membership care and community outreach, a far-reaching distribution of tasks and responsibilities among members, biblical preaching, sponsoring and commissioning missionaries throughout the world, and focus on the centrality of Christ and Holy Spirit transformation in the life of the believer. There are, however, some teachings and ministry practices that she would disapprove of, considering them unbiblical. But perhaps the clearest expression of Ellen White's Christian priorities is the prayer ministry of YFGC. That church is bathed through and through with prayer.[3] And many believe that prayer lies at the foundation of the church's incredible growth.

So what else can Adventists do by way of prayer to foster the work of God?

Prayer intercessors

Every time I have trained groups of churches for evangelism, regardless of the country, I have suggested that members join at least one of three prayer ministries. These are three different levels of prayer intercession. I call them prayer intercessors, prayer walkers, and prayer warriors. Let's look at the prayer intercessors first.

Prayer intercessors are the infantry of the prayer army. They are the foot soldiers, the basic foundation for prayer warfare in each congregation or institution. Without them, we cannot even hope for any breakthroughs in the spiritual realm. Let's assume these prayer intercessors are in a local church. What do they do? How does their ministry operate?

Get organized. The pastor, or a leading member with a burden for prayer, should make an announcement asking for prayer intercessors. Announce the date and time for a brief training and organizational meeting. This announcement would be ideal at the end of a stirring Sabbath sermon on prayer, followed by a call to commitment for prayer. In the last church I pastored, I preached a seven-sermon series on prayer. At the end of the last sermon, I simply invited people to come back in the afternoon, at four o'clock, in order to pray for an hour. I wasn't as well organized then as I would be today, so I didn't have resources or know exactly how to follow up. But the timing of this announcement was key. Over one hundred members, a third of the attending members, returned that Sabbath afternoon to pray.

Secure materials. Before the organizational meeting, training materials and resources should be secured—this book, for example. There are other valuable books on prayer, and many other materials are available.[4] One good source is the Revival and Reformation website at the General Conference of Seventh-day Adventists: http://revivalandreformation.org. There you will find a treasure trove of materials: PDF training documents, videos, books, and other useful resources for churches and institutions to start a serious prayer ministry.

Design a plan. Make sure you have a prayer plan for your prayer intercessors: when to gather for prayer, how and what to pray for, and what to avoid in corporate prayer. Do not make the training too long, and get the official intercessors to start praying right away—within a week or less of the initial training meeting (you, of course, will want to dedicate time for corporate prayer at the training as well). Anticipate having to do a follow-up training event a few months later. There will be key questions and suggestions by those participating.

Focus your prayer time. Too often, churches and institutions pray general prayers, prayers that would be difficult to know whether or not God has answered them because they are so vague. Praying that way is ineffective. The objective of the intercessors should be to focus on specific people and specific needs. For example, they pray for all the nonmembers attending the local church. Prayer intercessors should have a list of these attendees and their contact information. The list should be guarded carefully to protect the privacy of the individuals. Along with the names and contact information, specific items for which to pray should be listed. If you don't know what they need prayer for, ask those who know them, or if you know them well enough, ask them directly. Most people don't mind being prayed for.

Another group of people to pray for is those with special needs: the sick, those going through a challenging time in their lives, those who appear hopeless. An important list all prayer intercessors should have is a list of prayer promises from Scripture (see Appendix A). Refer to this list as you pray.

Set times and places to pray together. All prayer intercessors should pray *daily* for some or all of the people on their lists. They should do this in the privacy of their homes. But they should *also* get together to pray at least once or twice every week. They could pray every Sabbath, for example, right before or right after the church service. In one of the churches I pastored, we got together every Sabbath at seven o'clock in the morning to pray for specific individuals and situations. An additional time to pray would be at least once a month in someone's home or at the church. This could be an evening of fellowship and prayer for several hours, if necessary. As prayer intercessors develop spiritually and as they develop a greater hunger for God's power over the lives of those for whom they pray, they may choose to have the sessions more often.

Finally, all the intercessors in a given church should be involved as leaders during special times of prayer at the church. For example, they could lead out during a 40 Days of Prayer initiative (more on this in another chapter) or during a fasting and prayer weekend (next chapter). And if there is an evangelistic series coming up, intercessors should make special efforts to meet and pray, especially right before and after sermons when the preacher will prompt decisions for Christ, His teachings, and His church.

The second level of prayer ministry involvement in a local church or Adventist institution is prayer walking. We have discussed that at length in the previous three chapters already. The third level involves prayer warriors. These people will take prayer to the highest level.

Prayer warriors
My definition of a prayer warrior is "someone who has the gift of prayer and agonizes consistently before God on behalf of others until God's answer becomes evident." Hear Ellen White describe these prayer warriors:

The season of distress and anguish before us will require a faith that can endure weariness, delay, and hunger—a faith that will not faint though severely tried. . . . All who will lay hold of God's promises, as he [Jacob] did, and be as earnest and persevering as he was, will succeed as he succeeded. Those who are unwilling to deny self, to agonize before God, to pray long and earnestly for His blessing, will not obtain it. Wrestling with God—how few know what it is! How few have ever had their souls drawn out after God with intensity of desire until every power is on the stretch. When waves of despair which no language can express sweep over the suppliant, how few cling with unyielding faith to the promises of God.[5]

These are not only prayer intercessors participating at the first level of involvement. These are people who take prayer very seriously as a vital tool for the salvation of humanity, and they spend time in it accordingly. These are people who have a real passion and burden for prayer, the people who are closest to the throne of God, as it were. These are the Moseses, the Jobs, and the Jacobs who say to God: "I will not let You go unless You bless me!" (Genesis 32:26). These are the women who, like the persistent widow in Jesus' parable, "cry out day and night to Him" until God provides the answer (Luke 18:1–8).

In the local church context, this would be the third and highest level of prayer-ministry commitment. It is important not to give the impression that prayer warriors are "holier" than other prayer intercessors or other church members, in general. They simply have made a commitment to prayer that others are not ready to make or interested in making.[6] The prayer warriors would do everything the prayer intercessors would do *as well as* what the prayer walkers would do. But they would *also* get involved in ways the other two groups would not. There are exceptions to this, of course. Some prayer warriors cannot walk due to physical ailments, but if they daily pray, earnestly and faithfully, with a deep burden in their hearts for the salvation of others, they are prayer warriors. These are the people Satan fears: "Satan knows better than God's people the power that they can have over him when their strength is in Christ."[7] "Satan cannot endure to have his powerful rival appealed to, for he fears and trembles before His strength and majesty. At the sound of fervent prayer, Satan's whole host trembles."[8]

The following is a commitment page I used recently in Hong Kong, indicating all three levels of involvement I have used to help people decide where to get involved.

Prayer Evangelism

Below are three different ways to participate. You may choose to combine more than one way.

Level 1—Prayer Intercessors

1. Pray every day individually for evangelism in your church/community.

2. Gather with others after each Sabbath service to pray for 15 minutes over interests, contacts, friends, and the church's readiness for evangelism. Meet with the group once a month to pray for one hour.

3. Participate in the 40 Days of Prayer on the dates set by your church, and attend the Consecration Service, to pray for the pre-harvest and evangelistic meetings.

4. Join the special prayer gatherings on Sundays or other days *during* the evangelistic harvest meetings.

Level 2 – Prayer Walkers

1. Go through the training provided and read the instructions document.

2. Join a prayer-walking team and choose an area in the city to specifically pray for people you see on the street, in shops, apartment buildings, businesses, restaurants, MTR stops, etc.

3. Pray-walk two or three times each week plus on Sabbaths.

4. Join the Prayer Intercessors in the 40 Days of Prayer and the Consecration Service.

Level 3—Prayer Warriors

1. Choose a city block and pray specifically for each home and apartment building on that block. Regularly walk up and down that block several times a week, praying for it.

2. After praying for your block for one month, leave a Prayer Request Card on the doorknob of a specific home or apartment, or knock on the door and ask for prayer requests with the card. Come back later and pick up the card with the prayer requests. Pray for those requests.

3. A few weeks after you receive the prayer requests—unless the request is urgent or dated—and have prayed for them, stop by the homes, or apartments, knock, and ask how it has been going. Do this once a month so that the people are used to you stopping by asking about their prayer needs.

4. One week before either the pre-harvest meetings (archaeology and/or apologetics) or the evangelistic meetings begin, invite to the meetings the people you have met and have been praying for.

Please indicate with an X the level you have chosen to commit: _____ Level 1 _____ Level 2 _____ Level 3

Please complete the bottom part and turn it in. Thanks.

Name _____ E-mail _____

Address _____

Phone _____ Church Membership _____ Level Indicated _____

So what do prayer warriors do in addition to what intercessors and walkers do?

Focus on a specific territory and/or specific people. Whereas prayer intercessors may pray for the community in general, prayer warriors wrestle in prayer for specific areas in the city or specific people in need of rescue. For example, a group of prayer warriors may choose to prayer walk around a neighborhood that is known for drug trafficking or a part of the city known for prostitution. Obviously, these places involve the potential for greater danger, and that needs to be carefully considered. But these prayer warriors may have developed a real burden for the people trapped by Satan in these places. And their focused prayer is for them to be freed by Jesus. After all, Jesus said He came "to heal the broken-hearted" and "set at liberty those who are oppressed" (Luke 4:18). Cheryl Sacks, a prayer coordinator trainer in the United States, tells the story of a team that focused on a drug-infested area of the city, and within a month, the main crack house in the area burned to the ground. Within four months, all other crack houses in the neighborhood disappeared, and with them all the gangs![9] Earnest, faithful prayer warriors will make a real difference.

There are legal issues involved in the great controversy between good and evil. God can do more on behalf of others when we get involved in prayer. Why? Carrol Shewmake has articulated an answer this way: "God has purposely limited Himself in His intervention in human lives in order to preserve individual freedom. Otherwise Satan would accuse Him of *forcing* people to serve Him. But in God's plan, when the righteous pray for family, friends, and *even those they will never personally contact,* God then freely acts in the lives of those people in a way that He would not if we did not pray."[10]

Ron Halvorsen, the legendary Adventist evangelist, made it a practice to prayer walk sections of the city where he would conduct weeks-long evangelistic meetings. Pastor Ron was a prayer warrior and wrote a book about being one (cited in note 4). Because he grew up as a gang member in New York City, surrounded by the worst the city had to offer, his burden was drug dealers and prostitutes. One time, he had a series of meetings in Honolulu, Hawaii. The meetings were a great success, leading over 225 people to baptism. He attributed much of this success to the prayer walking he and others had done in the city. One of those baptized was a prostitute. She left that life behind to walk with Jesus! When she told Pastor Halvorsen she had been a prostitute, he asked where she had worked in the city. It turns out that the street she had frequented as a prostitute was the very street that Pastor Halverson had prayer walked day after day for the salvation of the lost!

Use a prayer request card. Prayer warriors who prayer walk their neighborhood, especially, should have a follow-up plan. Let's assume you are a prayer warrior. After praying for a few weeks or months for each home in your neighborhood and for each person you see in the park or in public places, you should plan to make direct contact with people. How do you do that?

You can design a Prayer Request Card that you would leave on the doorknobs of people's homes or apartments. If you cannot afford to make or to print a card, you can simply write a personal note, make copies of it, and leave it on people's doors. What should this card or note say?

Dear neighbor, my name is _____ and I live close by. I believe that God answers prayer, and I'd like to pray for you. If you have any need for prayer, please leave your prayer request on the back of this card/note at the door, and I will pick it up later without disturbing you. May God bless you.

You may choose to put two names on the card, yours and that of your prayer partner's, but not more than two names. You may also choose to add a Bible verse at the end, such as Psalm 116:1, Matthew 19:26, or Hebrews 13:5. Make sure you include the text, not just the Bible reference.

Of course, you can change the words for the card, but notice a few things about this example. By saying "I live close by," you're identifying with your neighbor, you're saying you are not a stranger. Saying "I believe God answers prayer" is better than saying, "God answers prayer"; people will accept the first statement better. Adding the statement "If you have any need for prayer" is less direct than saying only "I'd like to pray for you." And saying "I will pick it up later without disturbing you" answers the question people may have about how they would let you know of their requests, and it eases any concern your neighbor may have about talking to strangers. Of course, whatever you choose to say in the card or note needs to be prayerfully considered in the context of the community's culture.

Make very sure you keep track of where you leave these prayer request cards/notes. You will need to go back in the afternoon or evening to pick them up. You don't want to leave the cards on the doors for days. If you left the cards in the evening, go later at night or early in the morning to pick them up. You want to pick up the cards before the people leave again for work in the morning. When you go back to pick them up, be quiet, and do *not* knock on people's doors. Make sure you pick up *all* the cards you left in the neighborhood. Some doors will not have the cards anymore. That means people saw the card, took it, and chose *not* to leave a request. Most cards you pick up will not have prayer requests. That's OK. Even if you only have one card in a hundred with a prayer request, it is worth the effort!

Now, this is very important: check each card for a prayer request *before* picking up the next card. Why? Because you need to remember the address where that request came from. Write the address on the card itself and add that day's date before moving on. This is extremely important; otherwise, you will forget where that card came from, and you may never be able to get back to them again.

Follow up people's requests for prayer. Whatever prayer requests you receive, treasure them as precious in God's eyes, and pray for them earnestly. Pray for them as soon as you collect the cards and are back home. Pray for them constantly throughout the day, every day! Claim Bible promises for them. Think of this as a unique opportunity God is giving you to make an actual difference in that person's life. This is a door of entrance into their hearts. Paul prayed regularly for doors of entrance in the mission field (1 Corinthians 16:9; 2 Corinthians 2:12; Colossians 4:3; Acts 14:27).

Depending on the prayer request, wait a few weeks before you go back to the home of those who wrote prayer requests to see whether God answered the prayer yet, but don't wait too long. Sometimes, a person may have a request, such as, "My daughter will have surgery on Thursday." In that case, you should go back Friday or Sabbath to check to see how things went with their daughter. This will likely impress the neighbor, seeing that you're actually a person of your word. It will build trust in you as a servant of God.

For other requests, such as the need for a job, for more income, or for peace in the family, you should wait longer. But make sure you pray every day for God to provide these people with clear, tangible blessings.

What do you do when you go back?

Try going back at a time you're likely to find them home. If they are not there, try again later or the next day. If they are not home again, leave them a personal note. In the personal note, you may say something like this: "Dear neighbor, this is (your name). We've been praying every day for (mention the specific request) since you told us on the request card (put the date). We dropped by to check on how things are developing."

Do *not* leave your phone number or contact information yet, unless you already know them. That can become an easy excuse for someone to call you and say, "Never come to my door again!" The enemy of souls will always exploit people's weaknesses. Simply wait a couple of days and go back. Do the same a third time, if necessary. Try going at a different time of the day. It isn't until you have met the person face to face and have spent some time with them that you might consider exchanging personal information. Trust must be built first.

Remember that God will be with you as you seek to bless your neighbors. I once heard of a sister in the church who was absolutely frightened about prayer walking her neighborhood. We will call her Lynn. Lynn was very shy and was afraid of talking to strangers. The pastor assured her that what she needed to do was talk to *God* about people. So she finally went prayer walking. One day, while prayer walking, Lynn heard the Lord say to her: "Go and knock on that door." She cringed. "I don't want to knock on that door!" she protested. The Lord again impressed her to do it. She was afraid and began to despair, but she obeyed and knocked on the door. A lady opened the door. Lynn clammed up. She didn't know what to say.

She finally said, "Hello, I'm a prayer walker."

"Oh, that's nice," the lady of the house said.

"I walk every evening in this neighborhood praying for people," Lynn said. "Do you have a prayer request?" she finally asked with an awkward smile.

The woman started to cry. "My husband is in the hospital, and he's very sick right now. We don't know what is going to happen to him. Would you please pray for my husband?" Lynn offered a simple prayer of faith.

A few days later, Lynn was out prayer walking again. When she came close to that house, the door opened, and the lady inside waved at her, saying, "Hello, prayer walker!" Lynn went over to her. The lady opened the door wide for a man to come through and said, "I want you to meet my husband." They talked for a while, and the man thanked Lynn for praying for him. He had been healed. After this experience, Lynn was so excited to pray for her neighbors that she got business cards made, introducing herself as a Prayer Warrior! The card read: "Write a prayer request on the back." The word got around the neighborhood. Most of Lynn's neighbors were not practicing Christians, so when they were in trouble or needed guidance, they didn't go to a church or to a minister, they called Lynn, the prayer warrior!

Praying for others is often like planting seeds: it may take a while for a full plant to develop, but it will come. In 1973, archaeologists discovered date palm seeds in Masada, a mountain with a flat top in the hot desert of Judea,[11] where King Herod, at the time of Christ, had a palace. The seeds had lain in hot, dry jars for two thousand years. In 2005, a researcher by the name of Elaine Solowey carefully planted one of them to see what would happen. The seed grew into a date palm. The tree is more than four feet tall today, and it blossoms every year.

Our prayers, like the date palm seeds, will eventually bear fruit!

Questions for Group Discussion or Personal Reflection

1. Does it surprise you that the amazing success of the largest church in the world is due, at least in part, to the counsel of Ellen White?

2. What are the three levels of prayer ministry workable in a church, according to the author?

3. At which level of prayer ministry would you like to be involved?

4. What do prayer intercessors do to accomplish their ministry?

5. What do prayer warriors do that is different from what intercessors or prayer walkers do?

6. What practical counsel in this chapter did you find insightful for prayer ministries?

---

1. In the words of a Korean Adventist researcher, "Rev. Cho has exercised absolute power over his church." Song Won Moo, *A Paradigm for Cell Church Ministry in the Seventh-day Adventist Church in Korea* (DMin diss., Andrews University, 2010), 141. Cho retired in 2008, but he continues as pastor emeritus. In 2007, the church boasted a membership of 803,000. Perhaps the loss of membership was influenced by Dr. Cho's legal troubles (see next note). Still, with a membership of over half a million, it is by far the largest congregation in the world.

2. For years I had heard rumors to that effect, mostly about two Adventist pastors interviewing Dr. Cho. The story was finally corroborated when I read an article by Byard Parks in *Adventist Frontiers,* the magazine from the parachurch mission organization Adventist Frontier Missions, titled "Lessons From the Biggest Church in the World," *Adventist Frontiers* 18, no. 6 (June 2002).

As remarkable a Christian leader as Dr. Cho was for so long, he was not perfect. In 2014, "he was convicted of embezzling US$12 million (U.S.) from the church. He was given a suspended sentence of three years and was fined nearly $5 million. One of his sons was also convicted and was handed a three-year sentence." *Encyclopaedia Britannica Online,* s.v. "David Yonggi Cho," accessed August 12, 2020, https://www.britannica.com/biography/David-Yonggi-Cho.

3. For a thorough examination of the various ministries and priorities of YFGC, see Karen Hurston, *Growing the World's Largest Church* (Springfield, MO: Chrism, 1995). The author, an American, grew up in that church as the daughter of one of the early associate pastors and trainers for lead pastor David Yonggi Cho. For example, their Sunday worship service consists of *Silent Prayer,* Reading of Psalms, Doxology, The Apostles Creed, Hymn, *Prayer,* Scripture Reading, Choir, *Prayer,* Sermon, *Guided Concert of Prayer,* Appeal to Nonbelievers, *Prayer, Prayer of Application, Prayer for the Sick,* Hymn, *Offering Prayer,* Announcements, *Singing the Lord's*

Prayer, and *Prayer of Benediction* (emphasis added). That's just the worship service. There are innumerable prayer programs, such as the 5:00 A.M. daily prayer meetings, the all-night prayer sessions between 10:00 P.M. and 4:00 A.M., and the multiple programs offered at their Prayer Mountain retreat facility.

4. For a number of years, I was privileged to work with a great American evangelist by the name of Ron Halvorsen. He wrote a very inspiring book on prayer intercession by church members, which has been translated to other languages as well. The book is *Prayer Warriors* (Fallbrook, CA: Hart Research Center, 1995). A similar book but with a little different focus is Mark A. Finley, *10 Days in the Upper Room: Receiving the Gift of the Holy Spirit* (Nampa, ID: Pacific Press®, 2011). And another one would be *Praying for Rain: A Mini-Handbook for United Prayer,* available as a PDF from the Revival and Reformation website, http://revivalandreformation.org.

5. Ellen G. White, *The Great Controversy* (Washington, DC: Review and Herald®, 1911), 621.

6. This is a point well made by Ron Halvorsen. See his *Prayer Warriors,* 146–148.

7. Ellen G. White, *Testimonies for the Church,* vol. 1, (Mountain View, CA: Pacific Press®, 1948), 341.

8. White, 346.

9. Cheryl Sacks, *The Prayer-Saturated Church: A Comprehensive Handbook for Prayer Leaders* (Colorado Springs, CO: NavPress, 2007), 200, 201.

10. Carrol Johnson Shewmake, *When We Pray for Others: The Blessings of Intercessory Prayer* (Hagerstown, MD: Review and Herald®, 1995), 14; emphasis in the original.

11. See Don Jacobsen, *Just a Minute . . . and 30 Other Gentle Confrontations* (Hiawassee, GA: HighWalk Productions, 2014), 35. I know this to be true also because my former colleague at Southern Adventist University, Michael Hasel, is an archaeologist who knows the archaeologist who found the seeds, and he told me the story.

CHAPTER 14

Fasting and Prayer

After a very dramatic and life-changing conversion, a law clerk by the name of Charles Finney immediately became an evangelist in the Eastern United States. He had fallen in love with Jesus, and nothing could stop him from sharing the good news of salvation with others. Years after his conversion, he recalled that in those days, he felt God's Word "had wonderful power, every day," and as he shared God's Word with others, he "could not remember one whom [he] spoke with, that not soon after converted."[1]

Finney became very effective in soul winning. He prepared his sermons by praying with his Bible open on his knees. Thousands listened to his evangelistic sermons and turned their lives over to God. Multitudes came to Christ from dozens of cities and towns along the Hudson River in the State of New York. However, from time to time, he felt empty of the power of God. When that happened, Finney would "set apart a day for private fasting and prayer, . . . and would inquire anxiously after the reason for this apparent emptiness." But after a time of fasting and prayer, "and crying out for help," the power of God would return to him "with all its freshness."[2]

Can fasting, along with prayer, make such a difference in a person's prayer effectiveness? I have compiled some testimonies from people who shared the difference that fasting has made in their lives. After fasting and praying for her son, Becky wrote: "I saw a significant turn of (spiritual) interest in my sixteen-year-old son." Darlene, after an extended fast, said that "the Lord began to show" her the gravity of her sin, "like never before." Ralph shared that the further he progressed into the fast, the closer he experienced the presence of God. Don said that because of fasting, he now looks "to the Lord for guidance regarding watching TV," which means more time with God and his family. And he added, "I also learned to control my appetite."

Fasting is no magic pill to solve all problems, but it is a powerful tool in the hands of the Holy Spirit to change people's lives, especially of the person who fasts. "The absence of fasting," wrote a well-known Christian author, "is indicative of our comfort with the way things are. . . . [It] is the measure of our contentment with the absence of Christ."[3] Are we willing to sacrifice some comfort for a deeper experience with the Lord?

For some readers, this is familiar territory. You may have fasted in the past or may do so regularly today. For many others, fasting is something they have not yet experienced. Fasting is depriving yourself of something that pleases your senses for the sake of something better—namely, God and His purposes. Fasting is usually associated with not eating or skipping certain foods or meals, but it may involve more than that. In today's world of technology, fasting may very well imply laying aside watching television, movies, or online programming; setting aside the use of social media for a time; paying no attention to the multiple notifications received from news or sports outlets on our cell phones; or limiting the use of the internet. Remember, the battle fought between Christ and Satan is for control of our minds.[4] "The spirit of true fasting and prayer," writes the servant of the Lord, "is the spirit which yields mind, heart, and will to God."[5]

The benefits of fasting

What does fasting help us accomplish? It helps us to focus on God while stopping a myriad of distractions from that end. "Fasting helps to express, to deepen, and to confirm the resolution that we are ready to sacrifice anything, to sacrifice ourselves, to attain what we seek for the kingdom of God."[6] One reliable source put it very clearly: "The chief benefit to be obtained from fasting is a clarity of mind that comes with complete or partial abstinence from food and that enables a person to perceive God's will more distinctly."[7]

I can testify to the truth of this statement. Years ago, I was pastoring a church that was engaged in a fasting and prayer weekend (more on this later), seeking earnestly for the Lord to work in our lives. I had been counseling a young woman for a few months who was bulimic, anorexic, and a pathological liar, and who exhibited some demonic influence. She was in very bad shape emotionally and spiritually, and I felt that progress was not being made in spite of the constant praying of myself and others at the church. But a breakthrough came the weekend we fasted. She seemed very angry at what the guest speaker had said that Sabbath. His sermon was about the love of Jesus toward Mary Magdalene, and I was baffled by why she would find that objectionable. But then, a flash of insight came to my mind, and I heard myself blurt out: "You were sexually molested when you were young, weren't you?" I could hardly believe I had just said that! Besides, how would I know if this was the case? She turned pale and very quiet, and said, "How do you know that? My mother and my uncle (the abuser, as it turned out) are the only people in the whole world who know that." Well, I didn't know that. But I did know that Mary Magdalene was taken advantage of when she was young,[8] and I instinctively put two and two together. Acknowledging that fact cleared the way to recovery for that young woman. To this day, I am convinced I would never have had that insight had I not been fasting that weekend. My mind was unusually clear.

What God says about fasting

Both the Bible and the Spirit of Prophecy have much to say about fasting and prayer. In the Old Testament, the word *fast* comes from the Hebrew *tsom*, in reference to the practice of self-denial. "Most scholars believe that the practice of fasting began with the loss of appetite during times of great distress and duress."[9] This was a natural expression of grief, like when one is sick and does not feel like eating. The prophet Samuel led a fast when Israel needed surrender and spiritual revival (1 Samuel 7:3–6). Elijah fasted while under great stress bordering on depression (1 Kings 19:1–8). Ezra led the exiles to seek God with fasting and prayer for success on their enterprise and protection from harm (Ezra 8:21–23). Esther fasted and requested others to fast in order to plead for protection from those who sought to destroy her people, the Jews (Esther 4:15, 16). Daniel fasted from rich foods to have a clear mind and serve God well while in a foreign land (Daniel 1:8–13).

In the New Testament, Jesus fasted forty days as He prepared to begin His public ministry (Matthew 4:1, 2). Of course, forty-day fasts are not normative for Christians.[10] Jesus, apparently, was sustained supernaturally, as were Elijah and Moses during their forty-day fasts. But Jesus is an example for us regarding His willingness to forego simple pleasures for a closer connection with God and greater effectiveness in ministry. The early church fasted and prayed as they sought to understand God's will and whatever next possible mission steps God would have in mind for them (Acts 13:1–3; 14:23). Christ's disciples were admonished to fast in order to overcome their unbelief (Matthew 17:21). Paul and his associates fasted (2 Corinthians 6:5), and he also recommended that couples fast from marital sex during special seasons of prayer (1 Corinthians 7:5). The Bible also warns of circumstances when fasting can be ineffective: when we seek to connect with God while disconnecting—not caring—for the needs of others (Isaiah 58:3–8).

Many Adventist pioneers also fasted. After the Great Disappointment of 1844, a number of them redoubled their efforts to understand the Scriptures regarding last-day prophecies. So they fasted and prayed and studied until major breakthroughs were experienced in their understanding of the Word of God.[11] Early Adventists also fasted and prayed at other times.[12] Even today, Ellen White urges church leaders to set aside days for fasting and prayer.[13] She also recommended fasting and praying on behalf of those in the clutches of spiritualism and Satanic influences. She encourages in these cases that "if the saints of God with deep humility fast and pray, their prayers will prevail."[14]

Fasting and prayer when in crisis or during growth

There are times when churches and institutions should carefully consider calling their members and workers for fasting and prayer days. This is especially true when great challenges face the church or its people. For example, at the time of this writing, the coronavirus COVID-19 was in full display as a pandemic.[15] The virus sprang up in late December 2019 in Wuhan, China. In less than five months, it had become a pandemic, infecting close to 5 million people in more than 95 percent of the world. Sports and musical events of all types were canceled. Schools were closed. Entire countries went into complete lockdowns. The stock markets in major world financial centers experienced historic losses, leading to what could become the greatest global depression in a century. Many industries and businesses lost so much revenue they became irreparably affected. The world, comparatively speaking, came to a standstill. Many experts now say life won't be the same again.

Of course, all this impacted the Adventist Church as well. The General Conference Session, held only every five years, was postponed for a year, and multiple ancillary meetings were canceled. All travel by church leaders was suspended. In South Korea, where my wife and I live, all Adventist churches had to close. Some churches offered worship services online, but the lack of members physically attending church has caused a dramatic drop in tithes and offerings. Just one month after the churches closed, local conferences held emergency meetings to discuss the rapidly dwindling financial resources. A month later, we heard reports that conferences in various parts of the world were forced to cut pastors' salaries by a third, in order to survive. Where my wife and I serve, we also had to give up part of our salary. This is a genuine crisis, a health and financial crisis capable of crippling the world and the church. This dire scenario is a very good example of a time when the church needs to fast and pray together, asking for the urgent intervention of God.

When I was a church pastor, the last church I served experienced a major spiritual revival. Prayer became central in that church: during prayer meetings, committee meetings, outreach efforts, early morning gatherings, and times of special intercession. Large numbers of people—young adults, families, retirees, businesspeople, professionals, and youth—participated in corporate prayer. The Lord blessed the church's desire to seek after God as they asked for the Holy Spirit to bless and intervene in the lives of many in the congregation. Attendance in church services quadrupled in less than eighteen months. Giving—both tithes and offerings—increased tenfold. A clear majority of the members became active, involved in some type of ministry at the church. Evangelism became the central focus, leading to almost two hundred baptisms in five years. Obviously, the Holy Spirit was working. At this time of incredible spiritual and numerical growth, church leaders called for a weekend of fasting and prayer, seeking to experience even greater victories in the lives of our members and our guests who were interested in the Adventist message.

Fasting and prayer weekends

As it turned out, fasting and prayer weekends were organized every six to eight months in that church. The members had no prior experience doing this. How did they conduct these weekends?

First, there was careful planning and organization. A theme for each weekend was chosen. Someone known for his or her expertise in the theme was invited to be the guest speaker. Deacons and deaconesses undertook key responsibilities. Deacons took care of all physical facilities—restrooms, cleaning, water and juice distribution—during the three-day gatherings. Deaconesses were responsible for registration, supplies, materials for participants, and children's programming. A brief handout with instructions on how to fast was created and distributed. People were encouraged to fast, keeping in mind their health and experience. Some fasted more and some less. Elders helped lead prayer for special rooms (keep reading) and helped the pastor cover sessions that the guest speaker could not.

The fasting and prayer event lasted forty hours, from Friday afternoon through Sunday morning. That time was divided into ninety-minute sessions. In the evening, the last session ended at ten o'clock, and in the mornings, the first session began at six o'clock. That means about fifteen sessions per weekend. Obviously, one speaker could not be expected to speak fifteen times in forty hours, so the pastor and the elders led in about half of the sessions—those likely to be less attended. Below is a table showing a typical ninety-minute session:

Activity	Objective	Time Length
Congregational singing	Call for a new session; set the tone for the meeting.	10 minutes
Welcome and prayer	Start a new session.	5 minutes
Review of prayer cards	Identify with others' needs.	5 minutes
Message	Focus on God's Word according to the theme.	40 minutes
Corporate prayer	Talk with God together about the Holy Spirit and people's pressing needs. This was done in different ways each time.	20 minutes
Break	Take a walk, move around, meditate before the next session.	10 minutes

The prayer cards were anonymous and had three lines on which to write prayer requests. People were encouraged to write down their three most heart-felt petitions before God and then pin the cards along two of the eight walls encircling the sanctuary. At each session, more cards were added, and during the breaks, many people went to read those cards. They often found needs similar to their own and were moved to empathize with others' needs and to pray for them.

The entire church facility was filled with people praying. Additionally, there were rooms set aside for very special prayer needs. One was for those needing healing from broken relationships. Typically, that would mean people experiencing divorce or separation, people alienated by lack of mutual forgiveness, or people with problems with family relations. A second prayer room was designated for seeking victory over addictions—smoking, drinking, gambling, drugs, sex, or any other type of enslaving habit. These rooms were led by wise, sensitive lay leaders or retired pastors who were careful in dealing with these types of issues. The hope was that members who went to these special prayer rooms would find that others also struggled with similar issues and that they would empathize with and encourage one another. The third special room was set aside to pray for physical and emotional healing. This included people with physical handicaps, with lingering diseases, and those who suffered depression or had cancer.

The majority of those participating prayed with the main group. If there was a large group at a particular session—say, three hundred or four hundred in attendance—the entire group was divided into twelve smaller groups, one for each month of the year. Signs were previously set around the sanctuary, indicating the month number, and people went to their birth month to pray with others. They prayed short *audible* prayers because the objective of corporate prayer is to be blessed by listening to the prayers of our brothers and sisters, as well as to our own.

These fasting and prayer weekends were attended by a much larger number of people than was first anticipated. As more weekends were organized, people from other churches also decided to participate. On one of those weekends, we had up to eight hundred people join in. The entire membership of the church was only half that number. Many breakthroughs were seen in people's lives. Broken marriages were healed. Wayward youth experienced radical changes. People were physically healed. Relationships were mended. Decisions to follow Christ were made, even though evangelistic meetings were not necessarily taking place at the time.

The people most affected by these fasting and prayer weekends were young adults and young professionals. Most of them had never fasted before. They had never spent a weekend seeking after God. Many of them had well-paying jobs in areas of finance, the health industry, or the software industry. They were accustomed to caring only of themselves. They were not in a hurry to get married because their large salaries made their lives easy. Many of them drove foreign luxury cars, and some even owned boats and other recreational vehicles. But because they were younger and had more stamina than the older people, they were able to attend more sessions. Most people attended five or six of the fifteen sessions, but young adults attended an average of twelve or thirteen. By so doing, they enabled the Spirit of God to work deep in their lives. Many of the young adults changed their lifestyles radically. They traded their expensive vehicles for less expensive ones and started regularly giving tithes and offerings to the church. Some considered becoming missionaries. Others became involved in ministry, serving at the church and reaching out to their coworkers and nonmember friends, something they had not taken the time to do in the past. A number began to study the Bible with seekers. Prayer and fasting were the avenues God used to change the church's atmosphere.

Maybe your church is ready to plan a fasting and prayer initiative of this nature right away. Other churches may need to grow more spiritually for something like this to happen successfully. But why not pray for your church to be ready?

Here is the counsel of God: "Now and onward till the close of time the people of God should be more earnest, more wide-awake, not trusting in their own wisdom, but in the wisdom of their Leader. They should set aside days for fasting and prayer. Entire abstinence from food may not be required, but they should eat sparingly of the most simple food."[16]

If we make the time and the effort to seek God earnestly, He will reveal Himself in many wonderful ways. We will see concrete answers to our prayers. Let us go to Him in faith!

Questions for Group Discussion or Personal Reflection

1. Have you ever seriously fasted and prayed? What was your objective in doing so?

2. Fasting is not simply about abstaining from food. What other things should Christians consider abstaining from at times in today's world? Why?

3. Why would such a simple exercise—abstaining from food or other pleasures—accompanied by prayer, make such a difference?

4. What did you find surprising or unique about the fasting and prayer weekends conducted by the author's former church?

5. Do you think your local church and/or Adventist institution would be ready to experience something like this? What would it take for them to organize a fasting and prayer Sabbath or weekend?

1. See Helen Wessel, ed. *The Autobiography of Charles G. Finney* (Minneapolis, MN: Bethany House, 1977), 31, 29. For a description of Finney's wonderful conversion, you may also see my *Adventism's Greatest Need: The Outpouring of the Holy Spirit* (Nampa, ID: Pacific Press, 2011), 113–115.

2. Charles Finney, *Power From on High: What Is It and How to Obtain It* (Fort Washington, PA: Christian Literature Crusade, 2005), 13, 14.

3. John Piper, *A Hunger for God: Desiring God Through Fasting and Prayer* (Wheaton, IL: Crossway, 1997), 93.

4. See Danny Vierra, *The Power of Fasting and Prayer* (Victor, CA: Modern Manna, 2013), 17.

5. Ellen G. White, *Counsels on Diet and Foods* (Washington, DC: Review and Herald', 1938), 189.

6. Andrew Murray, *With Christ In the School of Prayer: Thoughts on Our Training for the Ministry of Intercession* (New York: Fleming H. Revell, 1895), 99, https://www.google.com/books

/edition/With_Christ_in_the_School_of_Prayer/kwI3AAAAMAAJ.

7. Siegfried H. Horn, ed., *Seventh-day Adventist Bible Dictionary*, vol. 8 of the Commentary Reference Series (Washington, DC: Review and Herald®, 1960), s.v. "Fasting."

8. Ellen G. White wrote, "Simon had led into sin the woman he now despised [Mary]. She had been deeply wronged by him." *The Desire of Ages* (Washington, DC: Review and Herald', 1898), 566.

9. Elmer L. Towns, *Fasting for Spiritual Breakthrough: A Guide to Nine Biblical Fasts* (Ventura, CA: Regal Books, 1996), 25.

10. In her book *Counsels on Diet and Foods*, Ellen White admonished: "You are not called upon to fast forty days. The Lord bore that fast for you in the wilderness of temptation. There would be no virtue in such a fast; but there is virtue in the blood of Christ," p. 189.

11. Ellen White recalls meeting with such pioneers as Joseph Bates, Father Pierce, Elder Edson, and James White: "We studied and prayed earnestly; for we felt that we must learn God's truth. Often we remained together until late at night, and sometimes through the entire night, praying for light, and studying the Word. *As we fasted and prayed*, great power came upon us. But I could not understand the reasoning of the brethren. My mind was locked, as it were, and I could not comprehend what we were studying. Then the Spirit of God would come upon me, I would be taken off in vision, and a clear explanation of the passages we had been studying would be given me, with instruction as to the position we were to take regarding truth and duty." "Establishing the Foundation of Our Faith," *Manuscript Releases*, vol. 3 (Hagerstown, MD: Review and Herald', 1990), 413; emphasis added.

12. See Ellen G. White, *Testimonies for the Church,* vol. 3 (Mountain View, CA: Pacific Press®, 1948), 451; and Ellen G. White, "Where Are the Nine?," *Advent Review and Sabbath Herald*, February 19, 1889, 1. One time they *should have fasted but didn't* do it was when they met for the 1888 General Conference Session. That session proved pivotal in the understanding of Christ's work on behalf of sinners, but many delegates were not ready for God's light on the matter. See Ellen G. White, *1888 Materials*, 831, 832.

13. "It is in the order of God that those who bear responsibilities should often meet together to counsel with one another, and to pray earnestly for that wisdom which He alone can impart. Talk less; much precious time is lost in talk that brings no light. Let brethren unite in fasting and prayer for the wisdom that God has promised to supply liberally." Ellen G. White, *Gospel Workers* (Washington, DC: Review and Herald®, 1915), 417.

14. Ellen G. White, *Testimonies for the Church*, vol. 1 (Mountain View, CA: Pacific Press®, 1948), 343, 344.

15. On March 13, 2020, when I first rewrote this section, there were 132,600 people infected, almost 5,000 had died, in 108 countries reporting. Information from Jessie Yeung, Joshua Berlinger, Adam Renton, Meg Wagner, Mike Hayes, and Veronica Rocha, "March 13 Coronavirus News," CNN, updated March 13, 2020, https://edition.cnn.com/world/live-news/corona virus-outbreak-03-13-20-intl-hnk/index.html, and Al Jazeera and News Agencies, "Coronavirus: Which Countries Have Confirmed Cases?," Al Jazeera, accessed March 13, 2020, https://www.aljazeera.com/news/2020/01/countries-confirmed-cases-coronavirus-200125070959786 .html. Ten days later, the numbers of the dead were 14,641 and those infected more than 336,000, in 173 countries or regions! In ten days, over 200,000 people got the virus! See Julia Hollingsworth, Jenni Marsh, Rob Picheta, Fernando Alfonso III, and Amir Vera, "March 22 Coronavirus News," CNN, March 22, 2020, https://edition.cnn.com/world/live-news /coronavirus-outbreak-03-22-20/index.html. By April 8, the number of those infected had risen to 1,511,104, and the dead to 88,338. The severity of the pandemic was seen in the exponential growth of cases and deaths, day by day, week after week. See *Washington Post* Staff, "Mapping the Worldwide Spread of the Coronavirus," *Washington Post*, accessed April 9, 2020,

https://apple.news/A_R4dopFQRQulXvHMhehAHA. And on May 17, there were 4,626,632 confirmed cases and 311,363 dead. See the COVID-19 Tracking Project at https://www.fox news.com/, accessed May 17, 2020.

16. Ellen G. White, "The Need of Earnest Effort," *Advent Review and Sabbath Herald*, February 11, 1904, 8.

CHAPTER 15

Other Prayer Strategies

I t is a solemn thing, and no small scandal in the Kingdom," wrote A. W. Tozer, "to see God's children starving while actually seated at the Father's table."[1] This is a shockingly true and terribly sad statement. I fear it has applied to my life all too often. I have begged God to make me a man of prayer, for I have wasted many opportunities to commune with Him over the years. At times, it has felt like having the prize within my grasp and then letting it go at the last minute through one of the many distractions offered by the enemy. Our lives are very weak without Jesus.

Only prayer, accompanied by the Word, can allow the fullness of God's Spirit to work freely in our lives. In fact, the Word itself begs us to pray. E. M. Bounds said it eloquently: "No insistence in the Scriptures is more pressing than prayer. No exhortation is more often reiterated, none is more hearty, none is more solemn and stirring, than to pray. There is no duty to which we are more strongly obliged than the obligation to pray. There is no command more imperative and insistent than that of praying."[2]

"Lord, teach us to pray" was the petition of the disciples (Luke 11:1). Some of us have more difficulty than others establishing good, wholesome habits. There is something in our sinful nature that knows what to do but doesn't do it (Romans 7:18, 19; Jeremiah 17:9). Everyone needs the encouragement and strength of others in order to grow spiritually (Hebrews 10:23–25), but some of us need it even more. And that is why it is so critical that we pray *together*.

Practical prayer initiatives

When I was the pastor of the church already mentioned, the church got involved in a multiplicity of prayer ministries. There was the *prayer chain*. Every member or family unit was connected to another. In times of crisis, one person called his or her contact person, prayed with them over the crisis at hand, and then the other person did the same with the next one in line. Today, this can be easily done, and more quickly, through social media. However, the advantage of *calling* someone was to verbalize praying together, instead of simply texting a need and moving on.

Prayer at worship became important for the church. The focus was on claiming Hebrews 4:15, 16: "For we do not have a High Priest who cannot sympathize with our weaknesses, but was in all points tempted as we are, yet without sin. *Let us therefore come boldly to the throne of grace*, that we may obtain mercy and find grace to help in time of need" (emphasis added).

Can you see the components of this great promise and appeal? First, our High Priest, our heavenly Pastor, can fully empathize with our weaknesses. In this respect, He is very much like us. "He learned obedience by the things which He suffered" (Hebrews 5:8), just as we must. Second, Christ was victorious! He never gave in to sin. He knew how to overcome it. Third, based on the first two points, we can come boldly before God's throne with the full expectation to receive help. And fourth, that help will arrive just in time—not before, not after—but just in time. Our members learned to live by this wonderful promise.

The midweek *prayer meeting* was recalibrated to become a true *prayer* meeting. I have been in too many churches that have "prayer *requests* meetings" or "let's-talk-about-prayer meetings" more than meetings where people pray. We did not always succeed in this area. Deep-seated habits are hard to break. But we focused on praying, not on talking about prayer.

The prayer initiative that really began to change things substantially was the *early morning leaders' prayer time*. The pastor and the elders met at five o'clock in the morning on Mondays. Some weeks later, it was expanded to other days of the week and was opened to every interested member. These were, of necessity, small gatherings—as few as three and as many as thirty—but prayer time became very meaningful those early mornings. We had a sense that God was listening.

Another initiative was called *the hour of power*. This preceded the early morning prayer times as the church grew to appreciate corporate prayer. During long spring and summer days, we held that hour on Sabbath afternoons—just prayer for sixty minutes. During the short fall and winter days, we met on Friday nights.

Prayer at committees and small groups became central. The church board set aside thirty minutes for corporate prayer before starting with the agenda. Other committees followed the same practice. The small group ministries made prayer a key aspect of their gatherings. Sometimes they prayed for a long time, members being deeply touched by the presence of the Holy Spirit.

Before every major evangelistic series of meetings, we got together in what we called *Ten Days in the Upper Room*. Those were days when we laid before the Lord the names and cases of people who had not yet committed their lives to

Jesus and specially petitioned for the mighty power of the Holy Spirit to descend on our reaping meetings.

We already talked about *prayer and fasting weekends*. In the same vein, an all-night *prayer vigil* could be considered, with one caveat: staying up all night really taxes the body. Prayer vigils should be considered only if the next day is a holiday or day off from work, or if the crisis faced by the church is so severe that it is the equivalent of staying up all night at the hospital when a loved one hovers between life and death.

There are many other ways in which an Adventist church or institution can focus on prayer. Implementing several of these plans is ideal because different people may resonate with different ways of approaching God.

There are a couple of more prayer initiatives I'd like to mention in this chapter, one of which I have yet to try.

Prayer community events

Countries that share a Christian heritage or those that are open to the Christian faith may profit from a prayer community event. What is that? In every community or district, there are unique challenges experienced by its citizens, whether it is crime, loss of jobs, raising children successfully, a tragedy affecting a number of families, the closure of a major company that employed many local people, or another issue. Sometimes the problems transcend the community, such as the 2020 coronavirus pandemic or a state of war. Whatever the issue or issues, they are a good reason to invite community leaders, churches, and the population in general for a day of prayer.

In the United States, the first Thursday of May every year is called the National Day of Prayer.[3] Many prayer events take place throughout the nation, involving civic as well as religious leaders. One year, the Prayer Ministries coordinator of the North American Division of our church decided to organize an event. She called it Breakfast With the Mayor. How did she do this?

First, she contacted the mayor with the proposal to organize a prayer breakfast that would pray for the police, the fire department, civic and religious leaders, and others in the city. The mayor was not particularly enthusiastic about it—she had never been involved in anything like this before—but neither was she opposed to it. They set a date and went to work.

The second thing they did was form an *interdenominational* steering committee. It was important to have on the committee people who truly believed in the benefit to the community this event could have. This group also spent considerable time praying together.

Then they asked the chamber of commerce to be in charge of the registration. It was important to know how many people would need a meal. This group was also responsible for charging a fee to those who would attend since the city had no budget for a prayer breakfast. Having the Adventist church pay for it seemed a bit too sectarian or self-serving. Even though the idea came from Adventists, the objective was to engage different faith and civic groups to be part of the process. They contracted a catering service in the city to prepare and serve breakfast.

They asked the county commissioner's office to be in charge of the venue. This way, more and more civic institutions got involved and naturally supported the initiative. They had the fire department supervise parking, and young couples from educational institutions became servers and greeters. They also created a website and a printed program. The program included very brief greetings from every major city institution, the reason why prayer for the nation was needed, quality musical pieces, prayer for local and national institutions at each breakfast table, and the singing of the equivalent of a national anthem in America, a song called "God Bless America."[4]

This account is mentioned here by way of example. The point is to be creative and to incorporate the help of other institutions and churches in the community. Prayer is something to which most everyone is open. Why not help organize an event in the community that brings it together and helps the Adventist church become known for engaging with the community in meaningful ways?

Forty days of prayer
An increasingly common prayer initiative in Adventist churches has to do with setting aside forty days of special prayer. This is usually forty days before a major event, such as the start of evangelistic meetings, a mission journey, or when the church needs to make a major decision. I have used this plan to help prepare churches for evangelism.

Why forty days? The number forty in the Bible is symbolic of preparation, a time of transition to a new life. For example, Jesus spent forty days praying and fasting before His public ministry (Matthew 4:1, 2); during the Flood, it rained forty days before God began anew with humankind (Genesis 7:17; 8:6); Moses spent forty days with God before he received the Ten Commandments (Deuteronomy 9:9–11).

Many around us—family, friends, neighbors, coworkers—can experience a significant turnaround in their lives when we systematically pray for them. This is the time to write down names and Bible promises and to pray for each person daily.

Adventist pastor Dennis Smith has made a specialty of this initiative. He has written a series of training books focusing on forty days of prayer. These are helpful resources.[5] In his books, he offers a reading of one to two pages for each day, followed by six or seven discussion questions for groups, and then a daily prayer focus. It is very simple and practical. Where I have seen this done, the churches have prepared a reading for each day—sometimes simply a Bible promise—followed by articulating each day their focus on prayer (what they're there for), and then spent time praying together. Again, I'd like to reiterate that corporate prayer is praying aloud, giving different people the opportunity to pray short prayers that others can hear. Corporate prayer is not, as some practice, praying silently, individually. That approach to prayer does not necessitate the gathering together of the church.

In Changhua, Taiwan, I was scheduled to conduct a series of evangelistic meetings. The church was small: only twenty to twenty-five people attended on Sabbath mornings, including some nonmembers. The head elder said that he didn't remember any evangelistic meetings in his church in the past twenty-one years! So, as suspected, the church was not quite ready for evangelism. However, led by Pastor Wang, the people were willing to learn. And we had two months to do limited preparation.

We planned one afternoon training session with them. We focused on five things to do over the next eight weeks: (1) get organized into several teams to prayer walk around the city; (2) reach out to missing members; (3) engage in forty days of focused prayer; (4) offer one community service event; and (5) pray especially for the non-Adventist young people coming to the English language school at the church. The little church did all that was required. And when it came to prayer, three teams prayer walked several times a week, and members met each evening for prayer at the church for the forty days leading up to the start of the evangelistic meetings.

When the eleven-night series of meetings started, fifty-one people came, half of them nonmembers. That's more than twice the number of Sabbath morning attendees! Attendance averaged forty-nine people every night. By the end of the series, nine people decided to be baptized and join the church, five of whom were involved with the English language school. Prayer works!

My friend Dwight Nelson, senior pastor of the Pioneer Memorial Church at Andrews University, is a big believer in prayer, especially corporate prayer. He likens individual prayer to a light, something that can illuminate even a large area. But he sees corporate prayer like a laser beam, able to drill a hole through steel. "If we would accomplish the great work before us, it is essential that we present to God fervent and effectual prayer. . . . If several should meet together with one accord, with hearts burdened for perishing souls, and should offer earnest, fervent prayers, they would prove effectual."[6]

Questions for Group Discussion or Personal Reflection

1. List the prayer programs that now exist in your local church or at the Adventist institution where you work. Could more be added and some discarded? Which?

2. Do you think it is possible for your local church or Adventist institution to plan to pray together early in the morning, or at least daily, assuming you don't already? What would it take to accomplish that? Or if this already exists, what would it take to become more meaningful?

3. Dream for a moment about what community prayer event Adventists could or should lead. What would it be like?

4. Has your church or institution been involved in doing a forty days of prayer plan? What have been the weaknesses? What about the strengths? How could this be done to expect a greater impact?

5. What other prayer strategies can you think of that have not been mentioned in this book?

---

1. A. W. Tozer, *The Pursuit of God* (Camp Hill, PA: Christian Publications, 1982), 9. Tozer was one of the most influential Christian writers of the last century, often called "a twentieth-century prophet."

2. E. M. Bounds, *The Complete Works of E. M. Bounds on Prayer* (Grand Rapids, MI: Baker, 1990), 381.

3. See, for example, the National Day of Prayer website for the special day planned for 2020: https://www.nationaldayofprayer.org.

4. The entire experience is written and published in a small booklet by Don and Ruthie Jacobsen, *Breakfast With the Mayor* (Hiawassee, GA: HighWalk Productions, 2014).

5. For example, *40 Days: Prayers and Devotions to Prepare for the Second Coming* (2013); *40 Days: Prayers and Devotions to Revive Your Experience With God* (2013); *40 Days: Prayers and Devotions on Earth's Final Events* (2012); *40 Days: Prayers and Devotions Reflecting on the Cross of Christ* (2015); *40 Days: Prayers and Devotions on God's Amazing Miracles* (2017). The first three books mentioned were published by Review and Herald®, the last two by Pacific Press®.

6. Ellen G. White, "Friendship With the World Is Enmity With Christ," *Advent Review and Sabbath Herald,* August 23, 1892, 1.

CHAPTER 16

Prayer and Evangelism

Nothing rankles the forces of darkness more than when the church of God is involved in direct evangelism and prayer to save souls. Satan's fury knows no limit then. I remember conducting a field school of evangelism in Cleveland, Tennessee. We were working with eight willing churches and about ten seminary students from Andrews University. But the work was hard, and the decisions for baptism were slow in coming. There was a woman at those meetings who sat on the last row but never stayed for the sermon appeal. She would make very strange noises, disrupting the sermon, and I started to see a pattern: when I mentioned in the sermons the power of God or the cleansing blood of Christ, she'd make those noises, rather involuntarily.

One night, I finally remembered who she was. Years earlier, while I was still teaching at Southern Adventist University, a local pastor had called me because this same woman was demon-possessed and was pleading for help. I went to the church, and about fifteen of us prayed for her for some time, but the demon was furious. She was in a classroom nearby, yelling and cursing the air blue. Two of us ventured her way, to see if we could appeal to her better nature. When she saw us, she lifted a massive metal desk many times the weight of her small frame, threatening to throw it at us.

We escaped that night. But now, Satan showed his true colors again. During the evangelistic meetings, one night, she decided to stay on. I finally had the chance to greet her and sit next to her to talk with her. I knew the Holy Spirit had not given up on her yet; otherwise, she wouldn't be coming, even if only to disrupt the meetings. All was fine, until, suddenly, completely out of context, she turned to me with consummate hatred in her eyes, and with the scariest voice I had heard to that time, she said to me: "If I had a knife, I would slit your throat right now!"

That night, Jesus' angels protected me again, for which I'm very grateful. But if you dare to tread on Satan's territory, expect trouble (1 Thessalonians 2:18; John 16:33). That's why prayer—sustained, dependent, intercessory prayer—is so critical when doing evangelism. You won't need it if you do evangelistic meetings to merely fulfill a conference expectation or because you think it's something that ought to be done to satisfy Adventist culture, but you will need serious prayer if you really mean to win souls for Jesus from the clutches of the devil.

God to the rescue

When I was the dean of the School of Religion at Southern Adventist University, I took a group of eighteen theology seniors to conduct evangelism in Ghana, West Africa. We were the first Adventist university in America to work with Pastor Robert Folkenberg Sr. and his new mission organization called ShareHim.[1] When we arrived, we knew we were in a different world. Most of my students and I already had international experience, so different sounds and smells and mannerisms from a completely different culture did not bother us. What did surprise us was the fierce fight between good and evil. We saw several demon possession cases. We heard from new Adventists who had been rescued from witchcraft. We listened to hair-raising stories about the powers of darkness and the marvelous deliverance available in Jesus. We also realized that some Adventist members, when under stress, still appealed to dead ancestors and other spirits for help.

In Ghana, we saw the battle between light and darkness on a daily basis in our work. Each of the students and I preached in different locations throughout Kumasi, Ghana's second-largest city, and most of us in open fields. The people were interested, and the local churches worked tirelessly on their behalf, and Satan was not pleased. It seemed to me that he resented our presence because he had, for so long, been without the direct challenge of Bible truth. It was supposed to be the dry season, and yet it often rained in the evenings—but only as we were getting ready to speak. And when I gathered the students in the hotel after our nightly meetings, they told the same story, except that we each preached at slightly different times. The rain did not start until the Adventist preacher *in that specific site* got up to preach!

The good thing was that despite Satan's serious efforts to disrupt, discourage, and annoy the evangelists in Ghana, as well as those interested in the message, the church members in West Africa knew how to pray. Every night, teams of seven to ten people prayed before, during, and after each evangelistic meeting. They prayed together for about two hours. I joined them a few times, and, oh, how they prayed! You could tell they understood the mighty struggle between good and evil. They prayed the promises of God with conviction and faith. But the struggle continued.

On the night I spoke about baptism, the rain came exactly at the time I made the call for people to come forward for baptism. It poured, and since we were in an open field, everyone scattered to take shelter under trees or in nearby buildings. They could still hear my voice because of the powerful speakers we had set up, but they could not indicate their desire for baptism.

Another night, I was supposed to speak on what the Bible teaches about the state of the dead. Over my forty years of ministry, I have learned that this subject deeply angers Satan. He doesn't want the truth to be known. So, that night, for the first and only time, the rain came two whole hours *ahead* of time. It was a deluge. All the open-air evangelistic sites had to cancel their meetings. Since we were scheduled to preach *every* night, we had no extra night to make up for the missing subject. So we decided to have an early morning session instead.

The next morning at three-thirty, our fourteen-year-old son, Christoffer, and I got up and walked about two miles to the preaching site, and I preached the Bible truth on the state of the dead. Everyone in that part of the city could hear my voice when preaching at five in the morning. To make a fascinating story short, from that day on, people began to make decisions. The power of the devil was broken. We baptized 82 from my site. There were maybe a total of five hundred simultaneous evangelistic meetings going on in the city. On the last Sabbath, in Lake Bosomtwe, twenty-five pastors baptized a total of 3,189 people over a period of six hours. There was great rejoicing.

Prayer triumphs over Satan's hatred

God won again, and it was in no small part due to the faithful intercession of the saints. My students and I also prayed every night and every morning. The devil lost, and he had lost big. His fury was revealed a few days later, however, when the Ghana Union leadership, responsible for inviting us to do evangelism there, and the coordinators of these meetings experienced a terrible road accident. The three conference officers plus two more leaders were traveling in one car when an oncoming vehicle veered in front of them, causing them to go off the road at high speed. Their vehicle tumbled over and over off the road into the jungle. I saw pictures of the vehicle: it was an indistinct mass of crunched-up metal, and it was difficult to see how anyone could come out of that accident alive. But all the leaders survived it.

About the time of the accident, when I returned home, I noticed my computer and all my drives had been stolen from my office. This was a personal tragedy for me, since all my class lectures, all my sermons, all the work I had done for over twenty years of ministry was on those discs and on that computer.

We called the police, and they came to dust for fingerprints. One of the campus security workers came with them. In the meantime, one of my students who had gone to Ghana learned what had happened. He came to my office and prayed earnestly for me, that the Spirit of God would "convict the thief to bring back the computer and the discs!" That was a bold prayer, I thought! We learned later that the thief was the young security officer who was in my office with the police, and that he had heard every word of that prayer. The young man went home under deep conviction and brought the computer back, turning himself in to the authorities.

That was not yet the end. A few days later, I was attending meetings in Silver Spring, Maryland, near Washington, DC, and I became very sick. I developed a fever of 105 °F (40.5 °C), had a terrible headache that would not go away, and vomited everything I ate or even drank. I became extremely dehydrated and very weak. Through earnest, pleading prayer, the Lord brought me back home, but for a time, I felt I would die there. I had never had the flu, and I thought this was maybe it, but I also wondered if it was malaria, because I was already hallucinating.

My wife rushed me to the hospital emergency room, where I lost consciousness. The doctor confirmed later that I had falciparum malaria, and had I been three hours later to the hospital, I would have been dead upon arrival. The problem was compounded by the fact that the hospital had no medication to fight malaria since they seldom see any malaria patients in the entire United States! So the word went out that Dr. Clouzet had malaria and was between life and death. Some two thousand people all over the country prayed for me during those days. On Sabbath, three days after being admitted to the hospital, minister friends from the university anointed me with oil and prayed for the Lord to save my life (James 5:13–15). That night, my wife thought I would die; I was so very sick. But the next morning, the specialist came to my room and told me that my blood work showed no traces of malaria. He thought that was very strange. I was discharged three days later and returned to teaching the following week.

Prayer saved me that day—*the Lord* saved me that day—and I am certain the angels of heaven will one day let me know about other instances when prayer saved my life. But don't miss my point: the great controversy between good and evil is never as fierce as when you get involved in leading others to Jesus. Nevertheless, Jesus is right there with you, for He loves the work of soul saving. That is why intercessory prayer is so necessary when doing evangelism.

The role of prayer in evangelism

It is impossible to underestimate the role of prayer in evangelism. It is like breathing. Without it, many convicted souls would never make the decision to trust Jesus and His Word. When the apostles healed the paralytic at the temple, the Lord used the miracle to lead five thousand more to faith in Him (Acts 3:1–4:4). Peter and John were subsequently arrested. In the meantime, the rest of the apostles prayed earnestly for them, "fearing that the cruelty shown to Christ might be repeated."[2] Once released, Peter and John joined the rest, and they prayed, fully conscious of the great controversy being waged over souls (Acts 4:23–31). "The disciples prayed that greater strength might be imparted to them . . . for they saw that they would meet the same determined opposition that Christ had encountered when upon the earth."[3] This may be a reason why Jesus explicitly asked His followers to pray for more laborers willing to be involved in the work of evangelism (Matthew 9:36–38). Note that Jesus never asked us to pray for more souls. He knows many more people are ready to respond to our message than we imagine (John 4:35). What is needed are members willing to "harvest" them.

For many years, I have been privileged to be involved with teaching or leading evangelism while teaching at Southern Adventist University, in the seminary at Andrews University, and even now in Asia.[4] I have conducted evangelism in four continents and even have been privileged to lead a satellite evangelistic series in North America that led some eight thousand people to baptism.[5] I know the struggle between good and evil for those who are lost is real, and years ago, I learned the essential role of prayer in that struggle.

When I was young in evangelism, we had evangelistic meetings in the deep south of the United States. The meetings were going well, and the church members were supporting the meetings, but the evangelist was discouraged. In his long experience, he said he had never seen so few making the decision to be baptized. Normally, a meeting of that size and nature should produce about twenty-five converts, ready for baptism by meetings' end. But there were only ten. The evangelistic meetings were five weeks long, and only one week was left. After listening to the evangelist's concerns, I called a meeting with my ministerial students who were part of the team. We agreed to pray twice a day. We prayed for about an hour in the morning, and about an hour at night, after each meeting. We claimed God's promises to save the lost, believing that where we were, the field was ripe for harvest, in spite of appearances, and we prayed for each interest by name and circumstance. On the last night of the meetings, thirty-four people were baptized—not ten, not even twenty-five. And one of the thirty-four enrolled to become a pastor only months later. He made his decision on the last night of the meetings. Much changed within that week of earnest prayer.

Over the last few years, in my personal prayers, I have asked God for a specific minimum number of people to be baptized each time I do evangelism. As alluded to before, if we don't pray for specific results, we won't know God is answering our prayers. Many, many times, the outlook was discouraging. Nonmembers were interested in the evangelistic meetings, but they would not make decisions to trust God and join His last-day church. Yet, time and again, I have seen the Lord come through. He did in New York, in Saint Louis, in North Carolina, in Chicago, in the Silicon Valley of California. He did in Peru, in South Africa, in Ghana. And He did in Japan, Mongolia, and Hong Kong. I don't cease to be astonished that He answers our prayers for souls so consistently![6]

My most recent evangelistic series to date was in Taiwan, mentioned in the previous chapter. The church was very small, only twenty to twenty-five attending members, but twice as many attended the evangelistic meetings. Half of them were non-Christian. However, no one was making decisions for baptism. Not one! I knew it would be harder for Taiwanese to make those decisions because of my experience with the Chinese living in California, and the big series we had done in Hong Kong only months before. But even the hard-working pastor and his head elder were shocked that no one was moving forward. We asked every participating member to earnestly pray. We even asked the interests to earnestly pray. We appealed publicly as well as privately for them to trust their lives to Jesus. Several had been coming to the church for years but had never decided to follow Jesus or join the church.

Finally, the day before the end of the series arrived. And again, no one made the decision to be baptized. I had never experienced this before, and I kept arguing with God that this could not be possible, that it didn't make any sense. The Word had been preached faithfully, and I knew that God had promised His Word would not return to Him void (Isaiah 55:10, 11). The members had cooperated and done their best, following every instruction on what to do. The church was ready to receive new members. Why not at least one soul? That night, before going to bed, I prayed that the Lord would do something different, something unusual so that at least one person would desire to join the church (I was originally praying for five to be baptized).

Sabbath came, the last day of the meetings, and I made one last appeal for baptism at the end of my sermon. Unexpectedly, a woman in her early forties whom I had never seen before stood up, signifying her desire to be baptized.

A few seconds later, a seventeen-year-old young man, the leader of a group of nonmember youth who were coming to church, stood up. His fifteen-year-old sister followed, and her friend followed her. Then, the friend's mother also stood up for baptism! Another two youths stood up; and finally, a couple in their early thirties stood up for baptism. Nine people! God answers prayer!

And how did God do it? He did something unusual. The first woman who stood up was not Chinese. She was a Filipino woman visiting a friend. She had attended an Adventist church for some time in the Philippines; however, she had never made her decision for baptism. God used this visitor to encourage others to follow through.

Praying for souls

Charles Finney remains one of the most well-known and successful evangelists in American history. Thousands became Christians because of his evangelistic preaching in the state of New York. But historians and researchers have learned that the secret to his success may not be so much his preaching as the prayer that surrounded his preaching. First of all, he prepared each sermon on his knees. He *prayed* his sermons through. And second, there was a man named Daniel Nash.

Father Nash, as he was called, stopped being a pastor at the age of forty-eight to give himself "totally to prayer for Finney's evangelistic meetings." Three or four weeks ahead of time, Nash would go to the town where Finney was to preach. He would find two or three like-minded Christian brothers to join him and begin to pray, pleading for the souls of those in the city. There were reports that these men would fast for days as they prayed, and that when people heard them groan in their room, agonizing for souls in prayer, they thought they were starving to death![7] They were simply crying out for the Holy Spirit to convert men and women.

This consistent and powerful intercession led Finney to win many souls. In one city, three thousand women worked in a textile factory, many of whom attended the meetings, yet *all* of them became Christians. Sometimes, people riding the train would be convicted to give their lives to the Lord as the train went by the station of the town where Finney was preaching! Finney's evangelistic meetings changed the entire city of Rochester. "The whole community was stirred," wrote one of the converts, who later became a pastor. "Religion was the topic of conversation in the house, in the shop, in the office, and on the street. The only theater in the city was converted into a livery stable; the only circus into a soap and candle factory. Grog shops [cheap bars] were closed; the Sabbath was honored; the sanctuaries were thronged with happy worshippers; a new impulse was given to every philanthropic enterprise; the fountains of benevolence were opened, and men lived to good."[8] A record hundred thousand people were converted in that city. And prayer was the key.

When I lead field schools of evangelism, we teach people to pray for souls. We encourage them to prayer walk. We teach intercessors how to be more effective. We require all participating churches to have a certain percentage of the membership be involved in one of the three prayer ministries discussed in chapter 13. We ask them to turn in a list of all their nonmember friends or church associates about three months before the final evangelistic series so we can start praying for interests by name. When the time of the series comes, prayer-and-visitation teams pray for people sitting in the rows assigned to the teams. We meet regularly to pray for those showing the most interest or struggling with decisions. We have special prayer sessions the very night or the next morning after people make important decisions, such as accepting Jesus as their Savior, keeping the Sabbath, or giving up addictions or unclean foods. We especially pray for them the moment they decide they want baptism, knowing the enemy of souls will try his hardest to discourage and derail them.

Without abundant prayer, evangelism simply does not work. But with prayer, believing in the power and grace of God, it often results in more convictions to surrender than anticipated.

John Hyde and evangelism

John Hyde was a true champion when it came to praying for the lost. A missionary to India, he was hard of hearing, making it difficult for him to learn a new language. He was assigned to work in the Punjab region, between today's India and Pakistan. The area had been very challenging for Christian missionaries. Hyde began to pray in earnest for the lost there, but it took twelve years before he saw answers to his prayers. By 1899, he was spending entire nights in prayer, feeling that prayer was the only hope for results in India.

In 1904, he and others founded the Punjab Prayer Union. Each member was asked five questions:

1. Are you praying for [the] quickening [of the Spirit] in your own life, in the life of your fellow-workers, and in the church?
2. Are you longing for greater power of the Holy Spirit in your own life and work, and are you convinced that you cannot go on without this power?

3. Will you pray that you may not be ashamed of Jesus?
4. Do you believe that prayer is the great means for securing this spiritual awakening?
5. Will you set apart one-half hour each day as soon after noon as possible to pray for this awakening, and are you willing to pray till the awakening comes?[9]

Those prayer leaders called for a convention in Sialkot later that year. Missionaries and local pastors arrived. Hyde and two others spent thirty days praying before the convention began. Many gave their lives entirely to God during the convention. "Much of what God has done in Pakistan and northern India in the past one hundred years can be traced back to the original Sialkot Convention and John Hyde."[10] From 1904 to 1909, the number of Christians in the Punjab region quadrupled from 37,695 to 163,994. During that decade, the Christian population in India increased by 69.9 percent, sixteen times that of the Hindu community.[11]

An international evangelist at the time, Dr. Chapman, admitted he didn't know what *real* prayer was until he prayed with John Hyde. Hyde had invited him to the prayer room during the convention. Chapman wasn't excited about it because he'd just traveled all night and was tired. A few people were in the prayer room. "I knelt down," he said, "and a strange feeling crept over me. Several prayed, and then Hyde began, and I remember very little more. I knew that I was in the presence of God Himself, and had no desire to leave the place; in fact, I do not think that I thought of myself or of my surroundings, for I had entered a new world, and I wanted to remain there." They were there for hours. Meals were forgotten. His fatigue was gone. And his concern about what to speak later that day had disappeared. They prayed from 8:00 A.M. till 3:30 P.M.!

Dr. Chapman was scheduled to preach at 4:00 P.M. John Hyde ushered him to the pulpit and assured him all would be all right and that he would go back to the prayer room to pray for him while he preached. Dr. Chapman recalled that he felt something like an electric shock passing through him as they parted. "It was easy to speak," he recalled, "though I was speaking through an interpreter." The Lord was with the speaker in such a way that the Indian translator was "overpowered by the Spirit of God" so that another had to take his place! Chapman concluded: "I know the Lord spoke that night. He spoke to me and spoke to many. I realized then the power of prayer; how often I had read of blessing in answer to prayer, but it was brought home to me that evening with such force that ever since, I try to enlist prayer warriors to pray for me whenever I stand up to deliver His messages."[12]

John Hyde began personally praying for one conversion a day in 1908. Over four hundred were converted that year as the direct result of prayer. The following year, he prayed for two conversions a day, and over eight hundred people became Christians. In 1910, he prayed for four conversions a day. And the Lord granted that request as well!

Everyone started calling the missionary "Praying Hyde." Hyde died the following year, but not without making a profound difference in the lives of thousands—now millions—as he prayed for the lost. M'Cheyne Paterson worked with Hyde, and he said, "I never met any man whose very presence seemed to help the weak to become strong, the sinful to repent, the erring to walk aright so much as John Hyde."[13]

Prayer must become front and center—the strategic centerpiece of any and all our plans. But when it comes to evangelism, prayer must become the air we breathe.

Questions for Group Discussion or Personal Reflection

1. What did you think about Dr. Clouzet's encounter with the demon-possessed woman while doing evangelism? Do you think that's common?

2. What do you think about the idea that Satan hates evangelism? What evidence comes from the story in West Africa that seems to support such an idea?

3. Should the church pray for a specific number of conversions/baptisms when engaged in public evangelism? Why or why not?

4. What did you think about Charles Finney's evangelism and Father Nash's intercession?

5. Review the impact John Hyde's prayers had in India. Is he an extreme case of being a prayer warrior?

6. What will it take for the church to share the burden for others' salvation that John Hyde had?

1. See the ShareHim website at https://sharehim.org/php/index.php. ShareHim coordinates seventeen-night-long public evangelistic meetings in Third World countries where the Adventist Church is strong in soul winning and where the laity is thoroughly engaged in direct evangelism. It appeals to groups from First World countries where the church is well established but the zeal to become involved in evangelism has diminished. A win-win situation, those from the developed countries benefit from witnessing and engaging in the powerful work of God reaching many for Christ, and those from developing countries benefit from the greater financial resources and willingness to serve exhibited by their international brethren.

2. Ellen G. White, *The Acts of the Apostles* (Washington, DC: Review and Herald®, 1911), 67.

3. White, 67, 68.

4. At Southern, I was the coordinator for field schools of evangelism and the director of the Evangelism and World Missions Institute. At Andrews, I was the director of the North American Division Evangelism Institute, charged, along with colleagues at the institute, with teaching all pastors taking the master of divinity degree how to do effective evangelism, which we did all over the country. See the Mission Disruption NAD Evangelism website at https://www.nadei .org/. The Evangelism Institute is a division organization that has a number of doctoral-degreed professors who aid the seminary in accomplishing the work of teaching pastors to do evangelism. Their specialties are in the area of public and personal evangelism, missional small groups, empowering laity for mission, church growth, apologetics, and church planting. In Asia, I have conducted three field schools to date, each six to ten months long (Tokyo, Ulaanbaatar, Hong Kong), plus other evangelistic meetings in Okinawa and Taiwan.

5. The evangelistic plan, known as NET11 (because it finished in October of 2011), was thirteen months long and involved a multipronged approach. Over seven hundred churches signed up to be part of the plan. We had member evangelistic training for personal evangelism, for prayer evangelism, for missional small groups, for laypeople to give Bible studies, for ministries during public ministries, and for spiritual mentors that would nurture new believers. We required all the churches to be involved in community services and ministries. We also focused on the spiritual growth of the members, holding weekend and weeklong spiritual emphases on the righteousness of Jesus and the Holy Spirit. In addition, we held two major five-night preharvest meetings. One was with me (the pastor-theologian) and a microbiologist on the subject of creation and evolution. The other was with me and a trained biblical archaeologist. These meetings were meant to generate interest among secular people in the Bible. Finally, we had a twenty-eight-night evangelistic series of meetings called Prophecies Decoded. We produced DVDs and materials for all the churches and gave away much literature and Bibles. The Lord made an important impact across the division during that year.

6. In Tokyo, we knew the work would be very difficult, but I kept praying for ten baptisms. It seemed impossible because we only had an average of thirteen nonmembers attending the meetings, and four of them had no Christian background whatsoever. But at the end of the months-long field school and a twenty-four-sermon evangelistic series, ten people decided to follow Jesus and be baptized. In Mongolia, we knew we would have more baptisms, but there were powerful forces against our evangelistic meetings, including many attendees who had been associated with spiritualist mediums. My prayer was for seventy souls. A week before the meetings' end, we had baptized only twenty-seven, and reaching seventy seemed impossible. But we kept praying. By the last day, seventy-three had joined the church—seventy by baptism and three by profession of faith. In Okinawa, the mission president wanted to establish a small Spanish-speaking church, since there are a few Spanish-speaking people in the Japanese island. However, the Spanish interests did not come regularly, but two Japanese women did. So we provided simultaneous translation from Spanish to Japanese. Both were baptized at the end. In

Hong Kong, I had prayed for fifty, but only forty-eight were baptized. However, several more were baptized only a few weeks later.

7. See Christopher E. Sorensen, "Prayer in Missions Strategy," in *Winning Hearts: Leading Buddhists to Faith in God*, ed. Gregory and Amy Whitsett (Silver Spring, MD: General Conference of Seventh-day Adventists, 2016), 205.

8. Eddie L. Hyatt, *2000 Years of Charismatic Christianity* (Lake Mary, FL: Charisma House, 2002), 127, 128. See also J Paul Reno, "Prevailing Prince of Prayer (Daniel Nash)," Hope Faith Prayer, https://www.hopefaithprayer.com/prayernew/prevailing-prince-prayer-daniel-nash/.

9. Wesley Duewel, *Revival Fire* (Grand Rapids, MI: Zondervan, 1995), 223, 224.

10. From "Revivals and Church History: Sialkot Convention—John Hyde," Sermon Index, December 31, 2010, http://www.sermonindex.net/modules/newbb/viewtopic_pdf.php?topic _id=36798&forum=40.

11. Duewel, *Revival Fire*, 227.

12. J. Pergwern Jones, "A Vessel Unto Honor," in *Praying Hyde: Apostle of Prayer*, ed. E. G. Carré (North Brunswick, NJ: Bridge-Logos, 1999), 54–56.

13. R. M'Cheyne Paterson, "A Master Fisher for Souls," in Carré, *Praying Hyde*, 111.

CHAPTER 17

A House of Prayer

In his research on growing spiritual churches, seminary professor Joe Kidder has outlined three types of Adventist churches when it comes to prayer. The first is *the prayerless church*. This is a church that doesn't take prayer seriously, one that limits prayer to the start and end of services, committee meetings, and the midweek prayer meeting. They pray like this because that is the historical expectation by the denomination. The second church is *the church with prayer*. This church considers prayer important enough to have a prayer ministry and assign prayer warriors to it. The problem is that the congregation at large still has no sense of urgency about prayer. The third church is *the church of prayer*, a church that puts prayer at the center of everything they do. This church earnestly and consistently surrenders to God and seeks the guidance of the Holy Spirit. This church has truly become "a house of prayer."[1]

And what is, exactly, a "house of prayer"? The term shows up twice in Isaiah 56:7 and is repeated by Jesus in Matthew 21:13 and Mark 11:17. The context in Isaiah is full of anticipation and hope. "My salvation is about to come, and My righteousness to be revealed," declares the Lord (Isaiah 56:1). Then, God refers to the Sabbath as this great blessing to come, and two groups of people who will be affected most: Gentiles and eunuchs (verses 3–6), once considered by Jews to be beyond salvation. "Even them I will bring to My holy mountain, and make them joyful in My house of prayer. . . . For My house shall be called a house of prayer for all nations" (verse 7). God is saying that His house is the place of intercession. In the Old Testament times, priests interceded for the people. Today, our High Priest Jesus Christ is interceding for the world (Hebrews 7:25) alongside His church, the priesthood of all believers (1 Peter 2:9; Revelation 1:6; 5:10). In other words, in God's mind, His church is primarily a house of intercession for the lost—even those considered the farthest from God.

The Adventist Church of the future will, in fact, resemble the church as it once was in the first century of the Christian era. How do we know? Ellen

White predicted it. She wrote that, under the last warning of the third angel, the impact of the mission work in the world would be similar to that seen on the Day of Pentecost. The Holy Spirit will be poured out in a manifestation of the power of God like He was in those early days. "During the loud cry,[2] the church, . . . will diffuse the knowledge of salvation so abundantly that light will be communicated to every city and town" in the world.[3] The last message of mercy to be given to the world by the Adventist Church before Christ's return will be "a revelation of His character of love."[4] And what will that look like?

> Servants of God, with their faces lighted up and shining with holy con-secration, will hasten from place to place to proclaim the message from heaven. By thousands of voices, all over the earth, the warning will be given. Miracles will be wrought, the sick will be healed, and signs and wonders will follow the believers. . . .
>   . . . Notwithstanding the agencies combined against the truth, a large number [will] take their stand upon the Lord's side.[5]

Think about it: the incomparable love of Christ, the power of the Holy Spirit, holy consecration among believers, miracles like in the days of the apostles, and a powerful last warning to the world to join God's last-day church causing many to answer the appeal and be reconciled to God (2 Corinthians 5:20). Do you think prayer in the church, both private and corporate, will have anything to do with such developments in the not-too-distant future?

To the prophet Jeremiah, in the midst of tragic times—when Judah was being sieged and taken captive to Babylon, and the people of God felt no hope for the future—God made a promise of restoration. He said, "Thus says the LORD who made it, the LORD who formed it [the earth] to establish it (the LORD is His name): 'Call to Me, and I will answer you, and show you great and mighty things, which you do not know' " (Jeremiah 33:2, 3). Note two things here. First, God emphasizes that the act of creation—the most astonishing feat in the history of the universe—is because of His name. He is Power. He can do what no one else can! And second, based on His can-do name, let's call on Him and expect Him to answer us!

At the start of this book, I proposed that prayer be not merely an add-on to the many strategic outreach plans we have in the church, but that prayer must become the *foundational* strategy. Much like with missionary John Hyde in India, our prayers should relentlessly press before God the need of a dying world—the need for the heart of God to move to action. Not because He is unwilling to act—oh, no, He is more than willing!—but because the issues in the great controversy demand our intervention and petitioning before our High Priest Jesus so that He can act based on a *moral* basis, not just based on power.

So if prayer becomes *the* strategy, what could a church of one hundred members look like when it comes to prayer ministries?

Prayer in the small church

Prayer in the small church must begin with the pastor or the lay leader in charge. That leader must cultivate a genuine personal prayer life that leads to victory over besetting sin, to a deep love for people, and to absolute confidence in the power of God. The leader, then, must be a genuine and ever-growing *Christian*, not merely a good Adventist. And if that is not the likely scenario in that small church, prayer intercessors in the church must be the catalysts for the leader's needed conversion or the arrival of a new leader with these characteristics. That leader, if married, must have a spouse who is equally interested in spiritual growth for herself or himself and the church. This is important. If the spouse is not reading off the same page as the consecrated leader, Satan may use that spouse as someone behind enemy lines to attack the spiritual leader or the concerns over which he or she prays.

Second, the church must develop a team of intercessors. Perhaps the church is too small to develop prayer warriors, as described in this book, but at least faithful intercessors are a must. In the small church, prayer intercessors do not limit their ministry to praying. They must extend it to leading. These prayer intercessors, at least some of them, should be given considerable latitude to influence the church. They are the ones who must get the church praying! In small churches, pastoral care and leadership are not always available, at least on a weekly basis. These intercessors, then, must take up a large share of that role. Obviously, it would be important that at least a few of these intercessors have not only the gift of prayer but also administrative and leadership gifts (see 1 Peter 4:7–10).

Third, I honestly believe a key objective for the small church should be to develop the life of faith. Only God can move mountains, but our faith in Him can move the hand of God! Churches of every type and size should prioritize the life of faith, but especially the small church. The reason is simple: small churches already know they have limited resources, talent, personnel, and opportunities for outreach. It is too easy for them to say: "We can't do it. If we had more members or more young people, or more money, maybe, but we don't." That is exactly where the enemy of souls wants us stuck: we cannot. The small church needs to learn to say: But God can! And that type of faith comes by prayer and the study of God's Word (Romans 10:13).

Of course, it goes without saying that a few prayer-walking teams should be organized in the church to prayer walk their community. If Sabbath morning attendance is sixty, why not try to have at least four teams? The more, the better.

I can think of a number of other prayer strategies that would strengthen a small church, but if the members get serious about these four points, they will soon begin to see remarkable results and will be able to even teach much larger churches what it is like to live under the banner of the Holy Spirit.

Prayer in the midsize church

What about the midsize church? For the purposes of definition, let us say the midsize church is between 250 and 400 members on the books. Most church growth experts say that it is the ideal size for a church to really grow and begin doing significant ministry in the community.

In some parts of the world, a church of that size will have one pastor assigned to it and have no other churches to care for. In many Adventist settings, the pastor will have several other smaller churches attached to his or her district, but this one church is likely to be the "mother" or main church, and the one where his or her ministry energies will be focused. In fewer settings, the pastor may only have this one church, and even an associate pastor to help with it. The same thing I wrote regarding the small church and the leader applies in this case, with one additional caveat: some of the intercessors must make it their special ministry to pray for the pastor's family.

In one of the churches I pastored in California, I was immensely privileged to have seven members of our church daily intercede specifically for myself, my wife, and our three children. This ministry became much more critical than most may realize. Since a church of that size has the resources and personnel for significant community impact and spiritual growth, the devil will particularly target the leadership of the church, rightly expecting a trickle-down effect to the detriment of the congregation and even the community. In my case, I took the initiative to select those seven intercessors, asking them if they would be willing to serve in this capacity. They all were willing, and fairly quickly, I could tell the difference their prayers made in my life, ministry, and family.

At one point, I was overwhelmed with burdens and had a sense of defeat that I carried for a few weeks. Something was not right, even though I kept spending time with God. At one of the church's retreats in the mountains, I stayed in a cabin with five other men from the church. One evening, we were praying together, kneeling in a circle, and knowing that we were friends and had full confidence in each other, I confessed that I was burdened in a strange way and could not seem to shake it off. I wondered aloud if some of my intercessors had stopped praying for my family and me. Two of the seven intercessors were kneeling in that circle that day and later acknowledged to me that they had neglected to pray as they had said they would. They then pledged to be faithful. In a few days, I could again tell the difference their prayers made.

In addition to prayer-walking teams and intercessors, a church of this size should have prayer warriors. See chapter 13 about them and in what way their ministry of prayer is enhanced above that of prayer intercessors and prayer walkers. In addition, this size church should seriously consider planting one or more churches in nearby communities. This church size is ideal for effective ministry. Getting much bigger tends to diminish ministry effectiveness and soul-winning results, although that does not always need to be the case.[6] That's why, when the midsize church keeps growing, a new church plant is in order. Much prayer intercession should go into these plans: for the lead church planter, for the core planting team, for the strategy and timetable leading to the planting of the new church, for the specific location and ministry target, for the community outreach strategy, and for the incubation period of the church-planting team.[7]

One last recommendation for the midsize church is to engage in a prayer and fasting weekend from time to time. A good example of how that could be planned is in chapter 14. Make sure you have clear, specific objectives as to why you want the congregation to be engaged in such a spiritual exercise. Fasting and prayer seem most appropriate when the church, the community, or even the nation is facing a major threat or challenge (such as the recent coronavirus challenge), or when a critical number of members are experiencing a profound renewal in their lives, or when major decisions need to be made by the congregation, decisions that might impact them for years to come.

Prayer in the large church
The size of a large church will vary with the context. A large church in Brazil or Korea may be over 1,000 members, whereas in Japan or France, it will be 250. Here, I'm referring, in general, to churches 750 members or more with multiple pastoral staff. Many times, large churches are associated with an Adventist institution such as a hospital or a university. What does a large church that focuses on prayer look like?

Again, what has been said about the smaller churches applies to the large church as well. Everything from pastoral leadership to prayer-walking teams to intercessors and warriors to church planting and to fasting and prayer weekends applies. However, there is an additional aspect that the large church needs to pay particular attention to, and that is evangelism.

Because of the many and varied ministries usually found in the large church, evangelism tends to be secondary. The assumption is that great Sabbath School classes, a vibrant media ministry, a well-run Pathfinder program, the Adventist school sponsored by the church, and even connections with or support of city-run community events make up for direct evangelism. But that is not the case. The issue is masked by the fact that the large church will (or should) always have a good number of baptisms every year. Of course, many of those are biological baptisms—children of members who attend the Adventist school. But new adult converts with no Adventist background are relatively few. The tendency is for pastors and lay leaders to think that organizing a well-oiled evangelistic initiative that leads to public evangelistic meetings is simply adding too much work for a church that is already engaged with many viable ministries. Besides, even though the church is large, a relatively small percentage of the members are involved, and they tend to be the same people.

That's where prayer comes in. This type of large church has become institutionalized. The members have lost their sense of *personal* mission engagement with nonmembers (outside of work, such as working in an Adventist hospital, for example), and they feel they are already doing a lot of things at the church, anyway. The church needs conversion. The culture of the church needs conversion. It needs to switch from being a mostly inwardly focused church that pays attention to good programming, excellent music, superb Sabbath School teachers, and other ministries to becoming an outwardly focused church that puts the lost first. That is not an easy conversion. And it will take a lot of consistent prayer *by the church*, and by more than a few prayer intercessors. The church needs to become a true "house of prayer."

A very important additional prayer ministry in the large church would be *daily corporate prayer*. This prayer ministry *must* become a priority to three key groups: the pastoral staff, the elders of the church, and the church intercessors and prayer warriors. If any of these three groups gives only tacit support to this daily prayer plan, it will only be a plan and will soon grow old and irrelevant. The daily corporate prayer can be in the early morning, during lunch at noon, or in the evening, but it should be daily or at least as many times during the week as possible.

My first impression when I visited the largest Adventist church in China (about seven thousand members) was that they were very committed to their daily morning prayer. They start at four o'clock in the morning. When I arrived, it was already after eight o'clock, and about a dozen people were still praying! Keep in mind that in China, local authorities keep cameras around most churches to monitor their activities. In this church, a dozen cameras were inside the church, as well as outside. Members were not intimidated by the fact that anyone could watch them pray.

When this group—twelve to thirty people, for example—meets to pray, this is not the time to recite member prayer requests or mention all who are sick. That is for another time and setting. This is the time for *strategic* praying. Such prayer objectives should be well-articulated and printed for all to see in the prayer room. And if they can be articulated in a quantifiable way, all the better. It will be easier to know when God has actually answered such prayers. Major objectives must be placed before the prayer group, and with each objective, include Bible promises, data on the issue, and relevant research from Ellen White's writings to inform such praying. Here is the *negotiating* core group of the church. These are the people who will move the hand of God with their faithful boldness in the name of Jesus!

You may wonder why I have not said much about the traditional midweek prayer meeting. Now I will. In more and more Adventist churches, the traditional prayer meeting has ceased to exist or is attended by the same very few, usually older people, week after week. Younger people would not be attracted to it, nor would many older ones. The reason is poor management and lack of focus. Ellen White has said something about that.[8] When the prayer meeting is simply one more perfunctory gathering lacking life and meaning, the pastor leads it in order to fulfill some unwritten expectations about what churches should do. Often there is more talk than prayer in prayer meetings. This should not be. There is nothing sacred about the traditional prayer meeting, just as there is nothing sacred to preaching a sermon every Sabbath (Ellen White says members should *not* expect a sermon every Sabbath, but they *should* be ready to share personal testimonies of God's goodness every Sabbath.[9])

In the Adventist context, prayer meetings were born among Millerites, who, having experienced a deepening consecration by the study of God's Word, resolved to spend regular time in prayer together. In other words, prayer meetings were the *result* of a deepening spiritual experience. Praying together needs to be fueled, in part, by a meaningful experience praying alone. Praying together will not replace private prayer, although God may use it to spark a renewed conviction *for* private prayer. Here is the point: *meaningful* prayer engagement is what counts. If this is happening in the midweek prayer meeting, praise the Lord! By all means, do not cease. But sometimes, a church needs new models and venues of engagement if the old ones have stopped being effective. Jesus Himself said something about that (Luke 5:36–38).

Prayer in the Adventist institution

I don't want to miss the Adventist institution, such a key aspect of Adventist life. Adventist institutions such as hospitals, publishing houses, boarding academies, or universities have a culture of their own. Talented and well-educated Adventists tend to gather about such institutions, and we all know that it is not about the pay, but that is part of the sacrifices one makes working for the church. In general, Adventist workers do a lot of work in these places, leaving little time for much else. Spiritual development is, of course, encouraged but not rallied about as it would be in the local church. Can there be meaningful prayer ministries in the Adventist institution?

The easiest place for that to happen is at educational institutions. The reason for that is the students. Since students are in formation, and our main responsibility is their spiritual development, prayer gatherings, fasting and prayer experiences, and student prayer plans are natural parts of the overall educational objective. Many of the practical things mentioned in this book could take place. One that does not usually take place is prayer walking. Yet prayer-walking teams could naturally spring from young people doing this with their friends if only someone would help them catch a vision for it and get them organized.

Prayer walking is also suitable for other Adventist institutions, as well. It seems like using part of the lunch hour could work well. Another option would be to have strategic prayer time, starting shortly *before* noon (with administrative leadership and encouragement). As I have mentioned, we do this in the Northern Asia-Pacific Division every working day.

Groups of prayer intercessors could form among colleagues, for instance, in Adventist hospitals. Under the leadership of the chaplain's office, intercession teams can be encouraged to pray for pressing needs. Wouldn't it be wonderful if from a number of these intercession groups could come regular stories of people healed by the intervention of God? Wouldn't that be something beautifully distinctive of Adventist hospitals? What about the idea of listing miraculous healings regularly in the hospital chapel? That would show that prayer is a central feature of the institution's ministry.

The key is either to have a few self-motivated people who will take the initiative to engage in prayer ministries or for institutional *leadership* to catch a vision for it and participate and encourage it among its workers. If the latter takes place, the advancement would be faster and the potential for powerful results better. If leadership does not catch a vision for something like this, it will take longer for the Holy Spirit to be able to move through major obstacles.

Change is possible because God hears our prayers

Have you heard the story of the Adventist woman who prayed for names in the phone book? Here is the story. A man by the name of Noah and his friend began to attend evangelistic meetings at an Adventist church in America. They had both seen a sign promoting evangelistic meetings and talked about it while drinking at a bar. Both men were also into occult practices, but, somehow, an interest welled up in their hearts to know more about the Bible and the time of the end.

Through the study of the Word at the meetings, the Holy Spirit led the two men to repentance and conversion. At the end of the meetings, both were baptized, along with fifteen others that day. After the baptism, one of the church members introduced herself to them as Sister Ford, welcoming them to the church, and expressing her great joy about their decision. Then, she told them something they never expected to hear: "I've been praying for you." Neither Noah nor his friend had ever met this woman before. How could she have been praying for them? Well, a few months before, Sister Ford was impressed to pray for the people in her town. Not knowing, exactly, for whom she should pray, she grabbed the phone book and chose fifteen names *at random* and prayed every day for them to come to know Jesus. It turns out that Noah was one of the fifteen names! In fact, eight of the seventeen people baptized that Sabbath were from Sister Ford's list! Half of the entire harvest![10]

The mission of the Adventist Church to reach a dying world is simply overwhelming. We cannot do it with our present resources, and my guess is that we will never have enough resources—people, money, or innate motivation to do it. But prayer is the first base of the mission diamond. That is what we must do first and always if we hope to round the bases and reach home. But we must take prayer in the church very seriously. We must believe that God, in His mercy and wisdom, will answer prayer!

Ellen White, in the last chapter of her book *Gospel Workers*, entitled "The Reward of Service," mentions that many in heaven will see others come to them to thank them for being instruments in God's hands to lead them to Jesus. I can imagine, in the context of intercessory prayer for souls, angels coming to introduce someone to us. Neither they nor we may have known each other on earth, but the angel explains:

> Remember when you and your group prayed for your community for so many years? This couple is here today because of those prayers. Jesus, your King and High Priest, counted on your prayers to have legal grounds to intercede on their behalf, and even though it took a while, and they went through serious trials, they gave their hearts to the Lord. Satan kept saying to the Lord, "You cannot forgive their sins, they haven't asked for that!" But Jesus would say, "I can forgive their sins because I have faithful servants asking on their behalf, and I have already paid for them with My blood at the cross." They want to thank you today for your faithfulness.

Many good things will come from earnest, faithful members praying for the Lord of heaven to intercede on behalf of the lost. Remember the early church: "After the descent of the Holy Spirit, the disciples were so filled with love for Him and for those for whom He died, that hearts were melted by the words they spoke and *the prayers they offered.* They spoke in the power of the Spirit; and under the influence of that power, thousands were converted."[11]

Hearts were melted by *the prayers they offered.* Thousands were converted. That can happen again. By God's grace, it *will* happen again.

Let's begin praying today.

Questions for Group Discussion or Personal Reflection

1. How does Ellen White predict the church will carry on its mission at the end of time?

2. Describe what the small church could experience in terms of prayer ministry.

3. Describe what the midsize church could experience in terms of prayer ministry.

4. What do you think about a prayer team focusing specifically on the pastor and his or her family? In what way would that help the congregation?

5. Describe what prayer ministries could be part of the large church. What impact would these have on others?

6. Describe the prayer life that is possible in an Adventist institution.

7. How much is prayer needed in the church or institution where you are? What will you personally do about it?

---

1. S. Joseph Kidder, *The Big Four: Secrets to a Thriving Church Family* (Hagerstown, MD: Review and Herald®, 2011), 94–96.

2. In the writings of Ellen G. White, the "loud cry" refers to the proclamation in the power of the Spirit of the last-day message of the angel of Revelation 18:1–4 to "come out of" Babylon and join God's remnant church. This message from the fourth angel (Rev. 18) is to join and amplify the message of the three angels of Revelation 14:6–12. See Norman R. Gulley, "Loud Cry" in *The Ellen G. White Encyclopedia,* ed. Denis Fortin and Jerry Moon (Hagerstown, MD; Review and Herald®, 2013), 950, 951.

3. Ellen G. White, "The Closing Work," *Advent Review and Sabbath Herald,* October 13, 1904, 7.

4. Ellen G. White, *Christ's Object Lessons* (Battle Creek, MI: Review and Herald®, 1900), 415.

5. Ellen G. White, *The Great Controversy* (Washington, DC: Review and Herald®, 1911), 612.

6. Ellen White, in general, advises not to join large churches. She gives a number of reasons for this, such as "members [do] comparatively nothing" and die spiritually by not getting involved in ministry (*Testimonies for the Church,* vol. 8 [Mountain View, CA: Pacific Press®, 1948], 244); they have "little interest in the salvation of souls" (*Testimonies for the Church,* vol. 6 [Mountain View, CA: Pacific Press®, 1901], 424); and it is too easy to deal with other members "as pharisaical strangers," since it is so large (*Testimonies for the Church,* vol. 3 [Mountain View, CA: Pacific Press®, 1948], 197).

7. All these items are typical of well-thought-through church-planting plans. The "incubation" period is a reference to the time spent by the core planting team planning, praying, learning about, and reaching out to the community *before* they begin meeting officially with the new plant. If you'd like to know more about how to plant a church for missional objectives, check Tom L. Evans, *Steps to Church Planting: From Inception to Launch* (Berrien Springs, MI: NAD Evangelism Institute, 2011); and Aubrey Malphurs, *Planting Growing Churches for the 21st Century: A Comprehensive Guide,* 3rd ed. (Grand Rapids, MI: Baker, 2004).

8. "The prayer meetings should be the most interesting gatherings that are held, but these are frequently poorly managed. Many attend preaching, but neglect the prayer meeting. Here, again, thought is required." *Testimonies for the Church,* vol. 4 (Mountain View, CA: Pacific Press®, 1948), 70. She also wrote that "formality and cold stiffness should be laid aside" at the prayer meetings. *Testimonies for the Church,* vol. 2 (Mountain View, CA: Pacific Press®, 1948), 578.

9. See *Testimonies for the Church,* vol. 7 (Mountain View, CA: Pacific Press®, 1948), 18, 19.

10. I first heard this story in 2006 from Pastor Robert Folkenberg Sr. when he was the leader of ShareHim.

11. Ellen G. White, *The Acts of the Apostles* (Washington, DC: Review and Herald®, 1911), 22; emphasis added.

Appendix A

Additional Bible Prayer Promises
and Other Quotes From the Spirit of Prophecy

God's willingness to answer prayer

1. *2 Chronicles 7:14.* "If My people who are called by My name will humble themselves, and pray and seek My face, and turn from their wicked ways, then I will hear from heaven, and will forgive their sin and heal their land."

2. *Psalm 116:1, 2.* "I love the LORD, because He has heard
   My voice and my supplications.
   Because He has inclined His ear to me,
   Therefore I will call upon Him as long as I live."

3. *Isaiah 65:24.* "It shall come to pass that before they call, I will answer; and while they are still speaking, I will hear."

4. *Jeremiah 33:2, 3.* "Thus says the LORD . . . 'Call to Me, and I will answer you, and show you great and mighty things, which you do not know.' "

5. *Matthew 7:7, 8.* "Ask, and it will be given to you; seek, and you will find; knock, and it will be opened to you. For everyone who asks receives, and he who seeks finds, and to him who knocks it will be opened."

6. *Hebrews 4:15, 16.* "For we do not have a High Priest who cannot sympathize with our weaknesses, but was in all points tempted as we are, yet without sin. Let us therefore come boldly to the throne of grace, that we may obtain mercy and find grace to help in time of need."

7. *1 John 1:9.* "If we confess our sins, he is faithful and just and will forgive us our sins and purify us from all unrighteousness" (NIV).

Whatever you ask in the name of Jesus

1. *Matthew 18:19, 20.* "Again, truly I tell you that if two of you on earth agree about anything they ask for, it will be done for them by my Father in heaven. For where two or three gather in my name, there am I with them" (NIV).

2. *Mark 11:24.* "Therefore I tell you, whatever you ask for in prayer, believe that you have received it, and it will be yours" (NIV).

3. *John 14:12–14.* "Very truly I tell you, whoever believes in me will do the works I have been doing, and they will do even greater things than these, because I am going to the Father. And I will do whatever you ask in my name, so that the Father may be glorified in the Son. You may ask me for anything in my name, and I will do it" (NIV).

4. *John 15:16.* "You did not choose me, but I chose you and appointed you so that you might go and bear fruit—fruit that will last—and so that whatever you ask in my name the Father will give you" (NIV).

5. *John 16:23, 24.* "In that day you will no longer ask me anything. Very truly I tell you, my Father will give you whatever you ask in my name. Until now you have not asked for anything in my name. Ask and you will receive, and your joy will be complete" (NIV).

6. *Acts 3:1, 2, 6, 8.* "One day Peter and John were going up to the temple at the time of prayer—at three in the afternoon. Now a man who was lame from birth was being carried to the temple gate called Beautiful, where he was put every day to beg from those going into the temple courts."

   "Then Peter said, 'Silver or gold I do not have, but what I do have I give you. In the name of Jesus Christ of Nazareth, walk.' . . . He jumped to his feet and began to walk" (NIV).

7. *Romans 10:13.* "Everyone who calls on the name of the Lord will be saved" (NIV).

8. *James 5:13–15.* "Is anyone among you in trouble? Let them pray. Is anyone happy? Let them sing songs of praise. Is anyone among you sick? Let them call the elders of the church to pray over them and anoint them with oil in the name of the Lord. And the prayer offered in faith will make the sick person well; the Lord will raise them up. If they have sinned, they will be forgiven" (NIV).

9. *1 John 5:14–16.* "This is the confidence we have in approaching God: that if we ask anything according to his will, he hears us. And if we know that he hears us—whatever we ask—we know that we have what we asked of him. If you see any brother or sister commit a sin that does not lead to death, you should pray and God will give them life. I refer to those whose sin does not lead to death. There is a sin that leads to death. I am not saying that you should pray about that" (NIV).

Prayer, perseverance, and faith

1. *Matthew 9:27–30.* "As Jesus went on from there, two blind men followed him, calling out, 'Have mercy on us, Son of David!'

   "When he had gone indoors, the blind men came to him, and he asked them, 'Do you believe that I am able to do this?'

   " 'Yes, Lord,' they replied.

   "Then he touched their eyes and said, 'According to your faith let it be done to you'; and their sight was restored" (NIV).

2. *Matthew 15:22, 28.* "A Canaanite woman from that vicinity came to him, crying out, 'Lord, Son of David, have mercy on me! My daughter is demon-possessed and suffering terribly.'

   "Jesus did not answer a word. So his disciples came to him and urged him, 'Send her away, for she keeps crying out after us.' . . .

   "Then Jesus said to her, 'Woman, you have great faith! Your request is granted.' And her daughter was healed at that moment" (NIV).

3. *Mark 11:22, 23.* " 'Have faith in God,' Jesus answered. 'Truly I tell you, if anyone says to this mountain, "Go, throw yourself into the sea," and does not doubt in their heart but believes that what they say will happen, it will be done for them' " (NIV).

4. *Luke 5:18–20, 24, 25.* "Then behold, men brought on a bed a man who was paralyzed, whom they sought to bring in and lay before

Him. And when they could not find how they might bring him in, because of the crowd, they went up on the housetop and let him down with his bed through the tiling into the midst before Jesus.

"When He saw their faith, He said to him, 'Man, your sins are forgiven you.'

" 'But that you may know that the Son of Man has power on earth to forgive sins'—He said to the man who was paralyzed, 'I say to you, arise, take up your bed, and go to your house.'

"Immediately he rose up before them, took up what he had been lying on, and departed to his own house, glorifying God."

5. *Luke 17:12–19.* "Then as He entered a certain village, there met Him ten men who were lepers, who stood afar off. And they lifted up their voices and said, 'Jesus, Master, have mercy on us!'

"So when He saw them, He said to them, 'Go, show yourselves to the priests.' And so it was that as they went, they were cleansed.

"And one of them, when he saw that he was healed, returned, and with a loud voice glorified God, and fell down on his face at His feet, giving Him thanks. And he was a Samaritan.

"So Jesus answered and said, 'Were there not ten cleansed? But where are the nine? Were there not any found who returned to give glory to God except this foreigner?' And He said to him, 'Arise, go your way. Your faith has made you well.' "

6. *Luke 18:1–8.* "Then Jesus told his disciples a parable to show them that they should always pray and not give up. . . .

"And the Lord said, 'Listen to what the unjust judge says. And will not God bring about justice for his chosen ones, who cry out to him day and night? Will he keep putting them off? I tell you, he will see that they get justice, and quickly. However, when the Son of Man comes, will he find faith on the earth?' " (NIV).

7. *1 Thessalonians 5:17.* "Pray without ceasing."

8. *Hebrews 11:6.* "But without faith it is impossible to please Him, for he who comes to God must believe that He is, and that He is a rewarder of those who diligently seek Him."

9. *James 5:16.* "The prayer of a righteous person is powerful and effective" (NIV).

Praying for the Holy Spirit

1. *Ezekiel 36:25–28.* "I will sprinkle clean water on you, and you shall be clean; I will cleanse you from all your filthiness and from all your idols. I will give you a new heart and put a new spirit within you; I will take the heart of stone out of your flesh and give you a heart of flesh. I will put My Spirit within you and cause you to walk in My statutes, and you will keep My judgments and do them. Then . . . you shall be My people, and I will be your God."

2. *Joel 2:28, 29, 32.* "And it shall come to pass afterward
    That I will pour out My Spirit on all flesh;
    Your sons and your daughters shall prophesy,
    Your old men shall dream dreams,
    Your young men shall see visions.
    And also on My menservants and on My maidservants
    I will pour out My Spirit in those days."

3. *Zechariah 4:6.* "This is the word of the LORD. . . . 'Not by might nor by power, but by My Spirit,' says the LORD of hosts."

4. *Zechariah 10:1.* "Ask the LORD for rain in the time of the latter rain."

5. *Luke 11:13.* "If you then, though you are evil, know how to give good gifts to your children, how much more will your Father in heaven give the Holy Spirit to those who ask him!" (NIV).

6. *Luke 24:46–48.* "Then He said to them, 'Thus it is written, and thus it was necessary for the Christ to suffer and to rise from the dead the third day, and that repentance and remission of sins should be preached in His name to all nations, beginning at Jerusalem. And you are witnesses of these things. Behold, I send the Promise of My Father upon you; but tarry in the city of Jerusalem until you are endued with power from on high.' "

7. *Acts 1:4, 5, 8.* "And being assembled together with them, He commanded them not to depart from Jerusalem, but to wait for the Promise of the Father, 'which,' He said, 'you have heard from Me; for John truly baptized with water, but you shall be baptized with the Holy

Spirit not many days from now.' . . . 'But you shall receive power when the Holy Spirit has come upon you; and you shall be witnesses to Me in Jerusalem, and in all Judea and Samaria, and to the end of the earth.' "

8. *Acts 1:12–14.* "Then they returned to Jerusalem from the mount called Olivet. . . . And when they had entered, they went up into the upper room where they were staying. . . . These all continued with one accord in prayer and supplication."

9. *Acts 2:1–4.* "When the Day of Pentecost had fully come, they were all with one accord in one place. And suddenly there came a sound from heaven, as of a rushing mighty wind. And they were all filled with the Holy Spirit."

10. *Acts 4:23, 24, 29–31.* "And being let go, they went to their own companions. . . . They raised their voice to God with one accord and said: 'Lord, You are God, who made heaven and earth and the sea, and all that is in them."

" 'Now, Lord, look on their threats, and grant to Your servants that with all boldness they may speak Your word, by stretching out Your hand to heal, and that signs and wonders may be done through the name of Your holy Servant Jesus.'

"And when they had prayed, the place where they were assembled together was shaken; and they were all filled with the Holy Spirit, and they spoke the word of God with boldness."

Praying for people

1. *Exodus 32:31, 32.* "Then Moses returned to the Lord and said, 'Oh, these people have committed a great sin, and have made for themselves a god of gold! Yet now, if You will forgive their sin—but if not, I pray, blot me out of Your book which You have written.' "

2. *1 Samuel 12:23.* "Moreover, as for me, far be it from me that I should sin against the Lord in ceasing to pray for you."

3. *1 Kings 13:6.* "Then the king answered and said to the man of God, 'Please entreat the favor of the Lord your God, and pray for me, that my hand may be restored to me.'

"So the man of God entreated the Lord, and the king's hand was restored to him, and became as before."

4. *Job 42:8.* "Now therefore, take for yourselves seven bulls and seven rams, go to My servant Job, and offer up for yourselves a burnt offering; and My servant Job shall pray for you. For I will accept him, lest I deal with you according to your folly; because you have not spoken of Me what is right, as My servant Job has."

5. *Matthew 5:44, 45.* "But I say to you, love your enemies, bless those who curse you, do good to those who hate you, and pray for those who spitefully use you and persecute you, that you may be sons of your Father in heaven."

6. *Luke 22:31, 32.* "And the Lord said, 'Simon, Simon! Indeed, Satan has asked for you, that he may sift you as wheat. But I have prayed for you, that your faith should not fail; and when you have returned to Me, strengthen your brethren.' "

7. *John 17:15–17, 20, 21.* "I do not pray that You should take them out of the world, but that You should keep them from the evil one. They are not of the world, just as I am not of the world. Sanctify them by Your truth. Your word is truth."

"I do not pray for these alone, but also for those who will believe in Me through their word; that they all may be one, as You, Father, are in Me, and I in You; that they also may be one in Us, that the world may believe that You sent Me."

8. *Ephesians 3:16–19.* "[I pray] that He would grant you, according to the riches of His glory, to be strengthened with might through His Spirit in the inner man, that Christ may dwell in your hearts through faith; that you, being rooted and grounded in love, may be able to comprehend with all the saints what is the width and length and depth and height—to know the love of Christ which passes knowledge; that you may be filled with all the fullness of God."

9. *Philippians 1:9–11.* "And this I pray, that your love may abound still more and more in knowledge and all discernment, that you may approve the things that are excellent, that you may be sincere and without offense till the day of Christ, being filled with the fruits of

righteousness which are by Jesus Christ, to the glory and praise of God."

10. *1 Timothy 2:1–4.* "Therefore I exhort first of all that supplications, prayers, intercessions, and giving of thanks be made for all men, for kings and all who are in authority, that we may lead a quiet and peaceable life in all godliness and reverence. For this is good and acceptable in the sight of God our Savior, who desires all men to be saved and to come to the knowledge of the truth."

11. *3 John 2.* "Beloved, I pray that you may prosper in all things and be in health, just as your soul prospers."

Ellen White's statements

1. *God longs to answer you.* "[God] longs to have you reach after Him by faith. He longs to have you expect great things from Him. He longs to give you understanding in temporal as well as in spiritual matters. He can sharpen the intellect. He can give tact and skill. Put your talents into the work, ask God for wisdom, and it will be given you."—*Christ's Object Lessons*, 146.

2. *The need to pray together.* "The Lord has promised that where two or three are met together in His name, there will he be in the midst. Those who meet together for prayer will receive an unction from the Holy One. There is great need of secret prayer, but there is also need that several Christians meet together, and unite with earnestness their petitions to God."—"Christians to Be Colaborers With God," *Advent Review and Sabbath Herald*, June 30, 1896.

3. *Revival will come by prayer.* "A revival of true godliness among us is the greatest and most urgent of all our needs. To seek this should be our first work. . . . By confession, humiliation, repentance, and earnest prayer, to fulfill the conditions upon which God has promised to grant us His blessing. A revival need be expected only in answer to prayer."—*Selected Messages*, book 1, 121.

4. *Satan trembles when we pray.* "Satan cannot endure to have his powerful rival appealed to, for he fears and trembles before his strength and majesty. At the sound of fervent prayer, Satan's whole host

trembles."—*Testimonies for the Church*, vol. 1, 346.

5. *Angels will obey to answer prayer.* "Ministering angels are waiting about the throne to instantly obey the mandate of Jesus Christ to answer every prayer offered in earnest, living faith."—*Selected Messages*, book 2, 377.

6. *Power and victory come from prayer.* "The greatest victories gained for the cause of God are not the result of labored argument, ample facili-ties, wide influence, or abundance of means; they are gained in the audience chamber with God, when with earnest, agonizing faith men lay hold upon the mighty arm of power.

    "True faith and true prayer—how strong they are! They are as two arms by which the human suppliant lays hold upon the power of Infinite Love."—*Gospel Workers*, 259.

7. *Take time to commune with God.* "Many, even in their seasons of devotion, fail of receiving the blessing of real communion with God. They are in too great haste. With hurried steps they press through the circle of Christ's loving presence, pausing perhaps a moment within the sacred precincts, but not waiting for counsel. They have no time to remain with the divine Teacher. With their burdens they return to their work.

    "These workers can never attain the highest success until they learn the secret of strength. They must give themselves time to think, to pray, to wait upon God for a renewal of physical, mental, and spiri-tual power. . . .

    "Not a pause for a moment in His presence, but personal contact with Christ, to sit down in companionship with Him—this is our need."—*Education*, 260, 261.

8. *Enoch knew how to walk with God.* "Enoch steadfastly maintained his communion with God. The greater and more pressing his labors, the more constant and earnest were his prayers. . . .

    "Communing thus with God, Enoch came more and more to reflect the divine image. His face was radiant with a holy light, even the light that shineth in the face of Jesus. As he came forth from these divine communings, even the ungodly beheld with awe the impress of heaven upon his countenance."—*Gospel Workers*, 52.

9. *Only work bathed by prayer will work.* "Only the work accomplished with much prayer, and sanctified by the merit of Christ will in the end prove to have been efficient for good."—*The Desire of Ages*, 362.

10. *We should pray for God to open the way.* "We should hold convocations for prayer, asking the Lord to open the way for the truth to enter the strongholds where Satan has set up his throne, and dispel the shadow he has cast athwart the pathway of those whom he is seeking to deceive and destroy."—"The Promise of the Spirit," *Advent Review and Sabbath Herald*, April 30, 1908.

11. *Believe God and He will answer!* "If the people of God would only exercise faith, He would work in a wonderful manner to accomplish this work. Hear the words of Christ: 'If two of you shall agree on earth as touching anything that they shall ask, it shall be done for them of My Father which is in heaven.' Precious promise! Do we believe it? What marvelous results would appear if the united prayers of this company were to ascend to God in living faith! Jesus stands ready to take these petitions and present them to His Father, saying, 'I know these persons by name. Send answers to their prayers; for I have graven their names on the palms of My hands.' "—*Evangelism*, 414.

12. *Now we must pray more than ever.* "We must be much in prayer if we would make progress in the divine life. When the message of truth was first proclaimed, how much we prayed. How often was the voice of intercession heard in the chamber, in the barn, in the orchard, or the grove. Frequently we spent hours in earnest prayer, two or three together claiming the promise; often the sound of weeping was heard and then the voice of thanksgiving and the song of praise. Now the day of God is nearer than when we first believed, and we should be more earnest, more zealous, and fervent than in those early days. Our perils are greater now than then. Souls are more hardened. We need now to be imbued with the spirit of Christ, and we should not rest until we receive it."—*Testimonies for the Church*, vol. 5, 161, 162.

Appendix B

Prayer-Walking Teams for Cities of One Million or More

The following is a long list of world cities with a population of one million or more as of July 1, 2018. The "2018 Population" number refers to the city proper unless it is followed by one asterisk (*), which indicates the number is of the metropolitan area number (larger cities), or by two asterisks (**), which indicates the number is the population of the urban agglomeration number (several cities in the same metro area). The numbers are in thousands. For example, Tokyo's population number is 37,468. That means 37,468,000 live in the largest city in the world today.

The number of prayer-walking teams indicated would be the *minimum* number for that city. Add a zero to that number for the *minimal ideal* number.

The source for this information is from The United Nations' world cities data booklet *The World's Cities in 2018*, https://www.un.org/en/events/citiesday/assets/pdf/the_worlds_cities_in_2018_data_booklet.pdf.

#	City	Country	Division	2018 Population	Prayer Teams	Expected 2030 Population
1	Tokyo	Japan	NSD	37,468*	375	36,574
2	Delhi	India	SUD	28,514*	286	38,939
3	Shanghai	China	CHUM	25,582	256	32,869
4	São Paulo	Brazil	SAD	21,650*	217	23,824
5	Mexico City	Mexico	IAD	21,581*	216	24,111
6	Cairo	Egypt	MENA	20,076*	201	25,517
7	Mumbai	India	SUD	19,980*	200	24,572
8	Beijing	China	CHIN	19,618**	196	24,282

9	Dhaka	Bangladesh	SSD	19,578*	196	28,076
10	Osaka	Japan	NSD	19,281*	193	18,658
11	New York-Newark	United States	NAD	18,819**	189	19,958
12	Karachi	Pakistan	SSD	15,400**	154	20,432
13	Buenos Aires	Argentina	SAD	14,967**	150	16,456
14	Chongqing	China	CHIN	14,838**	148	19,649
15	Istanbul	Turkey	MENA	14,751**	148	17,124
16	Kolkata	India	SUD	14,681*	147	17,584
17	Manila	Philippines	SSD	13,482*	135	16,841
18	Lagos	Nigeria	WAD	13,463**	135	20,600
19	Rio de Janeiro	Brazil	SAD	13,293*	133	14,408
20	Tianjin	China	CHIN	13,215**	132	15,745
21	Kinshasa	Dem. Rep. Congo	ECD	13,171**	132	21,914
22	Guangzhou	China	CHIN	12,638**	126	16,024
23	Los Angeles-Long Beach	United States	NAD	12,458**	125	13,209
24	Moscow	Russia	ESD	12,410	124	12,796
25	Shenzhen	China	CHIN	11,908**	119	14,537
26	Lahore	Pakistan	SSD	11,738**	117	16,883
27	Bangalore	India	SUD	11,440**	114	16,227
28	Paris	France	EUD	10,901**	109	11,710
29	Bogotá	Colombia	IAD	10,574**	106	12,343
30	Jakarta	Indonesia	SSD	10,517*	105	12,687
31	Chennai	India	SUD	10,456**	105	13,814
32	Lima	Peru	SAD	10,391*	104	12,266
33	Bangkok	Thailand	SSD	10,156**	102	12,101
34	Seoul	Republic of Korea	NSD	9,963**	100	10,163
35	Nagoya	Japan	NSD	9,507*	95	9,407
36	Hyderabad	India	SUD	9,482**	95	12,714
37	London	United Kingdom	TED	9,046**	90	10,228
38	Tehran	Iran	MEN	8,896	89	10,240

39	Chicago	United States	NAD	8,864**	89	9,424
40	Chengdu	China	CHIN	8,813**	88	10,728
41	Nanjing	China	CHIN	8,245**	82	11,011
42	Wuhan	China	CHIN	8,176**	82	9,611
43	Ho Chi Minh City	Vietnam	SSD	8,145**	81	11,054
44	Luanda	Angola	SID	7,774**	78	12,129
45	Ahmadabad	India	SUD	7,681**	77	10,148
46	Kuala Lumpur	Malaysia	SSD	7,564*	76	9,805
47	Xi'an	China	CHIN	7,444**	74	9,984
48	Hong Kong	China (Hong Kong)	CHIN	7,429**	74	7,987
49	Dongguan	China	CHIN	7,360**	74	8,279
50	Hangzhou	China	CHIN	7,236**	72	9,260
51	Foshan	China	CHIN	7,196**	72	8,350
52	Shenyang	China	CHIN	6,921**	69	8,569
53	Riyadh	Saudi Arabia	MENA	6,907	69	8,547
54	Baghdad	Iraq	MENA	6,812*	68	9,365
55	Santiago	Chile	SAD	6,680**	67	7,243
56	Surat	India	SUD	6,564**	66	9,711
57	Madrid	Spain	EUD	6,497	65	6,907
58	Suzhou	China	CHIN	6,339**	64	9,389
59	Pune	India	SUD	6,276**	63	8,442
60	Haerbin	China	CHIN	6,115**	61	7,597
61	Houston	United States	NAD	6,115**	61	7,254
62	Dallas-Fort Worth	United States	NAD	6,099**	61	7,073
63	Toronto	Canada	NAD	6,082*	61	6,793
64	Dar es Salaam	Tanzania	ECD	6,048**	60	10,789
65	Miami	United States	NAD	6,036**	60	6,664
66	Belo Horizonte	Brazil	SAD	5,972*	60	6,583
67	Singapore	Singapore	SSD	5,792**	58	6,342
68	Philadelphia	United States	NAD	5,695**	57	6,114

69	Atlanta	United States	NAD	5,572**	56	6,602
70	Kitakyushu-Fukuoka	Japan	NSD	5,551*	56	5,395
71	Khartoum	Sudan	MENA	5,534**	55	8,023
72	Barcelona	Spain	EUD	5,494	55	5,812
73	Johannesburg	South Africa	SID	5,486**	55	6,978
74	Saint Petersburg	Russia	ESD	5,383	54	5,630
75	Qingdao	China	CHIN	5,381**	54	6,684
76	Dalian	China	CHIN	5,300**	53	6,848
77	Washington, DC	United States	NAD	5,207**	52	5,868
78	Yangon	Myanmar	SSD	5,157**	52	6,389
79	Alexandria	Egypt	MENA	5,086	51	6,417
80	Ji'nan	China	CHIN	5,052**	50	6,546
81	Guadalajara	Mexico	IAD	5,023*	50	5,943
82	Zhengzhou	China	CHIN	4,940**	49	6,669
83	Abidjan	Côte d'Ivoire	WAD	4,921	49	7,136
84	Ankara	Turkey	MENA	4,919**	49	5,869
85	Chittagong	Bangladesh	SSD	4,816*	48	6,393
86	Sydney	Australia	SPD	4,792*	48	5,566
87	Melbourne	Australia	SPD	4,771*	48	5,736
88	Monterrey	Mexico	IAD	4,712*	47	5,621
89	Brasília	Brazil	SAD	4,470*	45	5,199
90	Jiddah	Saudi Arabia	MENA	4,433	44	5,388
91	Cape Town	South Africa	SID	4,430**	44	5,468
92	Addis Ababa	Ethiopia	ECD	4,400	44	7,352
93	Nairobi	Kenya	ECD	4,386	44	7,031
94	Phoenix-Mesa	United States	NAD	4,359**	44	5,081
95	Changsha	China	CHIN	4,345**	43	5,525
96	Xinbei	China (Taiwan)	NSD	4,325	43	4,683
97	Boston	United States	NAD	4,308**	43	4,581
98	Hà Noi	Vietnam	SSD	4,283**	43	6,362

99	Changchun	China	CHIN	4,241**	42	5,257
100	Kunming	China	CHIN	4,230**	42	5,335
101	Rome	Italy	EUD	4,210^	42	4,413
102	Shantou	China	CHIN	4,174**	42	5,083
103	Montréal	Canada	NAD	4,172*	42	4,573
104	Pôrto Alegre	Brazil	SAD	4,094*	41	4,416
105	Recife	Brazil	SAD	4,028*	40	4,509
106	Kabul	Afghanistan	ESD	4,012	40	5,737
107	Wulumqi	China	CHIN	4,011**	40	5,574
108	Tel Aviv-Jaffa	Israel	IF	4,011*	40	4,916
109	Hefei	China	CHIN	3,980**	40	5,218
110	Fortaleza	Brazil	SAD	3,977*	40	4,446
111	Shijiazhuang	China	CHIN	3,950**	40	4,872
112	Medellín	Colombia	IAD	3,934*	39	4,344
113	Kano	Nigeria	WAD	3,820**	38	5,551
114	Ningbo	China	CHIN	3,815**	38	5,169
115	Salvador	Brazil	SAD	3,754*	38	4,181
116	Ekurhuleni	South Africa	SID	3,741**	37	4,601
117	Taiyuan	China	CHIN	3,725**	37	4,628
118	Jaipur	India	SUD	3,717**	37	4,943
119	Casablanca	Morocco	MENA	3,684**	37	4,349
120	Yaoundé	Cameroon	WAD	3,656**	37	5,734
121	Nanning	China	CHIN	3,628**	36	4,734
122	Detroit	United States	NAD	3,600**	36	3,679
123	Xiamen	China	CHIN	3,585**	36	4,376
124	Curitiba	Brazil	SAD	3,579*	36	4,040
125	Berlin	Germany	EUD	3,552	36	3,606
126	Fuzhou	China	CHIN	3,532**	35	4,377
127	Lucknow	India	SUD	3,505**	35	4,628
128	Busan	Republic of Korea	NSD	3,467**	35	3,532

129	Wenzhou	China	CHIN	3,419**	34	4,416
130	Douala	Cameroon	WAD	3,412**	34	5,112
131	Ibadan	Nigeria	WAD	3,383**	34	4,956
132	Seattle	United States	NAD	3,379**	34	3,747
133	Nanchang	China	CHIN	3,373**	34	4,435
134	Changzhou	China	CHIN	3,372**	34	4,526
135	San Francisco-Oakland	United States	NAD	3,325**	33	3,501
136	Faisalabad	Pakistan	SSD	3,311**	33	4,401
137	Asunción	Paraguay	SAD	3,222*	32	3,920
138	San Diego	United States	NAD	3,212**	32	3,526
139	Campinas	Brazil	SAD	3,210*	32	3,627
140	Kozhikode	India	SUD	3,175**	32	4,993
141	Santo Domingo	Dominican Rep.	IAD	3,172**	32	3,913
142	Bekasi	Indonesia	SSD	3,159	32	4,332
143	Athens	Greece	TED	3,156**	32	3,163
144	Tangshan	China	CHIN	3,145**	31	4,371
145	Wuxi	China	CHIN	3,144**	31	3,818
146	Guiyang	China	CHIN	3,136**	31	4,029
147	Durban	South Africa	SID	3,134**	31	3,535
148	Milan	Italy	EUD	3,132*	31	3,209
149	Mashhad	Iran	MENA	3,097	31	3,650
150	Puebla	Mexico	IAD	3,097*	31	3,669
151	Kanpur	India	SUD	3,081**	31	3,715
152	Kumasi	Ghana	WAD	3,065*	31	4,681
153	Antananarivo	Madagascar	SID	3,058**	31	5,189
154	P'yongyang	DPR of Korea	NSD	3,038	30	3,345
155	Kuwait City	Kuwait	MENA	2,989**	30	3,622
156	Kampala	Uganda	ECD	2,986**	30	5,506
157	Dakar	Senegal	WAD	2,978**	30	4,339
158	Kiev	Ukraine	ESD	2,957	30	3,004

159	Malappuram	India	SUD	2,950**	30	4,976
160	Izmir	Turkey	MENA	2,937**	29	3,316
161	Lanzhou	China	CHIN	2,936**	29	3,692
162	Caracas	Venezuela	IAD	2,935*	29	3,164
163	Lisbon	Portugal	EUD	2,927*	29	3,085
164	Abuja	Nigeria	WAD	2,919**	29	5,119
165	Surabaya	Indonesia	SSD	2,903	29	3,413
166	Shizuoka-Hamamatsu	Japan	NSD	2,899*	29	2,883
167	Guayaquil	Ecuador	SAD	2,899**	29	3,511
168	Minneapolis-St. Paul	United States	NAD	2,889**	29	3,177
169	Zhongshan	China	CHIN	2,872**	29	3,302
170	Kochi	India	SUD	2,858**	29	4,064
171	Guatemala City	Guatemala	IAD	2,851*	29	3,640
172	Indore	India	SUD	2,822**	28	3,918
173	Nagpur	India	SUD	2,808**	28	3,534
174	Tampa-St. Petersburg	United States	NAD	2,807**	28	3,188
175	Dubai	United Arab Emir.	MENA	2,785**	28	3,315
176	Sana'a'	Yemen	MENA	2,779**	28	4,174
177	Thrissur	India	SUD	2,774**	28	4,221
178	Incheon	Republic of Korea	NSD	2,763	28	2,923
179	Denver-Aurora	United States	NAD	2,753**	28	3,141
180	Port Harcourt	Nigeria	WAD	2,731**	27	4,595
181	Cali	Colombia	IAD	2,726**	27	3,039
182	Taibei	China (Taiwan)	NSD	2,706**	27	2,844
183	Algiers	Algeria	MENA	2,694**	27	3,263
184	Manchester	United Kingdom	TED	2,690*	27	2,934
185	Sapporo	Japan	NSD	2,665*	27	2,612
186	Coimbatore	India	SUD	2,641**	26	3,542
187	Port-au-Prince	Haiti	IAD	2,637**	26	3,488
188	Birmingham	United Kingdom	TED	2,570**	26	2,802

189	Goiânia	Brazil	SAD	2,565*	26	3,056
190	Zibo	China	CHIN	2,555**	26	3,084
191	Las Vegas	United States	NAD	2,541**	25	3,173
192	Bandung	Indonesia	SSD	2,538	25	3,002
193	Ouagadougou	Burkina Faso	WAD	2,531	25	4,426
194	Vancouver	Canada	NAD	2,531*	25	2,834
195	Handan	China	CHIN	2,528**	25	3,423
196	Lusaka	Zambia	SID	2,524**	25	4,267
197	Depok	Indonesia	SSD	2,503	25	3,564
198	Weifang	China	CHIN	2,466**	25	3,318
199	Tashkent	Uzbekistan	ESD	2,464	25	2,835
200	San Juan	Puerto Rico	IAD	2,454*	25	2,419
201	Bamako	Mali	WAD	2,447	24	3,932
202	Accra	Ghana	WAD	2,439*	24	3,187
203	Huai'an	China	CHIN	2,420**	24	3,430
204	Beirut	Lebanon	MENA	2,385**	24	2,311
205	Pretoria	South Africa	SID	2,378**	24	3,219
206	Riverside-San Bernard.	United States	NAD	2,374**	24	2,804
207	Thiruvananthapuram	India	SUD	2,369**	24	3,474
208	Huizhou	China	CHIN	2,360**	24	3,126
209	Yantai	China	CHIN	2,359**	24	3,135
210	Toluca	Mexico	IAD	2,354*	24	2,909
211	Patna	India	SUD	2,352**	24	3,002
212	Shaoxing	China	CHIN	2,350**	24	3,200
213	Brisbane	Australia	SPD	2,338*	23	2,724
214	Damascus	Syria	MENA	2,320	23	3,387
215	Baltimore	United States	NAD	2,315**	23	2,490
216	Sendai	Japan	NSD	2,306*	23	2,301
217	Mbuji-Mayi	Dem. Rep. Congo	ECD	2,305	23	3,899
218	Tunis	Tunisia	MENA	2,291**	23	2,703

219	Baku	Azerbaijan	ESD	2,286**	23	2,659
220	Medan	Indonesia	SSD	2,285	23	2,749
221	Lubumbashı	Dem. Rep. Congo	ECD	2,281	23	3,771
222	Belém	Brazil	SAD	2,280*	23	2,546
223	Bhopal	India	SUD	2,278**	23	3,008
224	Luoyang	China	CHIN	2,236**	22	2,946
225	Brazzaville	Congo	WAD	2,230	22	3,292
226	Tangerang	Indonesia	SSD	2,222	22	2,884
227	Daegu	Republic of Korea	NSD	2,221	22	2,205
228	Barranquilla	Colombia	IAD	2,218**	22	2,499
229	San Antonio	United States	NAD	2,217**	22	2,661
230	Saint Louis	United States	NAD	2,213**	22	2,351
231	Naples	Italy	EUD	2,198*	22	2,207
232	Taoyuan	China (Taiwan)	NSD	2,190	22	2,423
233	Maracaibo	Venezuela	IAD	2,179*	22	2,574
234	Manaus	Brazil	SAD	2,171	22	2,537
235	Rawalpindi	Pakistan	SSD	2,156**	22	2,805
236	Havana	Cuba	IAD	2,136	21	2,178
237	Nantong	China	CHIN	2,123**	21	2,828
238	Agra	India	SUD	2,110**	21	2,774
239	Vadodara	India	SUD	2,110**	21	2,708
240	Gujranwala	Pakistan	SSD	2,110**	21	2,883
241	Portland	United States	NAD	2,104**	21	2,373
242	Baotou	China	CHIN	2,096**	21	2,608
243	Hiroshima	Japan	NSD	2,095*	21	2,031
244	Mogadishu	Somalia	ECD	2,082**	21	3,497
245	Visakhapatnam	India	SUD	2,076**	21	2,732
246	Peshawar	Pakistan	SSD	2,065**	21	2,896
247	Amman	Jordan	MENA	2,065	21	2,402
248	Tijuana	Mexico	IAD	2,058*	21	2,491

249	Xuzhou	China	CHIN	2,054**	21	2,554
250	Sacramento	United States	NAD	2,054**	21	2,384
251	Brussels	Belgium	EUD	2,050*	21	2,182
252	Kannur	India	SUD	2,048**	20	2,766
253	Liuzhou	China	CHIN	2,042**	20	2,641
254	Esfahan	Iran	MENA	2,041	20	2,461
255	Hohhot	China	CHIN	2,009**	20	2,709
256	Minsk	Belarus	ESD	2,005**	20	2,086
257	Grande Vitória	Brazil	SAD	2,003*	20	2,311
258	Perth	Australia	SPD	1,991*	20	2,299
259	Mecca	Saudi Arabia	MENA	1,967	20	2,379
260	Nashik	India	SUD	1,952**	20	2,638
261	Phnom Penh	Cambodia	SSD	1,952**	20	2,805
262	Multan	Pakistan	SSD	1,931**	19	2,552
263	Bursa	Turkey	MENA	1,916**	19	2,263
264	Austin	United States	NAD	1,915**	19	2,453
265	Vijayawada	India	SUD	1,911**	19	2,644
266	Yangzhou	China	CHIN	1,901**	19	2,385
267	Vienna	Austria	EUD	1,901	19	2,080
268	Baoding	China	CHIN	1,889**	19	2,355
269	Charlotte	United States	NAD	1,886**	19	2,520
270	Orlando	United States	NAD	1,882**	19	2,242
271	West Yorkshire	United Kingdom	TED	1,864*	19	2,026
272	Valencia	Venezuela	IAD	1,860*	19	2,144
273	Baixada Santista	Brazil	SAD	1,853*	19	2,055
274	Rabat	Morocco	MENA	1,847**	18	2,192
275	Conakry	Guinea	WAD	1,843	18	2,687
276	Linyi	China	CHIN	1,843**	18	2,327
277	Almaty	Kazakhstan	ESD	1,829	18	2,170
278	Quito	Ecuador	SAD	1,822	18	2,180

279	Bucharest	Romania	EUD	1,821	18	1,741
280	Taizhou	China	CHIN	1,818	18	2,374
281	La Paz	Bolivia	SAD	1,814**	18	2,174
282	Ludhiana	India	SUD	1,806	18	2,260
283	Haikou	China	CHIN	1,805**	18	2,253
284	Semarang	Indonesia	SSD	1,800	18	2,245
285	Hamburg	Germany	EUD	1,793	18	1,799
286	Turin	Italy	EUD	1,786*	18	1,834
287	Panama City	Panama	IAD	1,783**	18	2,247
288	Hyderabad	Pakistan	SSD	1,782**	18	2,323
289	León	Mexico	IAD	1,780*	18	2,075
290	Yancheng	China	CHIN	1,779**	18	2,231
291	Cleveland	United States	NAD	1,776**	18	1,852
292	San Jose	United States	NAD	1,776**	18	1,929
293	Warsaw	Poland	TED	1,768	18	1,800
294	Rajkot	India	SUD	1,767**	18	2,416
295	Daqing	China	CHIN	1,763**	18	2,247
296	Budapest	Hungary	TED	1,759	18	1,786
297	Aleppo	Syria	MENA	1,754**	18	2,993
298	Indianapolis	United States	NAD	1,753**	18	2,021
299	Lomé	Togo	WAD	1,746**	17	2,496
300	Davao City	Philippines	SSD	1,745	17	2,256
301	Montevideo	Uruguay	SAD	1,737*	17	1,819
302	Cincinnati	United States	NAD	1,733**	17	1,881
303	Adana	Turkey	MENA	1,730**	17	1,976
304	Pittsburgh	United States	NAD	1,718**	17	1,785
305	Putian	China	CHIN	1,712**	17	2,529
306	Lianyungang	China	CHIN	1,703**	17	2,249
307	Lyon	France	EUD	1,690**	17	1,847
308	Wuhu, Anhui	China	CHIN	1,685**	17	2,463

309	Madurai	India	SUD	1,676**	17	2,133
310	Zhuhai	China	CHIN	1,671**	17	2,120
311	Kollam	India	SUD	1,670**	17	2,557
312	Palembang	Indonesia	SSD	1,665	17	2,064
313	Kansas City	United States	NAD	1,663**	17	1,834
314	Glasgow	United Kingdom	TED	1,661*	17	1,778
315	Datong	China	CHIN	1,659**	17	2,102
316	Santa Cruz	Bolivia	SAD	1,641	16	2,068
317	Jiangmen	China	CHIN	1,640**	16	1,956
318	Meerut	India	SUD	1,636**	16	2,093
319	Novosibirsk	Russia	ESD	1,636	16	1,717
320	Matola	Mozambique	SID	1,635	16	2,418
321	Gaziantep	Turkey	MENA	1,632**	16	1,967
322	Benin City	Nigeria	WAD	1,628**	16	2,451
323	Varanasi	India	SUD	1,615**	16	2,036
324	Xiangyang	China	CHIN	1,607**	16	1,931
325	Shiraz	Iran	MENA	1,605	16	1,857
326	Anshan	China	CHIN	1,600**	16	1,857
327	Marseille	France	EUD	1,599**	16	1,695
328	Columbus	United States	NAD	1,598**	16	1,832
329	Karaj	Iran	MENA	1,585	16	1,687
330	Stockholm	Sweden	TED	1,583**	16	1,814
331	Tabriz	Iran	MENA	1,582	16	1,781
332	Sharjah	United Arab Emir.	MENA	1,571	16	2,065
333	Jilin	China	CHIN	1,569**	16	1,838
334	Quanzhou	China	CHIN	1,568**	16	2,132
335	Daejon	Republic of Korea	NSD	1,558	16	1,610
336	Auckland	New Zealand	SPD	1,557**	16	1,791
337	Córdoba	Argentina	SAD	1,548**	15	1,715
338	Jamshedpur	India	SUD	1,543**	15	1,974

339	Gaoxiong	China (Taiwan)	NSD	1,532	15	1,602
340	Makassar	Indonesia	SSD	1,530	15	1,900
341	Mosul	Iraq	MENA	1,527**	15	2,200
342	Raipur	India	SUD	1,521**	15	2,169
343	Ulaanbaatar	Mongolia	NSD	1,520	15	1,841
344	Gwangju	Republic of Korea	NSD	1,518	15	1,559
345	Harare	Zimbabwe	SID	1,515	15	1,845
346	Qiqihaer	China	CHIN	1,515**	15	1,809
347	Srinagar	India	SUD	1,515**	15	1,990
348	Munich	Germany	EUD	1,504	15	1,610
349	La Laguna	Mexico	IAD	1,490*	15	2,013
350	Rosario	Argentina	SAD	1,488**	15	1,711
351	Yinchuan	China	CHIN	1,483**	15	1,939
352	Yekaterinburg	Russia	ESD	1,482	15	1,546
353	Cixi	China	CHIN	1,480**	15	2,048
354	Ciudad Juárez	Mexico	IAD	1,480*	15	1,730
355	Virginia Beach	United States	NAD	1,478**	15	1,569
356	Calgary	Canada	NAD	1,477*	15	1,779
357	Aurangabad	India	SUD	1,476**	15	1,982
358	Grande São Luís	Brazil	SAD	1,460*	15	1,604
359	Xining	China	CHIN	1,452**	15	1,878
360	Jining	China	CHIN	1,450**	15	1,738
361	Muscat	Oman	MENA	1,447**	14	1,838
362	Can Tho	Vietnam	SSD	1,444	14	2,294
363	Kharkiv	Ukraine	ESD	1,436	14	1,404
364	Milwaukee	United States	NAD	1,435**	14	1,537
365	Hengyang	China	CHIN	1,433**	14	1,879
366	Qinhuangdao	China	CHIN	1,432**	14	1,907
367	Yichang	China	CHIN	1,432**	14	1,952
368	Medina	Saudi Arabia	MENA	1,430	14	1,744

369	Abu Dhabi	United Arab Emir.	MENA	1,420	14	1,739
370	Monrovia	Liberia	WAD	1,418**	14	2,120
371	Jabalpur	India	SUD	1,411**	14	1,763
372	Batam	Indonesia	SSD	1,401	14	2,065
373	Jodhpur	India	SUD	1,397**	14	1,866
374	Edmonton	Canada	NAD	1,397*	14	1,673
375	Natal	Brazil	SAD	1,395**	14	1,642
376	Huainan	China	CHIN	1,393**	14	1,677
377	Asansol	India	SUD	1,391**	14	1,744
378	Chaozhou	China	CHIN	1,389**	14	1,654
379	Belgrade	Serbia	TED	1,389**	14	1,423
380	Mandalay	Myanmar	SSD	1,374**	14	1,757
381	Zurich	Switzerland	EUD	1,371**	14	1,514
382	Ranchi	India	SUD	1,370**	14	1,817
383	Tiruppur	India	SUD	1,369**	14	2,018
384	Zhangjiakou	China	CHIN	1,367**	14	1,720
385	Tegucigalpa	Honduras	IAD	1,363	14	1,851
386	Ottawa-Gatineau	Canada	NAD	1,363*	14	1,535
387	Chon Buri	Thailand	SSD	1,361**	14	1,580
388	San José	Costa Rica	IAD	1,358**	14	1,595
389	Allahabad	India	SUD	1,355**	14	1,698
390	João Pessoa	Brazil	SAD	1,347*	13	1,502
391	Kananga	Dem. Rep. Congo	ECD	1,335	13	2,240
392	Amritsar	India	SUD	1,335**	13	1,685
393	Kathmandu	Nepal	SUD	1,330	13	1,939
394	Anyang	China	CHIN	1,328**	13	1,893
395	Raleigh	United States	NAD	1,327**	13	1,767
396	N'Djaména	Chad	WAD	1,323	13	2,122
397	Copenhagen	Denmark	TED	1,321*	13	1,442
398	Adelaide	Australia	SPD	1,320*	13	1,472

399	Gwalior	India	SUD	1,317**	13	1,727
400	Porto	Portugal	EUD	1,307**	13	1,357
401	Dhanbad	India	SUD	1,302ᴬᴬ	13	1,604
402	Kota	India	SUD	1,299**	13	1,799
403	Basra	Iraq	MENA	1,299	13	1,751
404	Homs	Syria	MENA	1,295	13	1,891
405	Bucaramanga	Colombia	IAD	1,295**	13	1,473
406	Maceió	Brazil	SAD	1,294*	13	1,440
407	Prague	Czechia	EUD	1,292	13	1,345
408	Taian	China	CHIN	1,290**	13	1,575
409	Fushun	China	CHIN	1,288**	13	1,416
410	Querétaro	Mexico	IAD	1,288*	13	1,558
411	Onitsha	Nigeria	WAD	1,285**	13	2,138
412	Taizhong	China (Taiwan)	NSD	1,283**	13	1,434
413	Taizhou, Jiangsu	China	CHIN	1,282**	13	1,622
414	Helsinki	Finland	TED	1,279**	13	1,386
415	Suqian	China	CHIN	1,276**	13	1,950
416	Samut Prakan	Thailand	SSD	1,272**	13	1,477
417	Sofia	Bulgaria	EUD	1,272**	13	1,279
418	Konya	Turkey	MENA	1,271**	13	1,535
419	Joinville	Brazil	SAD	1,270*	13	1,427
420	Suweon	Republic of Korea	NSD	1,265**	13	1,420
421	Nizhniy Novgorod	Russia	ESD	1,264	13	1,251
422	Kazan	Russia	ESD	1,254	13	1,307
423	Jacksonville	United States	NAD	1,244**	12	1,427
424	Qom	Iran	MENA	1,241	12	1,469
425	Cochabamba	Bolivia	SAD	1,237**	12	1,600
426	Port Elizabeth	South Africa	SID	1,231*	12	1,429
427	Zhanjiang	China	CHIN	1,231**	12	1,533
428	Mianyang	China	CHIN	1,228**	12	1,504

429	Yiwu	China	CHIN	1,227**	12	1,698
430	Hai Phòng	Vietnam	SSD	1,219**	12	1,698
431	Weihai	China	CHIN	1,216**	12	1,622
432	Zunyi	China	CHIN	1,216**	12	1,545
433	Chelyabinsk	Russia	ESD	1,216	12	1,252
434	Mombasa	Kenya	ECD	1,214	12	1,889
435	Niamey	Niger	WAD	1,214	12	1,988
436	Ahvaz	Iran	MENA	1,212	12	1,394
437	Nouakchott	Mauritania	WAD	1,205	12	1,925
438	Dongying	China	CHIN	1,205**	12	1,553
439	Providence	United States	NAD	1,205**	12	1,267
440	Dublin	Ireland	TED	1,201**	12	1,374
441	Nashville-Davidson	United States	NAD	1,199**	12	1,422
442	Ad-Dammam	Saudi Arabia	MENA	1,197	12	1,478
443	Florianópolis	Brazil	SAD	1,197*	12	1,378
444	Bareilly	India	SUD	1,195**	12	1,583
445	Barquisimeto	Venezuela	IAD	1,189*	12	1,352
446	Kaifeng	China	CHIN	1,186**	12	1,588
447	Rizhao	China	CHIN	1,186**	12	1,578
448	Fès	Morocco	MENA	1,184**	12	1,455
449	Antalya	Turkey	MENA	1,184	12	1,481
450	Omsk	Russia	ESD	1,184	12	1,183
451	San Luis Potosí	Mexico	IAD	1,179*	12	1,396
452	Maracay	Venezuela	IAD	1,178*	12	1,340
453	Durg-Bhilainagar	India	SUD	1,177**	12	1,465
454	Nanchong	China	CHIN	1,173**	12	1,563
455	Samara	Russia	ESD	1,171	12	1,154
456	Kisangani	Dem. Rep. Congo	ECD	1,167	12	1,903
457	Shiyan	China	CHIN	1,162**	12	1,533
458	Mysore	India	SUD	1,162**	12	1,504

459	Tripoli	Libya	MENA	1,158	12	1,272
460	Ganzhou	China	CHIN	1,158**	12	1,692
461	Salt Lake City	United States	NAD	1,147**	11	1,284
462	Zhuzhou	China	CHIN	1,145**	11	1,394
463	Aligarh	India	SUD	1,143**	11	1,548
464	Jiaxing	China	CHIN	1,140**	11	1,648
465	Memphis	United States	NAD	1,139**	11	1,241
466	Pointe-Noire	Congo	WAD	1,138	11	1,664
467	Yingkou	China	CHIN	1,138**	11	1,497
468	Pekan Baru	Indonesia	SSD	1,138	11	1,500
469	Freetown	Sierra Leone	WAD	1,136	11	1,605
470	Maoming	China	CHIN	1,136**	11	1,469
471	Chiang Mai	Thailand	SSD	1,135**	11	1,318
472	Haifa	Israel	IF	1,135*	11	1,281
473	Tiruchirappalli	India	SUD	1,134**	11	1,415
474	Rostov-on-Don	Russia	ESD	1,134	11	1,143
475	Mendoza	Argentina	SAD	1,133**	11	1,320
476	Amsterdam	Netherlands	TED	1,132**	11	1,219
477	Ufa	Russia	ESD	1,129	11	1,153
478	Moradabad	India	SUD	1,127**	11	1,539
479	Zhenjiang	China	CHIN	1,124**	11	1,397
480	Benxi	China	CHIN	1,122**	11	1,348
481	Mérida	Mexico	IAD	1,122*	11	1,342
482	Tanger	Morocco	MENA	1,116**	11	1,517
483	Bogor	Indonesia	SSD	1,115	11	1,402
484	Krasnoyarsk	Russia	ESD	1,111	11	1,187
485	Chandigarh	India	SUD	1,110**	11	1,413
486	San Salvador	El Salvador	IAD	1,107*	11	1,190
487	Chifeng	China	CHIN	1,105**	11	1,406
488	Maputo	Mozambique	SID	1,102	11	1,486

489	Jinzhou	China	CHIN	1,101**	11	1,354
490	Bhubaneswar	India	SUD	1,100**	11	1,482
491	Baoji	China	CHIN	1,098**	11	1,422
492	Guilin	China	CHIN	1,096**	11	1,329
493	Cologne	Germany	EUD	1,096	11	1,167
494	Puning	China	CHIN	1,095**	11	1,412
495	Tengzhou	China	CHIN	1,094**	11	1,514
496	Pingdingshan	China	CHIN	1,093	11	1,417
497	Ruian	China	CHIN	1,089**	11	1,456
498	Xiangtan	China	CHIN	1,089**	11	1,371
499	Nanyang	China	CHIN	1,088**	11	1,372
500	Kaduna	Nigeria	WAD	1,083	11	1,499
501	Guwahati	India	SUD	1,083**	11	1,365
502	Mexicali	Mexico	IAD	1,082*	11	1,296
503	Richmond	United States	NAD	1,081**	11	1,218
504	Yerevan	Armenia	ESD	1,080	11	1,114
505	Hubli-Dharwad	India	SUD	1,079	11	1,374
506	Tbilisi	Georgia	ESD	1,077	11	1,102
507	Huaibei	China	CHIN	1,076**	11	1,394
508	Louisville	United States	NAD	1,073**	11	1,188
509	Aguascalientes	Mexico	IAD	1,070*	11	1,276
510	Suzhou, Anhui	China	CHIN	1,068**	11	1,507
511	Astana	Kazakhstan	ESD	1,068	11	1,456
512	Da Nang	Vietnam	SSD	1,064	11	1,449
513	Liuan	China	CHIN	1,063**	11	1,611
514	Zaozhuang	China	CHIN	1,063**	11	1,250
515	Salem	India	SUD	1,062**	11	1,363
516	Perm	Russia	ESD	1,062	11	1,091
517	Islamabad	Pakistan	SSD	1,061	11	1,477
518	Changwon	Republic of Korea	NSD	1,060**	11	1,070

519	Kigali	Rwanda	ECD	1,058	11	1,568
520	Voronezh	Russia	ESD	1,056	11	1,091
521	Lille	France	EUD	1,054***	11	1,126
522	Jieyang	China	CHIN	1,049**	10	1,473
523	Managua	Nicaragua	IAD	1,048**	10	1,203
524	Bandar Lampung	Indonesia	SSD	1,047	10	1,326
525	Cartagena	Colombia	IAD	1,047	10	1,150
526	Xinxiang	China	CHIN	1,044**	10	1,266
527	Cuernavaca	Mexico	IAD	1,043*	10	1,232
528	Quetta	Pakistan	SSD	1,042**	10	1,420
529	Goyang	Republic of Korea	NSD	1,039	10	1,145
530	Yongin	Republic of Korea	NSD	1,039**	10	1,186
531	Antwerpen	Belgium	EUD	1,032*	10	1,084
532	Lilongwe	Malawi	SID	1,030	10	1,748
533	Jinhua	China	CHIN	1,024**	10	1,447
534	Aba	Nigeria	WAD	1,023**	10	1,527
535	Liuyang	China	CHIN	1,020**	10	1,624
536	Jalandhar	India	SUD	1,014**	10	1,304
537	Solapur	India	SUD	1,014	10	1,231
538	Volgograd	Russia	ESD	1,014	10	992
539	Uyo	Nigeria	WAD	1,012**	10	1,771
540	Oslo	Norway	TED	1,012**	10	1,187
541	Chihuahua	Mexico	IAD	1,012*	10	1,232
542	Odesa	Ukraine	ESD	1,011	10	1,005
543	Panjin	China	CHIN	1,009**	10	1,250
544	Jingzhou	China	CHIN	1,008**	10	1,206
545	Rotterdam	Netherlands	TED	1,008**	10	1,049
546	Mwanza	Tanzania	ECD	1,003	10	1,827
547	Teresina	Brazil	SAD	1,001**	10	1,108
548	Binzhou	China	CHIN	1,000**	10	1,371

Adventist division or field abbreviations
CHIN = China Field
ECD = East-Central Africa Division
ESD = Euro-Asia Division
EUD = Inter-European Division
IAD = Inter-American Division
IF = Israel Field
MENA = Middle East and North Africa Union Mission
NAD = North American Division
NSD = Northern Asia-Pacific Division
SAD = South American Division
SID = Southern Africa-Indian Ocean Division
SPD = South Pacific Division
SSD = Southern Asia-Pacific Division
SUD = Southern Asia Division
TED = Trans-European Division
WAD = West-Central Africa Division